20th Anniversary Edition

The Australian
Bed & Breakfast Book

2008

Australia's Best Accommodation Guide

"Includes the kind of details reminiscent of Anne Tyler's The Accidental Tourist"
Susan Kurosawa, The Australian.

"This book should come with a warning: read it and you won't want to stay home this weekend."
Voyeur - Virgin Blue.

"This beautifully presented handbook should accompany every tourist."
Traveltalk.

"A major reason why B&Bs are becoming increasingly popular."
RM Williams Outback.

"Solves all the inherent difficulties with a no-nonsense approach."
Australian Country Style.

"I'm a great fan of the weekend in the country – this guide could have all the answers."
Bookseller and Publisher.

Rupertswood Mansion, Macedon Ranges – Sunbury, Vic

THE AUSTRALIAN BED & BREAKFAST BOOK 2008
Australia's Best Accommodation Guide

Layout: Matt Thomas
Maps: Elizabeth Thomas
Editing and Spanish Translation: Ian Southern
Printing: Book Builders, Hong Kong
Paper: Printed on paper produced from Sustainable Growth Forest

Australia Distribution: Tower Books Frenchs Forest; Gordon and Gotch Frenchs Forest
UK and Europe Distribution: Vine House Distribution Ltd, Hampshire
New Zealand Distribution: Moonshine Press, Wellington
US Distribution: Pelican Publishing Company, Inc., Gretna, LA

Published October 2007
Editor Carl Southern

Inn Australia Pty Ltd
PO Box 330, Wahroonga, NSW 2076, Australia
Tel: +61 2 8208 5959 Fax: +61 2 9487 6650
Email: info@BBBook.com.au Web: www.BBBook.com.au

20th Edition
Copyright © October 2007 Inn Australia Pty Ltd

Includes Index
ISBN 978-0-9758040-3-2

We welcome your comments or suggestions

Cover Image:
The Verandah Lounge by **Colina Grant**, Constitution Hill, NSW

AUSTRALIA'S BEST ACCOMMODATION GUIDE

Accommodation with Outstanding Gardens
Pet Friendly Stays
Romantic Stays
Family Getaways
Accommodation with Easy Access
Breakaways with Wine Activities
Eco-Tourism
Self-Contained Cottages and Apartments
Bed & Breakfasts and Farmstays
Country Cabins and Beach Houses
Historic Inns
Guesthouses and Small Hotels

"We received the greatest hospitality, slept in the most wonderful bed and enjoyed the best breakfast in a long, long time. We will return!"
From one of our guests.

Acknowledgements

Publishing The Bed & Breakfast Book often seems like listening to the stories of painting the Sydney Harbour Bridge – no sooner is it painted than the painting starts again. With The Bed & Breakfast Book, no sooner is one edition finished then the next edited is started. It is a detailed and involved publication as all hosts are consulted before their accommodation descriptions and details are included. Many hosts are so eager to be included and update details sometimes many months in advance. Other hosts are less forthcoming and need a whole series of emails and telephone calls before their entry is finalised. But I do thank all hosts for their continued support of The B&B Book. It is their commitment to wonderful accommodation and generous hospitality that enables us to present a wonderful collection of some of the best accommodation Australia has to offer.

We often hear of the wide ranging effects of globalisation, both positive and negative, but in the last few years The Bed & Breakfast Book has truly gone global! Much gratitude must go to our in-house production team at Moonshine Press in New Zealand, particularly to Elizabeth Thomas who works tirelessly for The New Zealand Bed & Breakfast Book and to Matt Thomas who put this book together almost single handed. Editing hosts' entries needs a keen eye – thanks to Ian Southern in Spain for his meticulous skills.

For the last few years Bookbuilders have printed The Bed & Breakfast Book in China. To Adam Crouch in Sydney and Ron Cheung in Hong Kong I am indebted for their great support and never ending patience. As a small in-house publisher distribution is the hardest nut to crack, so special thanks to our distributors, Tower Books and Gordon and Gotch in Australia, Vine House in the UK, Pelican in the US and Moonshine Press in New Zealand.

To all hosts and guests who regularly contact us with their comments, suggestions and valuable feedback on the properties included - your contributions are priceless. Last, but never least, we are indebted to you - the travelling public who use the 'little green book' to choose your next family getaway, romantic interlude or a stopover when travelling. We thank you for your ongoing support of our B&B hosts,

Carl Southern

Contents

THE AUSTRALIAN BED & BREAKFAST BOOK 2008
Australia's Best Accommodation Guide

THE AUSTRALIAN BED & BREAKFAST BOOK 1987-2008

Whilst the short break and weekend getaway market shows no signs of slowing down, the impact of B&B hosts can not be understated. They seem tireless in their commitment to offering the best accommodation, stunning breakfasts with lashings of hospitality. In the 20 years since the Bed & Breakfast Book was first published by Jim and Janet Thomas, the B&B industry has seen a phenomenal growth. The B&B with a shared bathroom and breakfast with the hosts and their family is now the exception rather than the rule. B&B is the broad term to encompass a wide range of styles where breakfast in included as part of the tariff.

When first published, The Bed & Breakfast Book chose to highlight 'hospitality' as well as accommodation and to this day it remains integral to our publishing philosophy. Within the covers of this edition are hundreds of different and unique properties committed to ensuring your stay is not only comfortable but enjoyable, whether the property offers simple Traditional B&B or Homestay accommodation, or Deluxe Self Contained in a Rural Retreat, or a Holiday Home by the sea. B&B Book hosts today are tireless workers in so many ways – hosts, cooks, tour guide; not to mention cleaners, porters and taxi drivers.

Properties included in The Bed & Breakfast Book offer a Commitment to Generous Hospitality whether traditional hosted or self contained accommodation. Hosts agree to Quality Assurance and guarantee high standards. A Mark of a good host is their commitment to you as a guest from the moment of your first enquiry to the time you are leaving; and they welcome your feedback, whether the friendly thank you or a comment in The Visitors Book.

The development for B&Bs seems to be an ever upward and increasing level of service and quality without skimping on hospitality or value. Whilst standards are improving standardisation is on the wain, with many hosts opting not to be assessed by an 'independent assessor' but preferring the travelling public to be their standard. Many guests use our Guest Review Forms to comment upon the features which made their stay special.

On rare occasions your expectations may not be met, in which case you should discuss your concerns straight away with your host rather than write a letter after you leave. They should in most cases be able to rectify the situation immediately and to your satisfaction. Do tell us if you have had a wonderful stay, likewise we like to know if your stay has been disappointing. Our feedback from guests and hosts alike tells us that the B&B Book hosts are not only the most generous but also the most understanding of guest needs.

As Australia's love affair with gardens continues, so there is a trend for more properties run by garden lovers for garden lovers. Likewise, our ownership of pets is so high, that we see an increasing number of properties welcoming pets. Some hosts offer facilities for your larger pets such as horses or alpacas! There are also more eco friendly properties, accommodation at wineries and properties specialising in the indulgent and luxurious end of the market.

And ... "The difference between a hotel and a B&B ... you don't hug the hotel staff when you leave."

A Quick Guide

Properties included in The Bed & Breakfast Book offer wonderful accommodation, fantastic breakfasts and outstanding value. They are the ideal way to appreciate genuine Australian Hospitality. B&B hosts can suggest wonderful places to visit, recommend the best restaurants or even prepare a wonderful meal. Above all they promise superior hospitality and are committed to ensuring your stay is both enjoyable and memorable.

Each entry in the guide has been written by the hosts themselves and you will discover the special features of the accommodation through their eyes, and their warmth and personality through their writing.

Location: *Town or City and/or Suburb or Region* →	**Byron Bay Hinterland**
Name and style of accommodation →	**Green Mango Hideaway** *B&B*
	Susie Briscoe
Accommodation Address →	Lofts Road, off Coolamon Scenic Drive
	Coorabell
	NSW 2479
Distance to nearest town →	*12 km W of Byron Bay*
Telephone, Email, web →	Tel (02) 6684 7171
	relax@greenmango.com.au
	www.greenmango.com.au
Tariffs →	Double $165-$250
	Single $150-$220
Type of breakfast →	Full breakfast
Payment options →	Visa MC Eftpos accepted
Number and type of bedrooms →	2 King 2 Queen (4 bdrm)
Number and type of bathrooms →	Bathrooms: 4 Ensuite

Description → From the moment you walk down its leafy path, you'll be captivated by the tropical atmosphere of this peaceful B&B set in Byron's spectacular hinterland. With just four guestrooms, each with ensuite & verandah, you'll be escaping the crowds and yet be within minutes of fabulous shops & cafés and glorious beaches. The muslin-draped beds & Oriental decor, the sparkling palm-fringed pool & lush gardens with abundant birdlife, and the wonderful breakfasts all guarantee you a relaxing and memorable stay.

Accommodation

Accommodation included in the B&B Book covers a range of styles, each with uniquely different characteristics. Some properties offer simple and homely B&B accommodation, others offer grand suites or luxurious self contained facilities. Your bedroom will be comfortable, usually with a private or ensuite bathroom, and breakfast is usually included in your room rate.

Styles

Homestay: Guests share living or dining rooms with host
Bed & Breakfast or Traditional Bed & Breakfast: Guests share living and dining rooms with other guests
Farmstay: Accommodation on a working farm with farm activities
Self-Contained: Guests have private accommodation with kitchen, living and dining areas
Separate Suite: Guests have private accommodation with limited or no kitchen facilities. Dining and living areas may also be limited.
Guesthouse or Hotel: Larger style accommodation, often with a restaurant but retaining the warm hospitality found in B&Bs.
Luxury: Higher quality accommodation, often including many extras such as quality furnishings and bed linen and special toiletries.

Accommodation Description

Each listing entry and photograph in the guide has been provided by the hosts themselves through which you will discover the uniqueness of the accommodation. Entries are arranged alphabetically by states, then city or region.

Icons

❀ **Accommodation with Outstanding Gardens** – great if you are a garden lover

�",'" **Pets Welcome** – contact hosts first to check on facilities available

🧍 **Children Welcome** – contact hosts first. Some hosts have facilities for babies only, others for older children

👫 **Not Suitable for Children** – Accommodation for adults. Some accommodation is designed for romantic getaways, other properties might have unfenced water such as dams making it unsuitable for children

🍇 **Winery or Wine Activities** – Accommodation at a vineyard or where wine activities are possible

🚶 **Accommodation with Onsite Activities** – maybe horse riding, farm activities or tennis

☯ **Eco tourism** – Accommodation complying with or supporting Eco tourism

🍴 **Restaurant** – Accommodation next to or with a restaurant as part of the facilities

🏊 **Swimming pool** – great for a cool swim on a hot day

♿ **Wheelchair access** – suitable for less able or non ambulant guests

🚭 **No Smoking on property** – just fresh air

🅱 **Member of State B&B Association**

AAA Tourism
★★★★★ **AAA Tourism Assessed** – the stars!

💮 **Tourism Accredited** – the green tick issued by Australian Tourism Accreditation Association

Breakfast

After a good night's rest, breakfast is the meal that 'breaks' our 'fast' between night and day. Too often today, it is a meal that is neglected at worst or rushed at best. But to a B&B host a good breakfast is the most important meal of the day. Whether it is a traditional country breakfast of well cured bacon and farm fresh eggs or a platter of seasonal fruits, home made bread and preserves, it will be generous and is one of the pleasures of a good B&B. Your breakfast is included unless otherwise indicated.

Some B&Bs request an additional charge for a cooked breakfast. Some hosts also cater for special diets.

Continental or Light: Usually includes cereals, bread or toast, fruit or fruit juice, tea or coffee.

Full: A light breakfast plus a cooked course.

Special: Exceptional breakfast, often with several courses.

Provisions: Breakfast supplies provided.

Accommodation Only: Some self-contained accommodation does not provide breakfast.

Additional Meals

Some B&Bs, farmstays, rural B&Bs or guesthouses offer additional meals. Others offer barbecue packages or picnic hampers. You may need to request meals in advance or by arrangement (B/A).

Beds and Bedrooms

Entries show the number and size of beds, bedrooms and guests that can stay.
Beds for 1 person
Single (1 bed)
Twin (2 single beds)
King twin (2 large single beds).

Beds for 2 persons
Double (small)
Queen (large)
King (very large).

Bathrooms

Most accommodation provides ensuite or private bathrooms for your exclusive use. Older or historic B&Bs may offer private bathrooms for your exclusive use but off the hallway. Some B&Bs offer luxurious bathrooms - some with spas.
Ensuite: Exclusive use from your bedroom
Private: Exclusive use, usually off the hallway
Shared: Shared with other guests.

Reservations

We recommend that you book well in advance to confirm your accommodation. Book directly with your host by email or telephone. Advise dates of arrival and departure, time of arrival, the room/s you require, how many guests in your party, if you are travelling with children or pets or any special requirements. Some B&Bs have minimum stays during peak periods. You may need to pay a deposit in advance. Ask how much is due, when full payment is required and the cancellation policy. Most hosts accept credit cards.

Tariffs

B&Bs offer great value accommodation, particularly as your breakfast is included. Most include complimentary tea or coffee; some include a welcome afternoon tea on arrival, drinks in the fridge or chocolates and port. Rates are in Australian dollars for two persons (ie double) or 1 person (single) and vary according to the quality of the accommodation, the location, the facilities offered and seasonal variations. Low season or midweek bookings can offer good value particularly in popular tourism destinations. Some hosts offer discounts for extended stays. Rates are valid for the current year but are subject to change. Please confirm when booking. Some have another bed in the room, for a third adult or children sharing the same room, for an additional charge. A 10% Goods and Service Tax (GST), where applicable, is included in rates.

Check-In

Hosts are often flexible with check-in and check-out times. Check-in times are usually from 1.00 -3.00 in the afternoon with check-out 10.00-12.00 in the morning.

Conditions of Stay

Hosts welcoming guests to stay at their accommodation aim to provide not only you but subsequent guests similar experiences of wonderful accommodation and great hospitality. Most hosts keep their terms and conditions to a minimum; some may invite you to 'sign-in' on arrival and agree to their 'Conditions of Stay'. This could cover you as well as the host in case of an unforseen incident. Moreover it guarantees all guests that the accommodation will always offer the finest standards.

Comment from a Guest

"The little extra things made our stay special – the welcome chocolates and the champagne for our anniversary, the freshly baked break for breakfast . . . and the list goes on . . ."
Melina Dunn who stayed at Ossian Hall

B&B Gift Vouchers

B&B Book Vouchers are a great Way to Travel. Purchase before you travel and use them in exchange for staying at accommodation included in The Bed & Breakfast Book. They are also the perfect Gift for birthdays, anniversaries, or Corporate Gifts. You may purchase Bed & Breakfast Book Vouchers to any value. Each Voucher comes with a copy of The Australian Bed & Breakfast Book (worth $19.95). Include a postage and handling charge of only $15 per voucher.

B&B Book Orders

Order a copy of The Australian Bed & Breakfast Book or The New Zealand Bed & Breakfast Book as a gift for a friend or relative. Books are only $19.95 each plus postage and handling: $4.95 Australia, $15 international airmail.
Or mention this ad in the 2008 B&B Book and receive your book postage free.

Order Gift Vouchers or Books directly from:

The Bed & Breakfast Book
PO Box 330
Wahroonga
NSW 2076
info@BBBook.com.au
(02) 8208 5959

The Website - www.BBBook.com.au

Some guests prefer books – some the web. We like books but acknowledge the role of the web, which is why you can find all entries included in the Bed & Breakfast book on our comprehensive website at www.BBBook.com.au. You will find more information on each property, more photographs and direct links to each B&B host's own website. You will also find many more B&Bs which are included only on our website, including properties in:

ACT: Macgregor,
NSW: Ariah Park, Bega Valley - Wolumla, Blackheath, , Cowra - Mandurama, Forestville, Lake Macquarie - Cardiff South, Sydney - Paddington, Wauchope
Qld: Airlie Beach, Ballandean, Brisbane - Paddington, Brisbane - Shorncliffe, Cairns - Babinda, Maleny, Mossman - Julatten, Toowoomba,
SA: Port Elliot
Tas: Bellerive, Hobart , Rosetta,
Vic: Beechworth, Bairnsdale, Benalla, Castlemaine, Murchison, South Melbourne
WA: Ascot, Ferguson Valley, Kalgoorlie Boulder, Margaret River

Accommodation
www.bbbook.com.au/index.html *Browse By Maps*
www.bbbook.com.au/search.html *Search for a B&B*

More Information
www.bbbook.com.au/about_the_book.html *About the Book*
www.bbbook.com.au/faq.html *FAQs*
www.bbbook.com.au/buy_the_book.html *Buy the Book*
www.bbbook.com.au/contact.html *Contact Us*

Joining the Book
www.bbbook.com.au/newlisting.html *Registration Form*
www.bbbook.com.au/about_joining.html *Become a Member*
www.bbbook.com.au/services_hosts.html *Benefits for Members*

Other Countries
www.bnb.co.nz *New Zealand*

Members Only
www.bbbook.com.au/members.html *Members' Login*

B&BS FOR SALE

Are you looking to buy a B&B or even to sell your existing property?

Visit **www.Inn.com.au** and click on B&Bs For Sale.

The 2007 People's Choice Awards For Great Accommodation & First Class Hospitality

The People's Choice Awards for Great Accommodation is our way of praising the industry as a whole. Award Winners are selected for different styles of accommodation determined by the number of comment cards retuned to us.

Congratulations to the following 2007 Award Winners

New South Wales: Family B&B
Arrowee House, Kyoko Sakamoto &
Ray Fitzgerald, Gloucester, NSW.
"Fantastic place, lovely, friendly welcome, yummy breakfast. The Jewel of Gloucester."
Cordelia Hibbert, Saltash NSW.

New South Wales: Self Contained Retreat
Ossian Hall, Diane & Jim Swaisland,
Colo, NSW.
"We could not have found a better place to spend our wedding anniversary. Jim and Diane are certainly more than just hosts – our stay was exceptional."
Prav and Peter Biondi, Glenwood, NSW.

Victoria: Luxury Self Contained Retreat
Craigielea Mountain Retreat, Simone & Richard Graham, Cherokee, Vic.
"Absolute Relaxation – It's true, you only need bring yourself – and Partner!"
D Williams, East Melbourne, Vic.

Western Australia: B&B
BroomeTown B&B, Toni & Richard Bourne, Broome, WA.
"We have stayed in B&Bs all over the world and this one surpasses them all!!!!!"
Pam & John Lake, Dudley, NSW.

Queensland: Luxury B&B Cottages
Lake Weyba Cottages, Philip & Samantha Bown, Peregian Beach, Qld.
"We're lost for words – The place, the design, the tranquillity, the food, the hospitality, the lake, the cottage and the animals are all just perfect."
Jo & James, Nundah, Qld.

INTRODUCTION

Bienvenue sur le site du livre Bed & Breakfast, le guide du logement en chambres d'hôte le plus populaire en Australie. Première édition: 1989.

Les chambres d'hôtes (ou B&Bs) offrent une valeur exceptionnelle et sont une manière idéale d'apprécier la véritable hospitalité australienne. Les gîtes touristiques se sont investis pour vous assurer un agréable et mémorable séjour et pour vous proposer une hospitalité supérieure, que vous restiez une nuit ou une semaine. Ils offrent un accueil chaleureux, un excellent logement et des petits déjeuners succulents. Ils peuvent suggérer de magnifiques endroits locaux à visiter, recommander les meilleurs restaurants ou même préparer des recettes maison.

Les chambres d'hôtes comprennent une gamme de styles, chacune avec des caractéristiques exclusivement différentes. Certaines sont simples et confortables, d'autres sont grandes et luxueuses. Votre chambre à coucher sera confortable, généralement avec salle de bains attenante ou privée et le petit déjeuner est habituellement compris dans le tarif de votre chambre.

Hébergement chez l'habitant : Partage du salon et de la salle à manger avec l'hôte.
Chambres d'hôte : Partage du salon et de la salle à manger avec d'autres invités.
Séjour à la ferme : Hébergement dans une ferme en exploitation avec des activités de la ferme.
Indépendant: Hébergement privé avec cuisine, salon et salle à manger.
Suite séparée : Hébergement privé. Sans cuisine.
Maison d'hôte ou hôtel : Un style d'hébergement plus grand, souvent avec un restaurant.
Luxe: Un hébergement de plus haute qualité.

Descriptions des hébergements
Les descriptions sont écrites par les hôtes eux-mêmes. Classées par ordre alphabétique par état, puis par ville ou par région.

Petit déjeuner
Continental ou léger : Comprend habituellement des céréales, du pain ou des toasts, des fruits ou des jus de fruit, du thé ou du café.
Complet: Petit déjeuner léger plus un plat cuisiné.
Spécial : Petit déjeuner exceptionnel souvent avec plusieurs plats.
Provisions : Eléments du petit déjeuner fournis

Repas additionnels
Certains B&Bs prépareront des repas du soir sur arrangement (B/A).

Lits et chambres à coucher
Les données décrivent le nombre et la taille des lits, des chambres à coucher et le nombre d'invités qui peuvent séjourner.
Lits pour 1 personne: Simple (1 lit). Twin (2 lits simples). King twin (2 grands lits simples).
Lits pour 2 personnes: Double (petits). Queen (grands). King (très grands).

Salles de bain
Ensuite: Utilisation exclusive de votre chambre.
Privées: Utilisation exclusive dans le couloir.
Partagées: Partagées avec d'autres visiteurs.

Logos

- Piscine
- Jardin magnifique
- Vignoble ou activités vinicoles
- Restaurant
- Eco tourisme
- Activités sur site
- Accès chaise roulante
- Accueil enfant ou sur arrangement
- Animaux domestiques bienvenus
- Non fumeur
- Association B&B
- Tourisme évalué AAA
- Tourisme accrédité
- Bons de réservation B&B acceptés

Réservations
Les tarifs sont en dollars australiens pour deux personnes (double) ou 1 personne (simple) et comprennent le petit déjeuner, sauf indication contraire. Frais additionnels pour des personnes supplémentaires dans la chambre. Les tarifs varient selon la qualité, l'endroit, les équipements ou la saison et devraient être confirmés lors de la réservation. Réservez à l'avance par courrier, par e-mail ou par téléphone.

"La différence entre un hôtel et un B&B est que vous ne serrerez pas dans vos bras le personnel d'hôtel quand vous partez."

www.BBBook.com.au

15

Einleitung

Willkommen bei unserem Bed & Breakfast Buch, der beliebteste B&B-Führer Australiens, der 1989 das erste Mal erschienen ist.

Bed and Breakfasts (oder B&Bs) sind eine fantastische Unterbringungsmöglichkeit, die Ihnen die Gelegenheit bietet, die Gastfreundschaft Australiens wirklich zu genießen. Die B&B-Gastgeber sorgen dafür, dass Sie Ihren Aufenthalt genießen und viele schöne Erinnerungen mit nach Hause nehmen können. Außerdem verspricht ein B&B, außerordentliche Gastfreundschaft, ob für eine Nacht oder eine ganze Woche. Unsere B&B-Gastgeber begrüßen Sie mit ausgezeichneten Unterkünften und fantastischem Frühstück. Durch ihre Ortskenntnis können sie Ihnen hiesige Orte sowie die besten Restaurants empfehlen oder Ihnen sogar hausgemachte Speisen zubereiten.

B&Bs sind vielfältig und jedes hat seine eigene, einzigartige Atmosphäre. Einige sind einfach und heimelig, andere elegant und luxuriös. Ihr Schlafzimmer ist bequem und hat üblicherweise ein eigenes Badezimmer oder ein Badezimmer auf dem Flur, während das Frühstück üblicherweise in unseren Zimmerpreisen enthalten ist.

Privatunterkunft (Homestay): Gemeinsame Nutzung der Wohn- und Esszimmer mit dem Gastgeber.
Bed & Breakfast: Gemeinsame Nutzung der Wohn- und Esszimmer mit anderen Gästen.
Ferien auf dem Bauernhof (Farmstay): Unterkunft auf einem Bauernhof mit Aktivitäten.
Selbstversorger (Self-Contained): Private Unterkunft mit Küche, Wohn- und Esszimmer.
Separate Suite: Private Unterkunft. Keine Küche
Gästehaus oder Hotel: Größere Unterkunft, oft mit Restaurant.
Luxus: Qualitativ hochwertige Unterkunft.

Beschreibungen der Unterkünfte
Einträge werden von den Gastgebern selbst verfasst. Alphabetisch sortiert nach Staaten, dann Stadt oder Region.

Frühstück
Kontinental oder Leicht: Umfasst üblicherweise Cornflakes, Brot oder Toast, Früchte oder Fruchtsaft, Tee oder Kaffee.
Voll: Leichtes Frühstück plus gekochter Gang.
Special: Außerordentliches Frühstück, oft mit mehreren Gängen.
Lebensmittel: Frühstücksutensilien werden zur Verfügung gestellt.

Zusätzliche Mahlzeiten
Einige B&Bs bereiten nach Absprache Abendessen zu (B/A).

Betten und Schlafzimmer
Einträge zeigen die Anzahl und Größe der Betten, Schlafzimmer und Gäste, die übernachten können.
Betten für 1 Person: Einzelbett (1 Bett) Zwei Betten (2 einzelne Betten). Zwei Betten (2 große einzelne Betten).
Betten für 2 Person: Doppelbett (klein) Queen (groß). King (sehr groß).

Badezimmer

Im Zimmer: Ausschließliche Nutzung in Ihrem Schlafzimmer
Privat: Ausschließliche Nutzung eines Badezimmers im Flur.
Gemeinsame Nutzung: Gemeinsame Nutzung mit anderen Gästen.

Logos

- Swimmingpool
- Fantastischer Garten
- Weinbau oder Aktivitäten rund um den Weinbau
- Restaurant
- Öko-Tourismus
- Aktivitäten auf dem Gelände
- Rollstuhlgerecht
- Kinder willkommen oder nach Absprache
- Haustiere willkommen
- Nichtraucher
- B&B Verband
- Geprüft durch AAA Tourism
- Zertifiziert durch Tourism
- B&B Buch Gutscheine werden akzeptiert

Reservierungen

Preise sind in australischen Dollar für zwei Personen (Doppel) oder 1 Person (Einzel) und enthalten Frühstück, außer anderweitig angegeben. Zusätzliche Gebühr für zusätzliche Person im Zimmer. Preise variieren je nach Qualität, Standort, Anlage oder Jahreszeit und sollte bei Buchung bestätigt werden. Buchen Sie im Voraus per Post, E-Mail oder Telefon.

„Der Unterschied zwischen einem Hotel und einem B&B ist, dass man das Hotelpersonal bei der Abfahrt nicht umarmt.

www.BBBook.com.au

はじめに

オーストラリアで最も人気のあるB&B宿泊施設(一泊朝食付旅館)ガイドブック、ベッド・アンド・ブレックファスト・ブック(Bed & Breakfast Book)へようこそ。1989年初刊。

ベッド・アンド・ブレックファスト(B&B)は 優れた価値を提供しており、本当の意味でのオーストラリアの温かいもてなしをよく理解するには理想的な宿泊施設です。B&Bのホストは、あなたの滞在が楽しく印象に残るものであるように最大の努力を払っており、あなたの滞在期間にかかわらず上等なもてなしをお約束します。温かい歓迎、すてきな宿泊施設、素晴らしい朝食でもてなしてくれます。地元の観光スポットを提供したり、一流レストランの推薦あるいはホームメードの食事を準備してくれます。

B&B宿泊施設にはさまざまなスタイルがあり、それぞれ異なった独自の特徴があります。シンプルで家庭的なものから大きく贅沢なものまで多様です。快適なベッドルームには、通常、専用バスルームあるいはバスルームと一続きのベッドルームが付いており、宿泊料金には朝食も含まれています。

ホームステイ:ホストとリビングルームあるいはダイニングルームの共有。
ベッド・アンド・ブレックファスト:他のゲストとリビングルームやダイニングルームの共有。
ファームステイ: 家畜を飼育する労働農場での宿泊施設。
セルフコンテイン:キッチン、リビングルーム、ダイニングルーム付き専用宿泊施設。
セパレートスイート:専用宿泊施設。キッチン無。
ゲストハウスあるいはホテル:大抵、レストラン付き大型宿泊施設。
ラグジュアリー: 高級宿泊施設。

宿泊施設詳細
宿泊施設の詳細はホスト自身が記述しています。各州ごとに、市あるいは地域のアルファベット順に記載されています。

ブレックファスト
コンチネンタルあるいは軽い朝食:通常、シリアル、パンあるいはトースト、フルーツあるいはジュース、紅茶あるいはコーヒーなど。
フルブレックファスト:軽い朝食と調理したお食事コース。
スペシャル:大抵、数種類のコースが付いた特別な朝食。
食料提供:朝食の食料提供。

追加の食事
手配いただければ、夕食を提供するB&Bもあります(B/A)。

ベッドおよびベッドルーム
詳細にはベッドの数と大きさ、滞在できるベッドルーム数とゲスト数が表示されています。
一人用ベッド:シングルベッド(1ベッド)。ツインベッド(シングルベッド2台)。大型ツインベッド(大型シングルベッド2台)。
二人用ベッド:ダブルベッド(小型)。クイーンベッド(大型)。キングベッド(特大型)。

バスルーム
一続き：ご利用のベッドルームから専用で使用。
私用：廊下から専用で使用。
共有： 他のゲストと共有。

ロゴ

- スイミングプール
- 素晴らしい庭
- ぶどう酒醸造場あるいはワイン造り
- レストラン
- エコツーリズム
- 現地活動
- 車椅子乗車可
- 子供可あるいは要手配
- ペット可
- 禁煙
- B&B協会
- AAAツーリズム評価
- ツーリズム基準品質保証
- B&Bブック割引券認可

予約
二人用（ダブル）あるいは一人用（シングル）の料金はオーストラリアドルで表示されており、特に記載がない限りは朝食も含まれています。各お部屋の定員以上のゲストがご使用になる場合は、割増料金をいただきます。料金はB&Bの質、場所、施設あるいは季節によって異なりますので、ご予約の際にご確認ください。郵便、Eメールあるいは電話で事前にご予約ください。

「ホテルとB&Bの違いは、ホテルではご帰宅の際にスタッフを抱きしめることはしません。」

www.BBBook.com.au

소개

호주 1989년 첫 발간을 시작으로 한 인기 절정의 Bed & Breakfast (아침식사를 제공하는 민박집) 숙식 가이드에 어서 오십시요.

Bed and Breakfasts (B&Bs)를 통해 극진한 서비스의 진정한 호주인들의 삶의 모습을 바탕으로 친절한 대접 형태를 받게 된다. 하룻밤을 묵어도 상관이 없으며 주인네들의 진정어린 환대로 추억에 남는 여정으로 남게 될 베드 앤 브랙퍼스트는 집에서 정성이 담긴 아침식사 (이외 식사도 개별 스케줄로 가능)의 그득함과 아울러, 관광지 안내, 레스토랑 가볼만한 곳들도 정보로 아울러 받게 될 수가 있다.

B&B는 여러 스타일 형태로 제공되게 되며 단순하면서도 집 같은 정경일 수도 있고 고급스런 서비스 제공을 안내받는 곳의 형태로도 구성되게 되어 있다. 아늑한 침실 제공과 함께 욕실은 함께 사용하거나 개인 사용으로 나뉘게 되며 아침식사는 비용에 아울러 포함되게 된다.

홈스테이: 집주인과 거실, 식당을 함께 사용하는 성격의 구성.
Bed & Breakfast: 다른 숙식객과 거실, 식당을 공용 스타일로서 구성된다.
Farmstay: 농장일을 도와 주며 숙식을 제공하는 스타일.
Self-Contained (호별 독립식): 개인 전용의 주방, 거실, 식당 스타일.
Separate Suite (독립 스위트): 개인 전용, 주방 없음.
Guesthouse (고급 하숙집), 호텔: 레스토랑이 겸용된 대형 숙박식의 제공.
Luxury (고급): 고급 숙박식 제공 형태.

숙식 정보
집주인들로부터 직접 정보 제공의 형태로서 주, 도시 (지역)별로 알파벳 순으로 정연되어 있다.

아침식사
Continental (컨티넨탈), Light (경식): 콘 후레이크, 빵 (토스트), 과일 쥬스, 차, 커피가 제공된다.
Full (풀): 아침식사와 더불어 정식 코스를 제공한다.
스페셜: 코스로 이루어진 스페셜 형태의 아침식사.
제공: 아침식사 공급.

기타 식사 제공
B&Bs 중에서 저녁 식사를 따로 요청시 제공하는 곳도 있다 (B/A).

침대, 침실 구조
숙식인 명수, 침실 침대 갯수, 크기를 제공하는 정보가 담겨 있다.
1인 침대: 싱글 (침대 1). 트윈 (싱글 베드2). 킹 트윈 (2개의 대형 싱글베드).
2인용 침대: 더블 (소형). 퀸 (대형). 킹 (최대형).

욕실
스위트: 개인 침실 전용.
Private (개인용): 복도 위치 전용.
Shared (공용): 기타 숙식인과 공용 형태.

로고

- 🏊 수영장
- 🌼 근사한 정경의 가든
- 🍇 와인 양조장, 와인 공정
- 🍴 레스토랑
- 👁 생태학 관광
- 🧍 현장 활동
- ♿ 휠체어 전용
- 👪 어린이 참가 (개별 일정요)
- 🐕 애완동물 반입 가능
- 🚭 금연
- B&B 협회
- ★★★★★ **AAA Tourism** (관광사업) 사정
- ✓ **Tourism** (관광사업) 공인
- **B&B Book** 상품권 수령함

예약

호주달러 사용. 2인 (더블), 1인 (싱글)이 기본이며 아침식사가 포함
(예외의 경우 따로 안내)되는 요금율. 추가인의 경우 따로 차지가 되며
등급별, 위치별, 설치물 형태별로 요율의 형태가 달라지게 됨 – 예약시
안내 되게 되며 우편, 이메일, 전화로 예약이 가능하다.

" 베드엔브랙퍼스트가 호텔과 틀린 점 하나– 떠날 때의 잊지못할 포옹담
긴 정겨운 인사."

www.BBBook.com.au

简介

欢迎使用 Bed & Breakfast（《早餐住宿指南》）一书，这是澳大利亚最受欢迎的早餐民宿指南第一版于 1989 年出版。

Bed and Breakfasts（或 B&B）具有极为重要的价值，是感受真正的澳大利亚盛情的理想方式B&B 主人致力于确保您的入住令人愉快且值得纪念，并承诺提供最高级的殷勤招待，无论您住一晚或一周他们提供热情扬溢的欢迎、愉快的住宿和极好的早餐他们可以建议参观当地的好地方、建议最好的餐馆，甚或准备烹调的家庭美食

B&B 住宿包括各种形式，每种形式都有唯一不同的特色一些形式简单、平常，另一些形式则豪华、奢侈您的卧室通常很舒适，带有私人或套房浴室，早餐通常包含在房价内。

在当地居民家居住：和主人共用客厅或餐厅。
住宿和早餐：和其他客人共用客厅或餐厅。
农场住宿：在经营各种农场活动的农场住宿。
自主式：配备厨房、客厅和就餐区域的私人住宿
单独的套房：私人住宿无厨房。
宾馆或酒店：通常有餐馆的较大地方的住处。
华贵：较高品质的住宿。

住宿描述

所有项目均由主人自己编写按州、市或地区的字母顺序排列

早餐

欧陆式早餐或西式早餐：通常包括谷类食品、面包或烤面包片、水果或果汁、茶或咖啡。
全套早餐：西式早餐加上一道炒菜。
特别早餐：通常有几道菜的特别早餐
自助早餐：提供各种早餐供应品。

其它膳食

某些 B&B 将根据安排 (B/A) 准备夜宵

床和卧室

目录会显示床数与大小、可以入住的卧室及房客人数。
单人床数：单人房（1 张床）双人房（2 张单人床）超大双人房（2 张大单人床）。
两人床数：双人房（小床）大号房（大床）特大号房（最大床）

浴室

套房：从您的卧室专门使用。
私人：专用走廊。
共用：与其他客人共用。

标志

🏊 游泳池
❀ 美丽的花园
🍇 葡萄酒厂或葡萄酒活动
🍴 餐馆
☙ 生态旅游
🚶 现场活动
♿ 轮椅使用者进出
👫 儿童欢迎或根据安排
🐕 宠物欢迎
🚭 禁止吸烟
🐝 B&B 协会
★★★★★ AAA Tourism 经过 AAA Tourism 评定
✅ 通过旅游质量认证
B&B 获得 B&B 书籍凭证认可

订房

用澳大利亚元提供的是双人（双人房）或单人（单房）房价，并包括早餐，除非另外指明对客房中的其他人额外收费房价会根据品质、位置、设施或季节有变化，应该在预订时确认通过邮件、电子邮件或电话提前预订

"酒店和 B&B 之间的差别是，您在离开时无需拥抱酒店人员。"

www.BBBook.com.au

Introducción

Bienvenido a The Bed and Breakfast Book, la Guía más popular de Alojamiento B&B en Australia. Publicado por primera vez en 1989.

Los establecimientos de 'Alojamiento y Desayuno' (en adelante B&B, del inglés Bed and Breakfast) tienen un precio muy interesante y son la manera ideal de disfrutar de la autentica hospitalidad de Australia. El compromiso de los dueños de los B&Bs es asegurar que su estancia es a la vez agradable y memorable, y le prometen una hospitalidad de primera calidad, tanto si se aloja por una noche o como una semana. Ofrecen una calurosa bienvenida, estupendo alojamiento y fantasticos desayunos. Pueden sugerir maravillosos lugares para visitar, recomendar los mejores restaurantes o incluso preparar una comida casera.

Los alojamientos de B&B incluyen una variedad de estilos, cada uno con características singulares. Algunos son sencillos y acogedores; otros son esplendidos y lujosos. La habitación será comoda, normalmente con baño privado o en suite, y el desayuno generalmente está incluido en el precio.

Alojamiento en Casa (Homestay): Los huéspedes comparten la sala de estar y el comedor con los dueños de la casa.
Alojamiento y Desayuno (Bed & Breakfast): Los huéspedes comparten la sala de estar y el comedor con otros huéspedes.
Alojamiento en Granja (Farmstay): Alojamiento generalmente en una granja en funcionamiento con actividades agropecuarias.
Alojamiento con todos los Servicios (Self-Contained): Alojamiento privado con cocina y zonas de comedor y de estar.
Habitación Independiente (Separate Suite): Alojamiento privado. Sin cocina.
Casa de Huéspedes u Hotel (Guesthouse or Hotel): Alojamiento de mayores proporciones, frequentemente con servicio de restaurante.
Lujoso (Luxury): Alojamiento de calidad superior.

Descripción del Alojamiento
Las entradas de la Guía han sido redactadas por los propios dueños del alojamiento. Están ordenadas alfabéticamente por estado y después por ciudad o región.

Desayuno
Continental o Ligero (Continental or Light): Normalmente incluye cereales, pan o tostadas, fruta o zumo de frutas, y té o café.
Completo (Full): Un desayuno ligero más un plato caliente.
Especial (Special): Un desayuno excepcional, frecuentemente con varios platos.
Provisiones (Provisions): Se suministran provisiones para el desayuno.

Comidas Extras
Algunos B&Bs preparan cenas por encargo (B/A, "by arrangement" en inglés).

Camas y Habitaciones
Las entradas muestran el número de camas y su tamaño, el número de habitaciones y los huéspedes que pueden alojarse.
Camas para 1 persona: "Single" (1 cama); "Twin" (2 camas individuales); "King twin" (2 camas individuales grandes).
Camas para 2 personas: "Double" (mediana), "Queen" (grande) o "King" (muy grande).

Cuartos de Baño

Baño en suite (Ensuite): Uso exclusivo con acceso desde dentro de la habitación.
Baño privado (Private): Uso exclusivo con acceso desde el hall.
Baño compartido (Shared bathroom):   Compartido con otros huéspedes.

Logos

- Piscina
- Fantástico Jardín
- Bodega o actividades de vinos
- Restaurante
- Ecoturismo
- Actividades in situ
- Acceso para silla de ruedas
- Niños bienvenidos o con previo aviso
- Animales domésticos bienvenidos
- Prohibido fumar
- Asociación de B&B
- Evaluado por AAA Turismo (organismo nacional de los clubes de automov ilismo de Australia)
- Autorizado por Turismo
- Se aceptan Vales de Descuento de B&B Book

Reservas

Los precios se ofrecen en dólares australianos para 2 personas (habitación doble) o para 1 persona (habitación sencilla) e incluyen el desayuno, salvo que se indique lo contrario. Hay un cargo adicional por personas extras en la habitación. Las tarifas varían según la calidad del alojamiento, la localización, los servicios ofrecidos y la temporada, y es aconsejable confirmarlos al reservar. Haga su reserva por adelantado por correo postal, correo electrónico o teléfono.

"La diferencia entre un hotel y un B&B es que no das un abrazo al personal del hotel cuando te marchas."

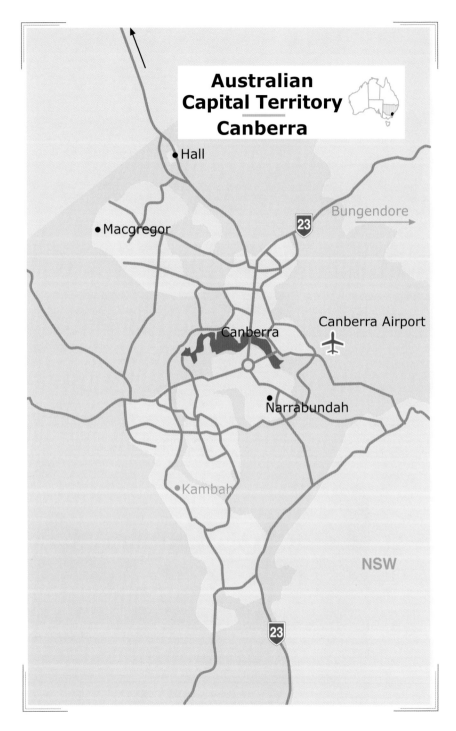

Australian
Capital Territory
Canberra

Hall

Macgregor

Bungendore

23

Canberra Airport

Canberra

Narrabundah

Kambah

NSW

23

Canberra - Hall

Surveyor's Hill Winery and B&B *B&B & Farmstay & Self Contained House*

Leigh Hobba
215 Brooklands Road
Wallaroo (near Hall)
NSW 2618
25 km N of Canberra

Tel (02) 6230 2046
or 0400 564 050
survhill@westnet.com.au
www.survhill.com.au

Double $145 Single $100
Children $20
Full breakfast
Dinner $65 for 3 courses including wine
Self catering & long stay discounts
Visa MC accepted
2 Queen 1 Double (2 bdrm) plus sofa bed
Bathrooms: 1 Private

B&B and Farmstay, in 1930 farmstead, 230 acre property with vineyards & olives, overlooking Murrumbidgee River, Brindabella Ranges. Easy drive to central Canberra. Guests enjoy exclusive use of the cottage, fully private, self contained, separate from hosts' residence. Open fire in loungeroom, electric heaters in all rooms ensure cosy warmth. Gourmet meals featuring farm and local produce and premium wines provided in cottage dining room. Excellent kitchen enables self catering. Generously discounted long stay and self catering rates are negotiable.

Canberra - Narrabundah

Narrabundah B&B *B&B & Homestay*

John & Esther Davies
5 Mosman Place
Narrabundah
ACT 2604
3 km SE of Parliament House

Tel (02) 6295 2837
or 0419 276 231
info@narbb.com
www.narbb.com

Double $120 Single $100
Continental breakfast
Dinner $40pp by arrangement
Discounts for stays of 4 days or more
Visa MC accepted
1 King/Twin (1 bdrm)
Bathrooms: 1 Ensuite

Comfortable, renovated home in quiet street. Conveniently located in relation to Canberra's main tourist attractions, such as Parliament House, National Gallery and War Memorial. Short drive to restaurants in Manuka. Close to public transport and to train station and airport. Air-conditioned (heating and cooling). Hosts are semi-retired and interests include history, genealogy, computing, music, gardening and embroidery. Miniature poodle in residence.

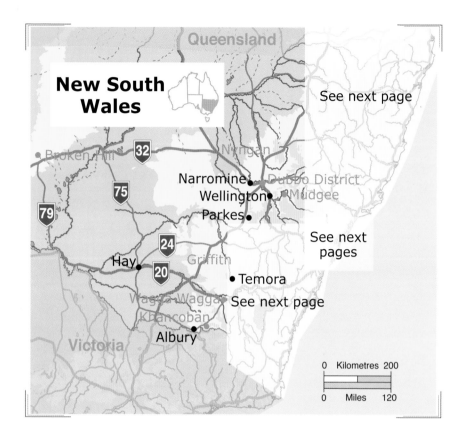

New South Wales

See next page

Broken Hill • ⟨32⟩ Nyngan

Narromine• Dubbo District
⟨75⟩ Wellington• Mudgee
Parkes•

⟨79⟩ See next
pages
⟨24⟩ Griffith
Hay• ⟨20⟩
• Temora
Wagga Wagga See next page
Khancoban
Victoria Albury•

0 Kilometres 200
0 Miles 120

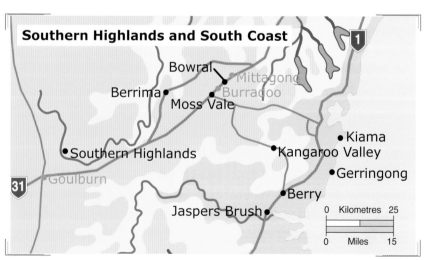

Southern Highlands and South Coast ⟨1⟩

Bowral
Mittagong
Berrima• Burradoo
Moss Vale

•Kiama
•Southern Highlands •Kangaroo Valley
•Gerringong
⟨31⟩ Goulburn
•Berry
Jaspers Brush• 0 Kilometres 25
0 Miles 15

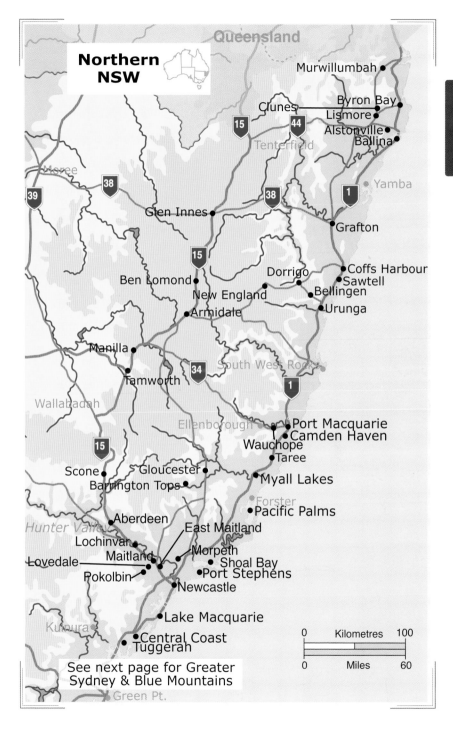

Northern NSW

Queensland

Murwillumbah
Clunes
Byron Bay
Lismore
Alstonville
Ballina
Tenterfield
Yamba
Moree
Glen Innes
Grafton
Coffs Harbour
Dorrigo
Sawtell
Ben Lomond
Bellingen
New England
Urunga
Armidale
Manilla
South West Rocks
Tamworth
Wallabadah
Ellenborough
Port Macquarie
Camden Haven
Wauchope
Taree
Scone
Gloucester
Myall Lakes
Barrington Tops
Forster
Pacific Palms
Aberdeen
East Maitland
Hunter Valley
Lochinvar
Morpeth
Lovedale
Maitland
Shoal Bay
Pokolbin
Port Stephens
Newcastle
Kurri
Lake Macquarie
Central Coast
Tuggerah

See next page for Greater
Sydney & Blue Mountains

Green Pt.

0   Kilometres   100
0   Miles   60

29

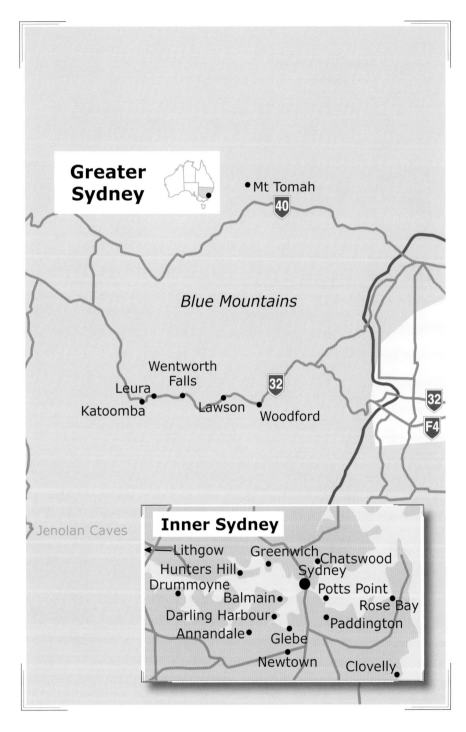

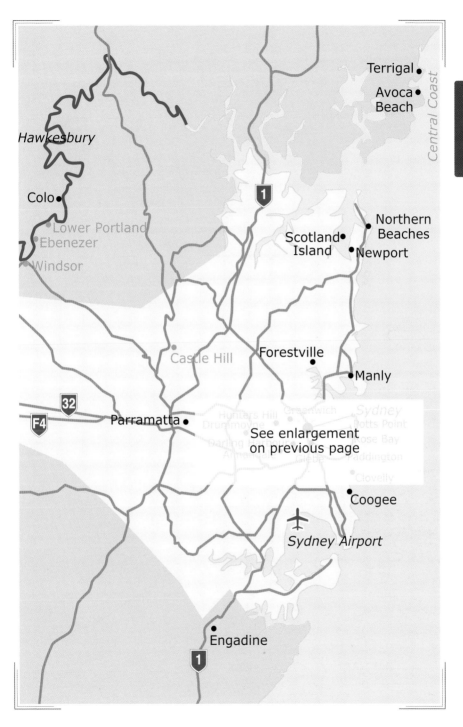

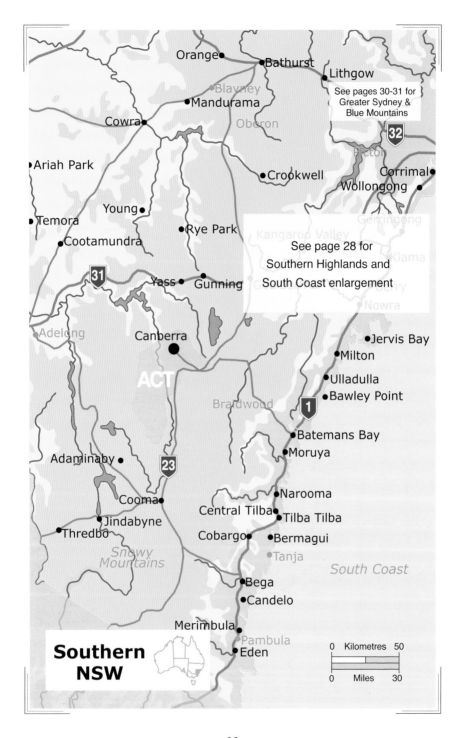

Orange
Bathurst
Lithgow
Blayney
See pages 30-31 for
Greater Sydney &
Blue Mountains
Mandurama
Oberon
Cowra
Picton
Ariah Park
Crookwell
Corrimal
Wollongong
Young
Gerringong
Temora
Rye Park
Kangaroo Valley
See page 28 for
Southern Highlands and
South Coast enlargement
Kiama
Cootamundra
Yass
Gunning
Nowra
Adelong
Canberra
Jervis Bay
Milton
ACT
Ulladulla
Bawley Point
Braidwood
Batemans Bay
Moruya
Adaminaby
Narooma
Central Tilba
Tilba Tilba
Cooma
Cobargo
Bermagui
Jindabyne
Thredbo
Tanja
South Coast
Snowy
Mountains
Bega
Candelo
Merimbula
Pambula
**Southern
NSW**
Eden

0   Kilometres   50

0   Miles   30

Get $50 off a 5 day rental with Avis

Rent a Group C (e.g Holden Astra) or above for 5 days or more
from the locations listed and you will receive $50 off the total time
and kilometre charges. Valid until 20th December 2008.
Please quote coupon number MPLA027.

Details and the offer is available from:

Artarmon	(02) 9439 3733	Ryde	(02) 9809 7577
Ashfield	(02) 9716 7052	Star City	(02) 9660 7666
Bankstown	(02) 9792 1714	Sydney Airport	(02) 8374 2847
Circular Quay	(02) 9241 1281	Taren Point	(02) 9540 1088
Hornsby	(02) 9489 7111	World Square	(02) 9261 0750
Kings Cross	(02) 9357 2000		
Parramatta	(02) 9630 5877		

AVIS

We try harder.

For all other bookings please call Avis Reservations on 136 333

Adaminaby - Selwyn Snowfields

Selwyn is the perfect place to learn to ski or snowboard with it's gentle progressing terrain and caring mountain staff. Our family friendly atmosphere will make you and your family feel right at home. With so much to do there's something for the whole family including skiing, snow boarding, snow tubing, tobogganing, or just playing in the snow!

In summer, after the snow has melted you can go horse trekking in the Kosciuszko National Park.
Roslyn Rudd, Reynella Homestead

∼

Adaminaby - Snowy Mountains

Reynella Homestead *Farmstay & Ski Lodge, Homestead*
Roslyn & John Rudd
669 Kingston Road
Reynella, Adaminaby
NSW 2629
5 km E of Adaminaby

Tel (02) 6454 2386 or 1800 029 909
Fax (02) 64542 2530
reynella@snowy.net.au
www.reynellarides.com.au

Single $115
Children on application
Full breakfast
Full three course dinner included
Lodge $115pp
Homestead (Horse treks) $95pp
Visa MC Diners Amex Eftpos accepted
2 King 1 Queen 4 Double 10 Twin 23 Single (19 bdrm)
Lodge style accommodation/shared bathrooms
Bathrooms: 5 Guest share

 AAA Tourism
 ★★★

Lodge accommodation on working sheep and cattle property - opportunities for some involvement. Largest horse trekking operation in Kosciuszko National Park. Operating from October to May. Stay in The Homestead only $95 per person, minimum 4 persons. Stay at the Ski Lodge in the winter only $115 per person, includes 3 course dinner. Ideal base for Skiing Accommodation. Superb food. BYO. Local fishing, bush walking, riding instruction. (Summer). Original operators - 36 years. Visit our website for dates and rates for treks.

Albury

Elizabeth's Manor *Luxury B&B & Self Contained House*
Larry & Betty Kendall
531 Lyne Street
Lavington, North Albury
NSW 2641
1.5 km W of North Albury PO

Tel (02) 6040 4412
Fax (02) 6040 5166
bookins@elizabethsmanor.com.au
www.elizabethsmanor.com.au

Double $160-$170 Single $130-$140
Children $22
Full breakfast
Dinner $44-$55
Visa MC Diners Amex Eftpos accepted
3 Queen 1 Double (3 bdrm)
Bathrooms: 3 Ensuite

AAA Tourism
★★★★★

Elizabeth's Manor would have to be the most luxurious and romantic adults only accommodation in Australia. On arrival guests will be presented with complimentary sparkling wine and chocolates. A gourmet breakfast can be served in your suite or the Gallery. Although we have a 'No Smoking' policy in the house, smoking is permitted anywhere outside. We also have a late check-out, twelve PM, a good excuse to try our new outside 'Therapeutic' heated spa.

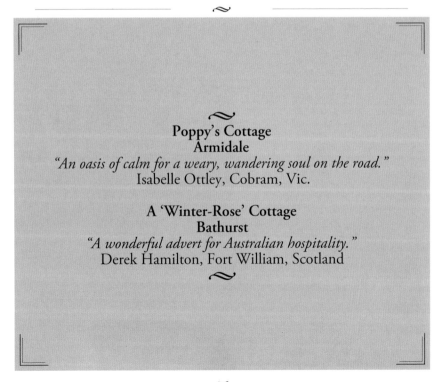

Poppy's Cottage
Armidale
"An oasis of calm for a weary, wandering soul on the road."
Isabelle Ottley, Cobram, Vic.

A 'Winter-Rose' Cottage
Bathurst
"A wonderful advert for Australian hospitality."
Derek Hamilton, Fort William, Scotland

Alstonville - Ballina

Hume's Hovell *Luxury B&B & Separate Suites* 🏊 ❀ 🧍 ♿ 👫 AAA Tourism ★★★★☆ 🏡
Peter & Suzanne Hume
333 Dalwood Road
Alstonville
NSW 2477
8 km S of Alstonville

Tel (02) 6629 5371
Fax (02) 6629 5471
stay@humes-hovell.com
www.bed-and-breakfast.com.au

Double $165-$231 Single $115-$160
Children $25
Full breakfast
Dinner $35-$45
Visa MC accepted
2 King/Twin2 King 3 Single (3 bdrm)
Bathrooms: 3 Ensuite 1 Private

'Hume's Hovell, one of the State's Best Short Break destinations' - NRMA Open Road Magazine review. Located south of Byron Bay, in the rolling green hills above Ballina, Hume's Hovell provides fine boutique accommodation amidst the trees of a Macadamia Plantation.

Spacious suites provide maximum privacy with luxurious comfort, featuring King size beds, air-conditioning, cosy lounges, TV/CD/DVD, guest toiletries, and special soaps. The Plantation Spa Suite is wheelchair friendly. Enjoy afternoon tea on arrival, plus complementary macadamias, plunger coffee, various teas, and chocolates in your suite.

Our rates include sumptuous breakfasts, afternoon tea, and in the evening savouries and pre-dinner drinks. Guests can then choose from dining at local restaurants, by candlelight in your suite or in the Poolside Pavilion (with prior arrangement). BBQs and Seafood Platters are other delicious popular alternatives.

Enjoy the beautiful beaches and World Heritage Wilderness Areas, stroll the country lanes, play tennis, swim in the salt-water pool, visit local galleries and markets. Do it all - or do nothing. For a secluded honeymoon, a place to unwind, or simply overnight, Suzanne and Peter will welcome you warmly.

Armidale

Armidale is set high on the Northern Tablelands halfway between Sydney and Brisbane. Mild summers, glorious autumn colours, soft, colourful springs and crisp winter days with occasional snowfalls provide many opportunities for seasonal activities.

Enjoy bushwalking in National Parks, horse riding, trout fishing, golfing, scenic helicopter flights and waterfalls. Wander through museums, galleries, Cathedrals, restaurants and coffee shops.
Marg Hadfield

~

Armidale

Poppys Cottage *B&B & Farmstay & Cottage, no kitchen*
Jake & Poppy Abbott
Malvern Hill
Dangarsleigh Road, Armidale
NSW 2350
6 km S of Armidale

Tel (02) 6775 1277
or 0412 153 819
Fax (02) 6775 1308
poppyscottage@bluepin.net.au
http://poppyscottage.com.au

Double $140 **Single** $110
Children $45
Special breakfast
Dinner $55 (3 course candlelit dinner
with complimentary bottle of wine)
Cot available
2 Double 2 Single (2 bdrm) main + ensuite: second = 2singles+dbl sofabed
Bathrooms: 1 Ensuite 1 Private

Armidale Award Winning B&B - an unforgettable warm, friendly, farmstay experience awaits you in this romantic, cosy atmosphere only 6km from historic Armidale. Nestled in enchanting cottage garden with friendly company of personality farm animals, the free-standing cottage allows guests to enjoy private ensuite accommodation. Beautiful gourmet breakfasts enjoyed beneath canopy of fruit trees, are a speciality. Option of delicious and intimate candlelit dinner with complimentary bottle of wine. Relax; enjoy country hospitality at its best: "warm, friendly and generous". Magnificent waterfalls nearby.

Armidale

Armidale Boutique Accommodation *Luxury Self Contained Cottages (3)*
Tracy & David Everett
134 Brown Street
Armidale
NSW 2350
0.5 km SW of Town Centre

Tel (02) 6772 5276
or 0402 058 504
Fax (02) 6772 5768
Tracy@ArmidaleBnB.com.au
www.ArmidaleBnB.com.au

Double $130-$200
Provisions first night
Extra person $45-$50
Visa MC Amex accepted
3 Queen 2 Double 2 Single (6 bdrm)
Belltrees: 3B/R; Camellia Court: 2B/R; The Elms: 1B/R
Bathrooms: 1 Private (1 in each cottage), Belltrees: 2nd separate toilet

AAA Tourism
★★★★

Three unique and very stylish self-contained properties, situated in the heart of Armidale. The cottages are provided with reverse-cycle air conditioning, "Belltrees" (our beautiful heritage property) also has a wood fire. Each kitchen is exceptionally well equipped and includes a quiet dishwasher. "Camellia Court" is contemporary in design and style, complete with leather lounges and a fabulous north-facing deck - wheelchair friendly too. "The Elms" is charmingly private with its own small garden protected from the elements, and is perfect for a single or couple.

Ballina

Landfall *B&B & Homestay*
Gaye & Roger Ibbotson
109 Links Avenue
East Ballina
NSW 2478
3 km N of East Ballina

Tel (02) 6686 7555
or 0428 642 077
Fax (02) 6686 7377
landfall@spot.com.au
www.bbbook.com.au/landfall.html

Double $100 Single $60
Full breakfast
Visa MC accepted
1 Queen 2 Single (2 bdrm)
Bathrooms: 1 Guest share

"Landfall" You're welcome in our home.

This home was the residence of Captain Tom Martin and his wife, Marjorie; he named this home "Landfall" when he retired to Ballina after many years at sea. "Landfall" is situated in East Ballina overlooking the golf course. You are invited to relax in our courtyard with its indoor solar heated pool and spa. "Landfall" is a "non smoking" home. We offer you friendly hospitality. The main part of our home is air conditioned as is the Queen Bedroom. Your hosts Gaye and Roger Ibbotson.

Ballina

The Yabsley B&B *B&B*
Judee Whittaker & David Clark
5 Yabsley Street
East Ballina
NSW 2478
3 km NE of Ballina

Tel (02) 6681 1505
or 0407 811 505
Fax (02) 6681 1505
yabsley@bigpond.com
www.yabsley.com.au

Double $135 Single $120
Full breakfast
Dinner 3 courses - $40pp
Visa MC accepted
2 Queen (2 bdrm)
Bathrooms: 2 Private

AAA Tourism
★★★★☆

The Yabsley is a two minute walk to Lighthouse Beach, Richmond River and Shaws Bay Lagoon. Also within easy walking distance to a hotel, a resort and three restaurants. The house has been refurbished and contains private guest suites, guest lounge and delightful courtyards. Watch the whales and dolphins or play tennis and golf. East Ballina gives access to day trips to Byron Bay, the Border Ranges or the Gold Coast. You can negotiate a superb meal of your choice cooked by David who specialises in seafood cuisine. Unfortunately we cannot cater for children.

Ballina

Brundah B&B *Luxury B&B*
Ros & Mal Lewis
37 Norton Street
Ballina
NSW 2478
In Centre of Ballina

Tel (02) 6686 8166
Fax (02) 6686 8164
stay@brundah.com.au
www.brundah.com.au

Double $189-$215
Single $145-$185
Full breakfast
Visa MC Diners Amex accepted
3 Queen 1 Single (3 bdrm)
Bathrooms: 3 Ensuite

AAA Tourism
★★★★☆

Brundah B&B . . . an elegant National Trust Heritage Home (circa 1908), set on half an acre of peaceful and secluded gardens. Take the time to sip afternoon tea or a cool drink on the wide verandahs, utilise the guest library, lounge or dining rooms all tastefully furnished for your comfort. Enjoy a large gourmet breakfast and on arrival complimentary afternoon tea or glass of wine. A short stroll will take you to the town centre, restaurants, river or beaches. Three Queen rooms each with ensuites. Hosts: Mal & Ros Lewis.

Batemans Bay

Chalet Swisse Spa *B&B & Guest House & Self Contained*
Herbert & Elizabeth Mayer
676 The Ridge Road
Surf Beach, Batemans Bay
NSW 2536
10 km S of Batemans Bay

Tel (02) 4471 3671
Fax (02) 4471 1671
info@chaletswissespa.com.au
www.chaletswissespa.com.au

Double $120-$295 Single $90-$255
Children $40
Continental breakfast
S/C cabins incl. linen $120-$245
Visa MC Diners Amex Eftpos accepted
2 King 6 Queen 9 Double 2 Twin
9 Single (17 bdrm) Deluxe 4.5*
2 King 6 Queen Lodge
Bathrooms: 17 Ensuite

AAA Tourism
★★★★

Situated on top of 'Hero's Hill' above Surf Beach our 85 ac Retreat & Health Spa offers you:- our own mineral spring water, fresh clean air, tranquillity, 120 degree ocean views from our Café-verandah, visits by birds and wallabies. Facilities: Indoor heated pool (28 degrees C), Spa, revitalising therapies and massages, rainforest walks, tennis, table tennis, archery. Guest lounge with large open fireplace, games corner. Friendly, widely travelled hosts. A place for you to relax, wind down and get pampered.

~

Bathurst

Bathurst is Australia's oldest inland city with many significant historic buildings. Vineyards, orchards and farms provide the region with fine food and wine. The Sommerville Collection is regarded as one of the top three collections of fossils, palaeontologic specimens and gemmology in the world.

Bathurst is an ideal base for exploring the Central West being about an hours drive from the Blue Mountains, Jenolan Caves, Cowra, Orange and many historic goldmining villages. Lyn Boshier, Elm Tree Cottage

Bathurst

Elm Tree Cottage *B&B & Self Contained House*

Lyn Boshier
270 Keppel Street
Bathurst
NSW 2795
In Bathurst

Tel (02) 6334 4844
elmtree@ix.net.au
www.bathurstheritage.com.au

Double $143-$165
Single $132-$143
Children $33
Breakfast by arrangement
3 adults $187-$198
Weekly rates on request
Visa MC Amex accepted
1 Queen 2 Single (1 bdrm)
Bathrooms: 1 Ensuite

Quiet and peaceful yet close to town Elm Tree Cottage offers warm country hospitality in the privacy of your own self contained cottage. Set in a beautiful garden, the sun streams in through french windows, Freshly brewed coffee and tea can be enjoyed in the walled garden overlooking the hills while the fountain plays gently in the background.

~

Bathurst

A Winter-Rose Cottage B&B *B&B & Cottage, no kitchen*

Anne Marie & Stewart Craine
79 Morrisset Street
Bathurst
NSW 2795
In Bathurst

Tel (02) 6332 2661
or 0428 455 540
Fax (02) 6334 3322
stay@winter-rose.com.au
www.winter-rose.com.au

Double $100-$120 **Single** $100
Full breakfast
Dinner from $25 B/A
Extra person $25 per night
Visa MC Diners Amex JCB accepted
3 Queen 1 Twin 2 Single (4 bdrm)
Bathrooms: 3 Ensuite 1 Private

Winter - Rose Cottage is the ideal base for touring the Central West for comfortable stays: guests with dogs, business stop-overs, and especially suitable for women travellers (get spoilt). You may choose from a cosy room in the main B&B or stay in the Cottage set in the lovely cottage-style garden (kitchenette available for extended stays). We use home grown products and home made jams for breakfast which you may eat by the wood fire in winter or in the garden in summer.

Bawley Point

Interludes at Bawley *B&B & Guest House*

Sandra Worth & Ken Purves
103 Forster Drive
Bawley Point
NSW 2539
26 km S of Ulladulla

Tel (02) 4457 1494
or 0418 665 735
interludes@bigblue.net.au
www.interludes.com.au

Double $130-$190
Full breakfast
Dinner by prior arrangement
Visa MC accepted
3 Queen (3 bdrm)
Bathrooms: 2 Ensuite 1 Private

Set in 26 acres of coastal bushland, Interludes boasts magnificent panoramic ocean views. Be lulled to sleep by the murmur of the sea and waken to a dazzling ocean sunrise, morning birdsong and the rustle of leaves in the trees. Enjoy the unsurpassed beauty of local beaches. Swimming, surfing, snorkelling, fishing or boating are all activities available to the energetic. Finish the day with a romantic candlelit dinner for two, enhanced by silvery moonlight gleaming on the water to the background song of the sea.

Bega Valley - Bemboka

Giba Gunyah Country Cottages *B&B & Farmstay & Self Contained House*

John and Ros Raward
224 Polacks Flat Road
Bemboka
NSW 2550
8 km E of Bemboka

Tel (02) 6492 8404
or 0438 674 449
Fax (02) 6492 8404
ggunyah@yahoo.com.au
www.gibagunyah.com.au

Double $140-$160
Family with 3 children $150
Full provisions
2 course dinner + wine on request $35pp
1 King/Twin 1 Queen 1 Twin (2 bdrm)
2 bedrooms in each cottage
Bathrooms: 2 Private 1 cottage has disabled access

AAA Tourism
★★★☆

Giba Gunyah cottages are perfect for that romantic weekend escape for two or for a longer, more relaxed family break. Set in more than thirty hectares of bush and rolling dairy farmland are two charming cottages furnished in country style. Cottages have 2 bedrooms, large bathroom, country kitchen, wheel-chair access, log fires, secluded fenced gardens, stunning views and prolific bird life. All linen is supplied and special little touches are provided to delight you. Your canine guests will love exploring new spaces, smells, and river.

Bellingen

Rivendell *B&B*

Janet Hosking
10 -12 Hyde Street
Bellingen
NSW 2454
0.2 km E of Bellingen

Tel (02) 6655 0060
or 0403 238 409
Fax (02) 6655 0060
rivendell@midcoast.com.au
www.rivendellguesthouse.com.au

Double $130-$150
Single $110-$150
Full breakfast
Visa MC Eftpos accepted
3 Queen 2 Twin (4 bdrm)
Bathrooms: 3 Ensuite 1 Private

 AAA Tourism ★★★★

In the heart of historic Bellingen, Rivendell is a beautifully decorated Federation home. Luxurious rooms furnished with antiques, fluffy bathrobes, open to shady verandahs and picturesque gardens. Take a refreshing dip in the freshwater pool, or in winter, relax by the log fire. After dinner enjoy complimentary port and chocolates. TV, stereo, books, games, magazines and tea/coffee making is provided in the guest lounge. "Lovely stay, fab food and cosy accommodation -we will be back! Thank you" Justin & Caroline UK.

~

Bellingen

Bellingen Heritage Cottages *Luxury Self Contained Cottage*

Gail & Gus Raymond
7 William Street
Bellingen
NSW 2454
0.25 km W of PO

Tel (02) 6655 1311
or 0428 551 311
Fax (02) 6655 1311
graymond@bigpond.net.au
www.auntylils.com.au

Double $150-$160
Single $140
Continental provisions
$25 extra person
1 King/Twin 2 Queen (3 bdrm)
Bathrooms: 1 Private

Aunty Lil's Cottage was built by the Raymond family circa 1910 and lovingly restored to the period with all comforts of home and beyond. Enjoy fascinating family memorabilia. Lots of pillows and feather doonas and warm cosy atmosphere. In heart of Bellingen in quiet street. Self contained - including lounge, dining, full kitchen, 3 bedrooms, bathroom, laundry and verandahs front and back. Cottage garden/off street parking. Minutes walking distance to Heritage and craft shops, restaurants, Bellinger River, Markets, and attractions. TV, DVD, VCR, sound system.

Bellingen - Urunga

Aquarelle Bed & Breakfast *Luxury B&B*

Helen & John
152 Osprey Drive
Urunga
NSW 2455
6.5 km S of Urunga

Tel (02) 6655 3174
or 0427 553 174
info@aquarelle.com.au
www.aquarelle.com.au

Double $135-$165
Single $115-$140
Full breakfast
Dinner winter months by prior
arrangement only
Visa MC Eftpos accepted
1 King/Twin 1 Queen (2 bdrm)
Bathrooms: 2 Ensuite

 AAA Tourism ★★★★☆

Aquarelle's two peaceful, elegant A/C suites suit the discerning traveller. Tall forests and a waterlily-covered lake surround the contemporary property, ensuring total privacy. Folding glass doors let you bring the outdoors into your private sitting room - gourmet breakfast accompanied by the call of the whip bird is an inspirational way to start your day. Fresh seasonal produce features on your daily breakfast menu, and we cater for special dietary requirements. "Sensational, refreshing and cleansing - we had an excellent stay." T & NE, Wagga Wagga.

Bermagui and Wallaga Lake

Bermagui offers the delights of a true Australian beachside holiday. Rock-pools to explore and safe beaches and swimming in our unique rock pool. Enticing and invigorating walks long enough to exhaust the liveliest youngster. Climb Mt. Dromedary to experience the stunning views from the summit.

The waterways of the Bermagui River, Wallaga Lake and Cuttagee Lake provide tranquil waters for fishing, boating, sailing, canoeing and a whole host of other water related activities.

Bev Bray

Bermagui

Bellbird Cottage *B&B*
Laurel & Edwin Lloyd-Jones
88 Nutleys Creek Road
Bermagui
NSW 2546
32 km S of Narooma

Tel (02) 6493 5511
or 0403 772 392
Fax (02) 6493 5511
bellbird@asitis.net.au
www.bellbirdcottage-bnb.com

Double $140 Single $110
Children $20-$40
Full breakfast
2 Queen 1 Twin (3 bdrm)
Bathrooms: 2 Ensuite
Twin room needs to share parent's bathroom

Tucked into a majestic spotted gum forest, Bellbird Cottage is a bird-lover's paradise allowing tranquil privacy. Close to local fresh fish and oysters, cafés, restaurants, wineries, galleries, golf, fishing, walks and beaches. Two comfortable suites with private entrances. Library: own sitting room/library with open fire and attic bedroom for 2 children. Courtyard: large suite opening to garden. Heaters, fans, electric blankets, refrigerators, TVs/videos. Home-baked afternoon tea. Full breakfast includes local produce. We share our home with a small dog. A warm welcome is assured.

Berrima

Berrima Guest House *B&B & Self Contained Apartment*
Wendy & Michael Roodbeen
Cnr Oxley & Wilkinson Streets
Berrima
NSW 2577
In Berrima

Tel (02) 4877 2277
Fax (02) 4877 2345
hillside@hinet.net.au
www.berrimaguesthouse.com

Double $160-$225
Single $120-$225
Full breakfast
Cottage $330-$420
Visa MC Eftpos accepted
1 King/Twin 5 Queen (6 bdrm)
Bathrooms: 6 Ensuite

 AAA Tourism
★★★★☆

Overlooking the historic Southern Highlands picturesque village of Berrima. Built around the original stone cottage tack room stables and old well. Circa 1843 this carefully restored boutique country guesthouse will enchant you. Start the day viewing the platypus in their natural habitat only 500m away, followed by a leisurely gourmet breakfast in the dining room or out on the deck. Stay in one of the five well-appointed centrally heated rooms or pamper yourself in the self contained studio including spa and gas log fire.

Berry - Jaspers Brush

Jaspers Brush B&B and Alpaca Farm *B&B & Farmstay*

Leonie and Ian Winlaw
465 Strongs Road
Jaspers Brush
NSW 2535
5 km S of Berry

Tel (02) 4448 6194
or 0418 116 655
Fax (02) 4448 6254
iwinlaw@ozemail.com.au
jaspersbrushbandb.com.au

Double $198-$220
Not child friendly
Full breakfast
Visa MC Amex accepted
2 Queen 2 Single (3 bdrm)
Bright and airy with views
Bathrooms: 2 Ensuite 1 Private

Come take breakfast overlooking one of nature's most spectacular creations.

Our property, located on the Berry escarpment, commands views that stretch from Jervis Bay to Gerringong, taking in the Shoalhaven River, Mt Coolangatta and the lush green pastures of the coastal plain.

The bedrooms, opening onto the wrap around verandah and the view, have private facilities, electric blankets, alpaca fleece doonas, heaters, ceiling fans and fresh flowers from the garden.

The house boasts an eclectic art collection and the guest lounge has an open fire with great art, travel, wine and garden books for browsing. A gourmet breakfast is served in the lounge overlooking the views and our herd of alpacas

Berry - Kangaroo Valley

Barefoot Springs *B&B & Homestay & Cottage, no kitchen*
Tim & Kay
155 Carrington Road
Cambewarra
NSW 2540
9.5 km SE of Kangaroo Valley

Tel (02) 4446 0509
Fax (02) 4446 0530
info@barefootsprings.com.au
www.barefootsprings.com.au

Double $160-$250 **Single** $150-$230
Full breakfast
Dinner BYO 3 course $50, 2 course $45
Visa MC accepted
4 Queen (4 bdrm)
Bathrooms: 4 Ensuite
Double spa in Cottages

B
arefoot Springs rests high on Cambewarra Mountain; between Berry, Kangaroo Valley and the Shoalhaven. Enjoy our mountain and coastline views, while strolling through 5 acres of beautiful gardens. Many tourist destinations within a 20 minute drive. Accommodation within our homestead is a Queen bedroom with en-suite, or three studio cottages, each with double spa, wood fire, TV/DVD, air con. and kitchenette. Full breakfast is served overlooking panoramic views. Our 37 acre property boasts waterfalls, creeks and natural rainforest, and abundant native wildlife.

~

Berry - Kangaroo Valley

Wombat Hill B&B *Luxury B&B & Farmstay & Self contained cottage*
Trish and Ken Jessop
1010 Kangaroo Valley Road
Bellawongarah
NSW 2535
10 km W of Berry

Tel (02) 4464 1924
trishandken@wombathillbandb.com
www.wombathillbandb.com

Double $190-$230
Pre school children $25, school age $40
Full breakfast
Extra adult $65, Pets $25
Visa MC accepted
2 Queen (2 bdrm)
Q/S b'room plus single sofa bed in living room
Bathrooms: 2 Ensuite Each unit has its own bathroom

E
njoy luxury, perfect peace and quiet, expansive mountain views, acres of glorious gardens, friendly farm animals, great wildlife, scrumptious breakfasts. Close to Berry and Kangaroo Valley, 2 hours from Sydney, and 2.5 hours from Canberra. We can recommend local activities and venues for your enjoyment. Everyone welcome, including children and pets. We welcome horses and alpacas too. Each unit has comfortable, modern amenities with Q/S bedroom, bathroom, living area with single sofa bed, A/C, fans, electric blankets, books, magazines, TV/VCR/DVD player, CD player, private deck, separate entry. (Full kitchen in cottage).

Berry - South Coast NSW

Broughton Mill Farm Guesthouse Berry *Luxury B&B & Guest House*

Rick Gainford & Jennifer Clapham
78 Woodhill Mountain Road
Berry
NSW 2535
1 km N of Berry

Tel (02) 4464 2446
or 0439 965 354
bmfberry@bigpond.net.au
www.broughtonmillfarm.com.au

Double $200-$245 **Single** $150-$195
Children during holiday periods or
if entire guesthouse is booked
Full breakfast Dinner by arrangement
Groups catered for
Visa MC Eftpos accepted
 2 King/Twin2 King 2 Queen 2 Single (5 bdrm)
Luxury suites with bathrooms and sitting rooms
Bathrooms: 5 Private 4 suites have baths, one is a double spa bath

  AAA Tourism ★★★★★

Nestled in picturesque countryside with sweeping views of the escarpment the Guesthouse is set in 3 1/2 acres of grounds. Just one kilometre from Berry and 5 minutes from the beach. Solar heated swimming pool, tennis court, chickens and vegetable and fruit gardens. Luxury accommodation with generous space and all facilities provided in a purpose built Guesthouse added to a 100 year old farmhouse. Common areas include dining, lounge sunroom and library. Functions are catered as well.

Blue Mountains

Mount Tomah Botanic Garden showcases both native and exotic plants from around the world. This cold-climate collection for the Botanic Gardens Trust Sydney has over 40,000 plants and is set against the stunning backdrop of breathtaking views that run all the way back to Sydney up to the Hunter Valley.

Discover remnant rainforest, themed plant displays that highlight biodiversity and adaptation such as the Gondwana Walk or the Rock Garden with plantings grouped by continent of origin.

Bill & Gai Johns, Tomah Mountain Lodge

Blue Mountains - Katoomba

Melba House *Luxury B&B*
Marion Hall
98 Waratah Street
Katoomba
NSW 2780
0.5 km E of Katoomba

Tel (02) 4782 4141
or 0403 021 074
stay@melbahouse.com
www.melbahouse.com

Double $195-$249 Single $185-$239
Full breakfast
Visa MC Eftpos accepted
1 King/Twin1 King 2 Queen (3 bdrm)
2 Spa Suites and 1 Shower Ensuite
Bathrooms: 3 Ensuite
2 Spas & Showers and 1 Shower

I magine your own log fire and spa, central-heating, electric blankets, large comfortable suites with own sitting and dining areas, sumptuous breakfasts, that's historical 4.5* Melba House. Quiet and secluded yet close to many restaurants, galleries, antique and craft shops and walking tracks. Also, close to the best-loved attractions of Katoomba and Leura. See our website www.melbahouse.com. "Of the B&Bs around the world we have stayed, this is our best experience, it's exquisite" (W. Dallas Texas). Stay 3 consecutive nights Midweek and only pay for 2.

Blue Mountains - Lawson

Araluen *B&B*
George & Gai Sprague
59 Wilson Street
Lawson
NSW 2783
15 km E of Katoomba

Tel (02) 4759 1610
relax@araluen.com.au
www.araluen.com.au

Double $145-$225 Single $95-$135
Children by arrangement
Special breakfast Dinner $35-$55
Golf package; Walkabout tour or
picnic hamper by arrangement
Visa MC accepted
3 Queen (3 bdrm)
Bathrooms: 3 Ensuite one with spa-bath

"P erfect balance of pampering and privacy." Large, superbly furnished home overlooking mountain bushland. "Perfect beds," modern ensuites, one with double spa-bath. Sumptuous breakfasts. Sunny living room; romantic log-fire. Quiet reading room. Huge games room (pool/billiards, piano, DVD library). Heating/cooling throughout. Prize gardens. Secluded waterfalls nearby. (Candlelit dinners/picnic baskets by arrangement.) Handy all Blue Mountains attractions. Attractive golf packages. "Excellent hosts." "Ideal getaway for up to 3 couples." Reviewed Australian Good Taste Dec 2001. SM Herald Reader Recommendation 16/03/02. Qantas Magazine Oct 2003.

Blue Mountains - Leura

Woodford of Leura *B&B*
John & Lesley Kendall
48 Woodford Street
Leura
NSW 2780
0.75 km E of Leura

Tel (02) 4784 2240
or 0427 410 625
Fax (02) 4784 2240
woodford@leura.com
www.leura.com

Double $135-$195
Single $100-$150
Full breakfast
Visa MC Eftpos accepted
1 King/Twin1 King 2 Queen
1 Double 2 Twin 1 Single (4 bdrm)
Bathrooms: 4 Ensuite

An award-winning retreat located in one of Leura's quietest country lanes and set in tranquil, spacious gardens framed by towering pines. This stately and enchanting home offers both suites and standard rooms, all with en-suites. Woodford is renowned for its sumptuous breakfasts and offers complimentary afternoon tea on arrival. It also features central heating, an indoor heated 4-person spa/jacuzzi and cosy guest lounge with log fire. Ideally located in a whisper-quiet setting midway between the historic village and golf course on the escarpment.

Blue Mountains - Leura

Broomelea *B&B*
Bryan & Denise Keith
273 Leura Mall
Leura
NSW 2780
0.5 km S of Leura

Tel (02) 4784 2940
or 0419 478 400
Fax (02) 4784 2611
info@broomelea.com.au
www.broomelea.com.au

Double $154-$215
Single $130-$190
Full breakfast
Visa MC Diners Amex Eftpos
JCB accepted
3 Queen 2 Twin (4 bdrm)
Bathrooms: 4 Ensuite

AAA Tourism
★★★★☆

A beautiful 1909 mountain home for guests who would like more than simply a bed and a breakfast. We offer spacious ensuite rooms with 4 poster beds, open fires, lounges, TV, Video, CD Players, a freshly prepared gourmet breakfast each morning and most importantly local knowledge. Broomelea is perfectly located in the Living Heritage precinct of Leura just a 10 minute stroll to famous cliff top walks with great views or our beautiful village with numerous restaurants and galleries.

Blue Mountains - Leura

Bethany Manor Bed & Breakfast *B&B*
Greg & Jill Haigh
8 East View Avenue
Leura
NSW 2780
0.8 km NW of Leura

Tel (02) 4782 9215
Fax (02) 4782 1962
bmanor@optusnet.com.au
www.bethanymanor.com.au

Double $130-$205
Single $110-$185
Full breakfast
Visa MC accepted
3 Queen (3 bdrm)
Bathrooms: 3 Ensuite

   AAA Tourism ★★★★☆

L ooking for a welcoming place to call home when visiting the World Heritage Blue Mountains? Bethany Manor is a Federation style home set on over an acre of parklike grounds, with tennis court. Your ensuite bedroom incorporates a spa-bath and verandah access while the Garden View room provides the perfect setting for enjoying a sumptuous breakfast in any season. Centrally heated with a wood fire in the guest's lounge. We're an easy walk to Leura village with its speciality shops, restaurants and railway station.

~

Blue Mountains - Lithgow

Majic Views B&B *B&B & Self Contained Apartment*
Allan & Jeanie Cupitt
157 McKanes Falls Road
Lithgow, NSW 2790
6 km E of Lithgow

Tel (02) 6353 1094 or 0409 244 791
0421 647 898
Fax (02) 6353 1094
relax@majicviews.com.au
www.majicviews.com.au

Double $125-$165 Single $95-$125
Children $15-$20
Continental breakfast Full breakfast B/A
Dinner $15-$25 B/A
Visa MC Eftpos accepted
2 King/Twin 3 Queen 3 Single (4 bdrm)
Large rooms all with views
Bathrooms: 2 Private Ensuite by arrangement

Q uiet, private rural setting on 5 acres with 'Majic Views' across the valley to the Blue Mountains Escarpment. Contemporary styled home, with the main accommodation offering 1 Queen and 1 Kingtwin bedroom, living area with CD, TV, VCR, DVD, kitchenette, luxury three way bathroom with spa and a private barbecue area. Suitable to families with additional bedding available. Private access. Central to Jenolan Caves, the Zig Zag Railway and Blue Mountains attractions. Discounted rate to seniors. Private bathroom available by arrangement.

Blue Mountains - Mount Tomah - Bells Line of Road

Tomah Mountain Lodge *B&B*
Bill & Gai Johns
25 Skyline Road
Mount Tomah via Bilpin
NSW 2758
14 km W of Bilpin

Tel (02) 4567 2111
or 0419 908 724
tomahlodge@ozemail.com.au
www.tomahmountainlodge.com.au

Double $220 **Single** $190
Full breakfast
Dinner $55pp
Visa MC Amex Eftpos accepted
1 King/Twin 2 Queen (3 bdrm)
Bathrooms: 3 Ensuite

  AAA Tourism ★★★★☆

T omah Mountain Lodge is situated in the World Heritage Blue Mountains National Park and offers comfortable, executive style accommodation. Mount Tomah is over 1000 metres above sea level with extensive mountain views. This secluded setting is only two minutes drive to Mount Tomah Botanic Garden, and a short drive to the historic gardens at Mount Wilson. The lodge offers spacious & comfortable lounge rooms with log fires. Gourmet three course candlelit dinners are a speciality.

Blue Mountains - Springwood

Southall *B&B*
Tanya & Wayne Lyons
353 Great Western Highway
Springwood
NSW 2777
1 km S of B&B

Tel (02) 4751 8212
or 0425 297 474
Fax (02) 4751 3080
yourhosts@southall.com.au
www.southall.com.au

Double $275-$295
Full provisions
Visa MC Eftpos accepted
1 Queen (3 bdrm)
Self contained suites
Bathrooms: 3 Ensuite

T he property was built by George Moore who was the mayor of Sydney in 1886. The property is heritage listed and is nestled away in a quiet large allotment providing complete privacy. The property has been a Vicarage, a Girls finishing school, a boys Grammar school and a private Maternity Hospital before becoming a beautiful Romantic Retreat B&B. The whole property is for the enjoyment of Guests, who can sit around the Courtyard, enjoy a cup of tea on the verandahs, or sit in the garden areas.

Blue Mountains - Wentworth Falls

Whispering Pines' Chalet Fontanelle *Luxury Separate Suite & Chalet & Cottages*

Maria & Bill McCabe
178 Falls Road
Wentworth Falls
NSW 2782
8 km E of Katoomba

Tel (02) 4757 1449
or 0412 144 917
Fax (02) 4757 1219
wpines@bigpond.com
www.whisperingpines.com.au

Double $190-$490 **Single** $150-$450
Continental provisions
Cottages $150-$440
Visa MC Diners Amex Eftpos
JCB accepted
1 King 2 Queen (3 bdrm)
Multiple room suites in separate wings of the Chalet
Bathrooms: 3 Ensuite Double spa in one suite

   AAA Tourism ★★★★☆

Enjoy the delights of our luxurious heritage-listed Chalet Fontanelle set in 4 acres of rambling woodland gardens, and perched on the escarpment at the head of the most spectacular waterfall in the beautiful Blue Mountains. Over 600,000 acres of unspoilt wilderness on our doorstep for you to explore. Our suites are warm and spacious with private lounges, fireplaces and luxury appointments.

Blue Mountains - Wentworth Falls

Den Fenella Lodge *Self Contained House*

Bill & Maria McCabe
c/- 178 Falls Road
Wentworth Falls
NSW 2782
2 km S of Wentworth Falls

Tel (02) 4757 1449
or 0412 144 917
Fax (02) 4757 1219
wpines@bigpond.com
www.whisperingpines.com.au

Double $180-$280
Children $25
Accommodation only
Extra person after first two $25
Visa MC Diners Amex Eftpos JCB accepted
2 Queen 2 Single (3 bdrm) Spacious - 2 upstairs, 1 downstairs
Bathrooms: 1 Ensuite 1 Family share Double corner spa bath and showers

Built in traditional mountains' style, this ultra-modern 3 bedroom lodge has every amenity and luxury essential for you to enjoy your holiday. The main bedroom opens onto the front deck and has an enormous ensuite with double corner spa bath. Two large bedrooms upstairs allow others to escape to their own private retreat. Fireplace, central heating/air conditioning, stereo system, surround sound home entertainment room, natural gas BBQ, large modern kitchen and dining room for 8 people. Very close to the National Park walking trails.

Blue Mountains - Wentworth Falls

Monique's Bed & Breakfast Establishment *B&B & Self Contained House*

Ian Williamson
31 Falls Road
Wentworth Falls
NSW 2782
0.4 km S of Wentworth Falls

Tel (02) 4757 1646
Fax (02) 4757 2498
moniques@ram.net.au
www.moniques.com.au

Double $100-$180
Single $80-$160
Children under 16 free
Full provisions
Whole Cottage $300-$390
1 King 1 Queen 1 Double 1 Single (3 bdrm)
King & Queen rooms have an extra single bed
Bathrooms: 3 Ensuite Cast iron bath in Wentworth

Guests stay in the private, self-contained cottage. There are three bedrooms (king, queen/twin, double), each with ensuite, a large comfortable lounge/dining room with enclosed log fire, TV/DVD/VHS&CD, a fully-equipped kitchen and a sunny terrace. The French Provincial style house and cottage are set in a quiet, mature garden. Features include: *generous provisions for self prepared breakfast *suitable for couples, groups of friends, family *walking distance to village shops and cafés *log fire, heating, electric blankets *close to famous bushwalks *attractive rates longer-stay.

~

Blue Mountains - Wentworth Falls

Blue Mountains Lakeside *B&B & Self Contained Apartment*

Michaela Russell
30 Bellevue Road
Wentworth Falls, NSW 2782
1 km N of Wentworth Falls

Tel (02) 4757 3777
or 0410 443 322
Fax (02) 4757 3444
stay@lakesidebandb.com.au
www.lakesidebandb.com.au

Double $165-$240 **Single** $135-$190
Children over 12 $30
Full breakfast
Dinner Reflections S/C Spa Suite
Breakfast avail. at small extra charge
Ask about our mid-week specials
Visa MC accepted
2 Queen 1 Double (2 bdrm) Lake Suite B&B, Reflections S/C Spa Suite
Bathrooms: 2 Ensuite Double spa in Reflections Suite

Blue Mountains' only WATERFRONT Bed & Breakfast. "At the edge of the Lake in the Heart of the Mountains." Looking for somewhere special with a log fire and spa? Choose the traditional Lake Suite with delicious cooked breakfasts with home grown produce or the new self contained Reflections Spa Suite with living room, kitchenette and verandah - both with amazing Lake views. Try a soothing in-house massage. Complimentary boats and trout fishing available. Birdwatchers paradise. Minutes to Echo Point. "An amazing piece of paradise." Michael and Ashley. (From our Visitors' Book).

Blue Mountains - Woodford

Braeside *B&B*
Robyn Wilkinson & Rex Fardon
97 Bedford Road
Woodford
NSW 2778
19 km E of Katoomba

Tel (02) 4758 6279
or 0414 542 860
Fax (02) 4758 8210
Braeside.BandB@bigpond.com
www.bluemts.com.au/braeside

Double $120-$140
Single $80-$90
Children from $15
Full breakfast
Dinner available $20-$30pp
Visa MC Diners Amex accepted
1 King/Twin 1 Queen 1 Double (3 bdrm)
Bathrooms: 2 Ensuite 1 Private

  AAA Tourism ★★★★

Braeside offers a quiet escape as well as being central to the attractions of the upper and lower Blue Mountains. Three bedrooms are available to suit a variety of needs including singles sharing, family groups with children and couples looking for a quiet escape. Flexible arrangements include providing an evening meal with a little notice. The guests lounge has an open log fire for cooler weather. Set in large parklike gardens Braeside offers a home away from home. No smoking inside.

~

Byron Bay and Hinterland

Nestled in the hills behind Australia's most easterly point of Byron Bay is a sub-tropical hinterland with a diverse and beautiful landscape. Drive through lush rolling hills dotted with macadamia orchards, stop at quaint villages and visit the Nightcap National Park with bush walks and waterfalls. Come and share this experience and soak up the atmosphere of peace, tranquillity and relaxed hospitality.
Suzanne McGuinness, Suzanne's Hideaway, Clunes.
Julie Snow, Seaview House

Byron Bay

Victoria's at Ewingsdale & Victoria's at Watego's *Luxury Guest House*

Victoria McEwen
Marine Parade & McGettigans Lane
Byron Bay
NSW 2481
2 km E of and 6 km W of Byron Bay

Tel (02) 6684 7047
or (02) 6685 5388
Fax (02) 6684 7687
indulge@victorias.net.au
www.victorias.net.au

Double $250-$699
Full breakfast
Visa MC Diners Amex
Eftpos JCB accepted
10 Queen (10 bdrm)
Bathrooms: 10 Ensuite

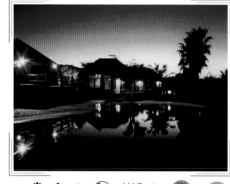

    AAA Tourism ★★★★★

Only minutes from Byron Bay, is the multi-award winning "Victoria's At Ewingsdale". This stately country manor is situated on 4 acres of landscaped gardens, and features panoramic ocean, mountain and rural views. "Victoria's at Wategos", is a stunning Tuscan style guest house, nestled in an exclusive ocean front valley at beautiful Wategos beach, just under the famous Cape Byron lighthouse. Experience personalised service in our small and exclusive boutique retreats, dedicated to providing the best in first class hospitality, quality and style.

Byron Bay

Seaview House *Luxury B&B*

Amanda & Julian
146 Lighthouse Road
(acess via Lee Lane)
Byron Bay
NSW 2481
1.5 km N of Byron Bay

Tel (02) 6685 6468
Fax (02) 6685 6468
seaviewhouse_byronbay@ozemail.com.au
www.seaviewbyron.com

Double $250-$500
Single $200-$300
Full breakfast
Dinner by prior arrangement from $100
Whole house is available by request
Visa MC Diners Amex Eftpos accepted
3 Queen (3 bdrm)
Bathrooms: 3 Ensuite

Seaview House is set high on Lighthouse Road with all rooms offering fabulous panoramic sea views to the Nightcap Ranges and across the Bay. Comfortable rooms offer TV, DVD, fridge, coffee & tea making facilities and air conditioning, private decks and ensuite ensuring a leisurely relaxed stay. Breakfast on the upper deck, served each morning, leisurely strolls to town, to the Beaches and a rainforest walk to the Lighthouse, ensure a wonderful stay at Seaview. In house Beauty Therapist available to enhance your stay.

Byron Bay Hinterland

Green Mango Hideaway *B&B*
Susie Briscoe
Lofts Road,
(off Coolamon Scenic Drive)
Coorabell
NSW 2479
12 km W of Byron Bay

Tel (02) 6684 7171
relax@greenmango.com.au
www.greenmango.com.au

Double $165-$250
Single $150-$220
Full breakfast
Visa MC Eftpos accepted
2 King 2 Queen (4 bdrm)
Bathrooms: 4 Ensuite

From the moment you walk down its leafy path, you'll be captivated by the tropical atmosphere of this peaceful B&B set in Byron's spectacular hinterland. With just four guestrooms, each with ensuite & verandah, you'll be escaping the crowds and yet be within minutes of fabulous shops & cafés and glorious beaches. The muslin-draped beds & Oriental decor, the sparkling palm-fringed pool & lush gardens with abundant birdlife, and the wonderful breakfasts all guarantee you a relaxing and memorable stay.

Candelo - Bega Valley

Bumblebrook Farm *B&B & Homestay & Farmstay & Self Contained Apartment*
Alan and Wendy Cross
Kemps Lane
Candelo
NSW 2550
20 km SW of Bega

Tel (02) 6493 2238
Fax (02) 6493 2299
stay@bumblebrook.com.au
www.bbbook.com.au/bumblebrook.html

Double $100-$115
Single $80-$115
Children under 13 free
Full provisions
Visa MC accepted
1 King/Twin 1 Queen
3 Double 4 Single (4 bdrm)
Bathrooms: 4 Ensuite

AAA Tourism
★★★☆

A 100 acre beef property with magnificent views and lovely bush walks, fronting Tantawangalo Creek. We have four well equipped self-contained units. Breakfast is a "cook-your-own" from our fresh farm ingredients. Children are welcome and can often help feed the farm animals. With prior notice guests are welcome to a friendly, candlelit, family dinner in the homestead. BBQs are provided by the creek and in the rustic playground near the units. Beaches and National Parks nearby. Pets welcome with prior arrangement.

Central Coast - Terrigal
AnDaCer Boutique B&B *Luxury B&B*
Gaby Schaudinn
28 Serpentine Road
Terrigal, NSW 2260
4 km W of Terrigal

Tel (02) 4367 8368
Fax (02) 4367 8368
stay@terrigalretreat.com.au
www.terrigalretreat.com.au

Double $140-$330
Full breakfast
Dinner by arrangement
Romantic Weekend Accommodation
Package from $330 per night
Visa MC accepted
3 Queen (3 bdrm)
Luxury linen and posturepedic mattresses
Bathrooms: 3 Ensuite
Unwind and rejuvenate in the therapeutic outdoor spa (jacuzzi)

   AAA Tourism ★★★★☆

If you are looking for a romantic getaway close to Sydney, An'da'cer House Retreat provides the perfect destination with luxury boutique B&B accommodation. Stay in a secluded and relaxing resort-style atmosphere set in beautiful gardens surrounded by tranquil coastal acreages. An'Da'Cer House Retreat offers three individual luxury Suites; two with direct access into the garden and pool area via private gardens. The breakfast conservatory, with its casual and inviting appeal, overlooks the pool and garden and is a delightful spot to sit while indulging yourself with the fabulous breakfasts served each morning.

Central Coast - Tuggerah
Greenacres B&B *Separate Suite*
Elizabeth & John Fairweather
8 Carpenters Lane
Mardi
NSW 2259
1 km W of Tuggerah

Tel (02) 4353 0643
or (02) 4353 0309
greenacres-bb@tpg.com.au
www.greenacres-bb.com

Double $125-$160
Single $110-$145
Children $15 each per night
Full provisions
1 Queen 1 Double (1 bdrm)
Bathrooms: 1 Ensuite

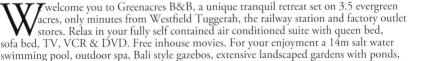

We welcome you to Greenacres B&B, a unique tranquil retreat set on 3.5 evergreen acres, only minutes from Westfield Tuggerah, the railway station and factory outlet stores. Relax in your fully self contained air conditioned suite with queen bed, sofa bed, TV, VCR & DVD. Free inhouse movies. For your enjoyment a 14m salt water swimming pool, outdoor spa, Bali style gazebos, extensive landscaped gardens with ponds, fountains, waterfalls, dam, bushwalking trails. Enjoy hand feeding our Silver Perch fish. Dog/cat enclosure located next to the suite.

Central Tilba - Tilba Tilba - Narooma

The Two Story B&B *B&B*

Ken & Linda Jamieson
Bate Street
Central Tilba
NSW 2546
In Central Tilba

Tel (02) 4473 7290
or 1800 355 850
Fax (02) 4473 7992
stay@tilbatwostory.com
www.tilbatwostory.com

Double $120 **Single** $100
Full breakfast
Visa MC Eftpos accepted
2 Queen 1 Double 1 Single (3 bdrm)
Bathrooms: 3 Ensuite

A warm welcome awaits you from Aussie hosts Ken and Linda Jamieson at the Two Story B&B. Nestled in the foothills of Mt Dromedary situated in the National Trust Village of Central Tilba. Our building is 113 years old built in 1894 and was originally the Post Office and residence, it has great character and views overlooking a superb valley of rolling hills and lush greenness, enjoy the atmosphere, warmth, and a glass of Tilba Port in front of our log fire. Our weather is temperate and beaches are close by. The Craft Village of Central Tilba is extensive, businesses include: leather shop, tea rooms, alpaca shop, cheese factory, woodturning gallery and more. A short scenic drive takes you to a local winery, short drives to Bermagui and Cobargo, bushwalking, fishing and swimming. We offer our guests off street parking, a choice of continental and full cooked breakfasts with tea/coffee facilities, in a totally relaxed atmosphere of pleasant old world charm and a non smoking environment. Enquire about our package: 2 nights at The Two Story B&B and 3 nights at our self-contained unit at Bateman's Bay. Situated 300km south of Sydney.

Cobargo

Old Cobargo Convent *B&B & Homestay & Self Contained House*
Bob & Dianne Saunders
Wandella Road
Cobargo
NSW 2550
0.5 km W of Cobargo

Tel (02) 6493 6419
or 0413 362 812
Fax (02) 6493 6419
oldconvent@asitis.net.au
www.cobargoconvent.com.au

Double $120-$140 Single $75-$90
Special breakfast
Dinner $25
Extra person in Schoolhouse $30-$35
Visa MC accepted
4 Queen 2 Twin (6 bdrm)
3 in B&B & 3 in S/C
Bathrooms: 3 Ensuite 2 Private

Experience the ambience of yesteryear, built in 1917 our historic Old Convent is restored and with antiques. French doors lead onto the verandah where you can admire unspoilt rural views. Choose from 3 tastefully decorated bedrooms or the fully self contained Old Schoolhouse, peaceful and private with 3 bedrooms, claw footed bath, wood heater and loads of charm and character. Only a short stroll to the historic working village of Cobargo with much of its original architecture and many unique shops.

Coffs Harbour

Coffs harbour is the idyllic holiday paradise is renowned for its' great weather, water sports, international golf courses, seafood, historic harbour and marina, and a casual lifestyle.

Located mid-way between Sydney and Brisbane on the sub-tropical North Coast of NSW with beautiful golden beaches, fine restaurants and an abundance of activities and adventure.

Take a cruise and go whale or dolphin watching, view the Solitary Islands Marine Reserve, or drive inland for white water kayaking or visit the World Heritage area and Dorrigo National Park.
Coffs Coast Tourism.

Boambee Palms Bed & Breakfast
Luxury B&B
Marcus & Colleen Blackwell
5 Kasch Road
Coffs Harbour, NSW 2450
6 km S of Coffs Harbour

Tel (02) 6658 4545
or 0417 787 790
Fax (02) 6658 4545
info@boambeepalms.com.au
www.boambeepalms.com.au

Double $160-$250 Single $130-$250
Full breakfast
Visa MC Amex accepted
1 King/Twin2 King 2 Queen (5 bdrm)
Super King with Double Spa and separate shower
Bathrooms: 4 Ensuite 1 Private
Two with luxurious Double Spas

AAA Tourism
★★★★☆

The perfect adults only escape. Everything a guest could wish for is here, 4 acres of lush landscaped gardens abundant with bird life. Facilities include floodlit tennis court, large sub tropical pool with BBQ area. There are five well appointed King and Queen ensuite rooms some with double spas. All rooms have private entrances, outside seating areas, air conditioning TV, CD, DVD, mini fridges, bathrobes, tea/plunger coffee, hair dryers.

Breakfast is a lazy 3 course gourmet affair served on the balcony overlooking the landscaped gardens on individual tables. Start with fresh juices, seasonal tropical fruits, a choice of cooked breakfasts - maybe potato pancakes topped with smoked salmon and dill and sour cream sauce whets your appetite or Turkish bread with avocado, bacon and topped with a poached egg or perhaps a traditional English breakfast followed by muffins and toast good coffee and a selection of teas. Of course the rainbow lorikeets are on hand to keep you entertained. We can also offer a range of meal options if you don't want to go out in the evening such as a cold local seafood platter.

Coffs Harbour - Sawtell

Sawtell Beach Break B&B *B&B*

John & Veronica
20 Honeysuckle Street
Sawtell
NSW 2452
8 km S of Coffs Harbour

Tel (02) 6658 1039
or 0429 807 896
0411 581029
Fax (02) 6658 1039
sawtellbandb@optusnet.com.au
www.bbbook.com.au/
SawtellBeachBreakBB.html

Double $85-$130
Continental breakfast
Visa MC accepted
1 Queen (1 bdrm)
Bathrooms: 1 Ensuite

View from Garden - Direct Access to Beach

AAA Tourism ★★★

Sawtell Beach Break B&B is the perfect place to relax. Your stylish queen size room with ensuite offers you a wonderful night's sleep, or put your feet up in your own private sitting room with TV/DVD player & bar fridge. Direct beach access to stunning Sawtell Beach & easy walking distance to Sawtell's award winning cafés and heritage listed cinema. Golf, tennis, fishing & more are all on offer. A tempting continental breakfast is also offered for the perfect start to your day.

Coffs Harbour - Sawtell

Creekside Inn (formerly Alamanda Lodge) *B&B*

Jenni & Graham Croot
59 Boronia Street
Sawtell
NSW 2452
0.1 km S of Sawtell

Tel (02) 6658 9099
jenni@creeksideinn.com.au
www.creeksideinn.com.au

Double $115-$170
Single $100-$140
Special breakfast
Visa MC accepted
4 Queen 1 Twin (4 bdrm)
Bathrooms: 4 Ensuite

AAA Tourism ★★★★☆

Creekside Inn is a 4 1/2 star B&B where you can sit by the creek, take a stroll to beaches, play golf, tennis, lawn, bowls, fish or surf. Enjoy a coffee or meal at one of the cafés and restaurants across the street in beautiful Sawtell. Your hosts Jenni & Graham Croot invite you to relax in one of our four theme guest rooms. We serve afternoon tea on arrival and a gourmet breakfast. Courtesy transfers from Coffs Harbour Airport and Railway Station.

Coffs Harbour Northern Beaches
Headlands Beach Guest House *B&B & Guest House*

Valerie & Terry Swan
17 Headland Road
Arrawarra Headland
NSW 2456
5 km N of Woolgoolga

Tel (02) 6654 0364
or 0417 240 440
0417 249 500
Fax (02) 6654 0308
info@headlandsbeach.com.au
www.headlandsbeach.com.au

Double $135-$160
Single $110-$135
Full breakfast
Visa MC accepted
3 Queen (3 bdrm)
Well appointed rooms with TV, radio, ceiling fans, heating
Bathrooms: 3 Ensuite

  AAA Tourism ★★★★☆

Headlands Beach Guest House offers guests absolute beach frontage with relaxed, warm and friendly coastal style living. Located 20 mins north of Coffs Harbour on the Solitary Islands Marine National Park and 5km from Woolgoolga. A fully equipped kitchen is available for guests to use along with the BBQ poolside. Guest lounge and dining room overlook the guest pool, Mullawarra Beach and Arrawarra Headland. Complimentary afternoon tea on arrival. Surfing beaches, headland and beach walks are at

Corrimal - Wollongong
Corrimal Beach Bed & Breakfast *B&B & Homestay*

Sue & Daryl Thomson
56 Dobbie Avenue
East Corrimal
NSW 2518
10 km N of Wollongong

Tel (02) 4283 2899
Fax (02) 4283 2899
dthom999@bigpond.net.au
www.corrimalbeach.com

Double $250-$390 **Single** $220-$360
Full breakfast
Dinner 2 or 3 course on request
Alfresco dining if requested
Visa MC accepted
2 Queen 2 Single (3 bdrm)
All have ensuites & private courtyards
Bathrooms: 3 Ensuite

Enjoy a quiet weekend escape in a modern architecturally designed home, 45min south from Sydney airport, 2h from Canberra, and minutes from central Wollongong. A short walk to the Illawarra cycleway or Corrimal beach, where you can stroll along the beach, surf, fish or just sunbake. 10 eighteen-hole golf courses and 10 bowling clubs within 30min drive. Close to many fine restaurants, renowned gardens and picturesque beaches. Board a train to exciting Sydney or visit the Southern Highlands. All rooms have TV, Ensuite and courtyard.

Crookwell

Nestled on top of the Great Dividing Range, an hour from Canberra and only two and a half hours from Sydney is the picturesque town of Crookwell - a secluded rural hideaway, which has been protected from the harshness of modern-day intrusions.

Crookwell experiences the seasons in all their glory. Autumn is a blaze of colour - winter sees rolling hills blanketed in white powdery snow and the perfect excuse to snuggle up next to a roaring log fire. Masses of exquisite blossoms, bulbs and flowers herald spring and a gentle summer allows you to escape the harsh heat and humidity of coastal regions. Great for Abercrombie and Wombeyan Caves

Mary and Geoff Ashton, Markdale Homestead

~

Crookwell

Markdale Homestead *B&B & Farmstay & Self Contained House*

Geoff & Mary Ashton
462 Mulgowrie Road
Binda
NSW 2583
40 km NW of Crookwell

Tel (02) 4835 3146
or (02) 8212 8599
Fax (02) 4835 3160
g_ashton@bigpond.com
www.markdale.com

Double $100-$220 Single $50-$110
Children under 2 free
Full provisions Dinner $25-$40
Phones and WiFi Internet
Visa MC accepted
2 Queen 3 Double 7 Twin (12 bdrm)
4 Stone House, 2 Annexe, 6 Sh Qt
Bathrooms: 1 Ensuite 4 Guest share 2 Stone House, 1 Annexe, 2 Shearers' Quarters

Food for the soul. A stunning landscape, 6000 acres, trout stocked streams, solar heated pool and all weather tennis. The Markdale Homestead and Garden combine the talents of two Australia Icons; Edna Walling, garden designer, and Professor Wilkinson, architect. Live in two adjoining, self contained, beautifully renovated, stone houses. Both have central heating, open fire, sitting room, kitchen, laundry, TV, CD Player, phone and internet access. Or stay in the comfortable Shearers' Quarters at cheaper rates.

Dorrigo

Dorrigo is where the mountains reach the sky. Perched on the dramatic eastern escarpment of the Great Dividing Range and only 40 km from the coast, Dorrigo offers spectacular scenery, bushwalking and abundant bird life.

Dorrigo is the gateway to the most accessible World Heritage Rainforest in New South Wales with spectacular scenery with easy walking tracks leading to a different world beneath the canopy of waterfalls and lush subtropical rainforest.

Di McDonald

Dorrigo

Lisnagarvey Cottage *Luxury B&B & Self Contained Cottage*
Mark & Elaine Martin
803 Whisky Creek Road
Dorrigo
NSW 2453
8 km W of Dorrigo

Tel (02) 6657 2536
or 0428 228 160
Fax (02) 6657 2053
bookings@lisnagarvey.com.au
www.lisnagarvey.com.au

Double $145
Single $120
Full provisions
Accomodation only rates available
1 Queen (1 bdrm)
Bathrooms: 1 Private Bath and shower

 AAA Tourism ★★★★

Nestled amidst the lush green hills of the Dorrigo Plateau and just 8 minutes to town is a beautifully renovated, luxury, one bedroom dairy bails with loads of character, charm, privacy and spectacular views over the plateau and Dorrigo township. Relax and enjoy the views from your private deck or curl up with complimentary port and chocolates in front of the wood fire. A gourmet breakfast basket can be supplied or you can choose to self cater. Fully self-contained.

Eden

Historic Eden is now a popular whale watching destination with migrating whales pausing to feed offshore here during October. Dolphin and Whale watching cruises are popular.

The fishing charter operators know where to catch 'a big one' or your can scuba dive on one of the wrecks that litter the coast.

Eden is centrally located for excellent bushwalking in the National Parks. One of the more popular is the Light to Light walk where you can walk along the rugged coast from Boyds Tower to Greencape Lighthouse.

Gail and David Ward, Cocora Cottage B&B

~

Eden

Crown & Anchor Inn B&B *B&B & Historic Inn*
Mauro and Judy Maurilli
239 Imlay Street
Eden
NSW 2551
0.2 km SE of Eden Central

Tel (02) 6496 1017
Fax (02) 6496 3878
info@crownandanchoreden.com.au
www.crownandanchoreden.com.au

Double $150-$190
Single $120-$160
Full breakfast
10% discount for 3 nights or longer
Visa MC accepted
5 Double (5 bdrm)
Bathrooms: 5 Ensuite

  AAA Tourism ★★★★

As seen on "Getaway" the "Today Show" and "Surfing The Menu." Step back in time. Experience romantic early Australian charm in an original 1840's Inn. Breathtaking ocean and bay views, antiques and open fires. Watch the whales from the veranda or the back deck during October and November. Central to Eden and wonderfully quiet; walk to restaurants, beaches and the working wharf. Enjoy a champagne watching the sun-set over the waters of Twofold Bay. Watch the sun-rise whilst breakfasting on the sunny veranda.

New South Wales

Eden

Cocora Cottage *B&B*
Gail and David Ward
2 Cocora Street
Eden
NSW 2551
0.5 km S of Centre of Eden

Tel (02) 6496 1241
or 0427 218 859
0409 961 241
info@cocoracottage.com
www.cocoracottage.com

Double $130-$155 Single $115
Not suitable for children
Full breakfast
Visa MC accepted
2 Queen (2 bdrm)
Working fireplace (1) Bay views
Bathrooms: 2 Ensuite with spas

AAA Tourism ★★★★

Heritage listed Cocora Cottage was the original Police Station in Eden. It is centrally located in a quiet area close to Eden's famous Killer Whale Museum, the Wharf and Eden's fine restaurants. Breakfast is served upstairs with spectacular views down to the Wharf and across Twofold Bay to the foothills of Mt Imlay. Both bedrooms have a Queen sized bed, an ensuite with a spa, a television and wireless internet. The front bedroom features the original open fireplace while the back bedroom offers bay views.

Gerringong

Tumblegum Inn
Christine & Ian Field
141C Belinda Street
Gerringong
NSW 2534
In Gerringong

Tel (02) 4234 3555
or 0422 880 727
Fax (02) 4234 3888
tumbleguminn@hotmail.com
www.tumbleguminn.com.au

Double $100-$130
Single $90-$110
Full breakfast
Visa MC accepted
2 Queen 1 Twin (3 bdrm)
Bathrooms: 3 Ensuite

AAA Tourism
★★★★

With rolling green hills that lap to pristine beaches, Gerringong reminds visitors of Ireland. Tumblegum Inn is a newly-built Federation style home featuring antique furnishings and warm hospitality. Two queen and one twin share bedrooms each contain ensuites, electric blankets, fans, clock radios and remote TV. Separate guest lounge has fridge, tea and coffee facilities, and home baked goodies. Only 1 1/2 hour south of Sydney, local attractions include beach side golf course, saltwater pools, boutique wineries, Minnamurra Rainforest and Kiama blowhole. Older children welcome, no pets. Winner, Illawarra Tourism Award for Accommodation.

Glen Innes

Queenswood - The Quiet One *B&B*

The Sim Family
82 Wentworth Street
Glen Innes
NSW 2370
0.5 km S of Town Centre

Tel (02) 6732 3025
or 0428 121 929
www.bbbook.com.au/
queenswoodthequietone.html

Double $90-$100 **Single** $75-$85
Children over 6 welcome $30-$35
Full breakfast
Dinner $25-$30 B/A
King with ensuite $105-$110
1 King 1 Queen 1 Twin (3 bdrm)
Bathrooms: 1 Ensuite 1 Guest share

Formally the residence of 'Queenswood Girls Grammar' opened in 1899, now an old style family home which welcomes you. Conveniently situated in town opposite the Bowling Club. Comfortable beds, electric blankets and room heaters, wood fires plus fully cooked breakfast. Experience our mild summers, invigorating winters (occasional snow), glorious spring and autumn. Visit the only Celtic Stones in Australia, National Parks. Fossicking, fishing and frolicking for everyone. Reservations please. Children over six welcome, not suitable for little children. No pets. Dinner by arrangement. BYO. Off street parking.

~

Glen Innes - Ben Lomond

Silent Grove Farmstay B&B *B&B & Homestay & Farmstay & Self Contained House*

John & Dorothy Every
Silent Grove
Ben Lomond
NSW 2365
32 km N of Guyra

Tel (02) 6733 2117 or 0427 936 799
Fax (02) 6733 2117
silentgr@northnet.com.au
www.silentgrovefarmstay-bandb.com.au

Double $85 **Single** $45-$50
Children $15 Full breakfast
Dinner $18
S/C Cottage (2 Adults 3 Children) $95pn
Visa MC accepted
1 Queen 1 Double 2 Single (3 bdrm)
Bathrooms: 2 Guest share

Enjoy country hospitality in a peaceful rural setting, short detour by sealed road from the New England Highway. Working sheep and cattle property. Farm activities. 4WD tour (fee applies). Panoramic views, scenic walks, yabbying (seasonal), tennis court, trout fishing, occasional snow fall. Easy access to New England, Gibraltar Range, Washpool National Parks. Glen Innes Australian Stones. Smoking outdoors. Have a cat. Winner of 2001 Big Sky Regional Tourism Hosted Accommodation. Campervans welcome. "Lovely peaceful atmosphere, friendly hospitality couldn't be better." WC.

Gloucester

Nestled in the foothills of the Bucketts Mountains and acclaimed for its friendliness and serene surroundings, Gloucester, base camp to World Heritage Barrington Tops.

Boasting a range of outdoor activities including fishing, horse riding, 4WD tours, canoeing, visit the Folk Museum or Gloucester Gallery to learn more about local history and culture, call into the Visitor Information Centre and pick up a copy of the Farm Trail map.

Events in Gloucester include the Shakespeare on Avon Festival, Mountain Man Tri Challenge, Rodeos, Country Music camps and community markets.
Kyoko Sakamoto, Arrowee House B&B

Gloucester - Barrington Tops

Arrowee House B&B *B&B & Homestay & Separate Suite*
Kyoko Sakamoto
152 Thunderbolts Way
Gloucester
NSW 2422
1 km N of Gloucester

Tel (02) 6558 2050
Fax (02) 6558 2050
information@gloucester.nsw.gov.au
www.gloucester.org.au/arrowee

Double $130 **Single** $65
Children 1-11 $1 per year
Children 12-16 $25
Full breakfast
Dinner $35 pp
Extra adult $65
Visa MC accepted
3 Queen 6 Single (4 bdrm) Baby cot available
Bathrooms: 1 Ensuite 1 Guest share 3 Private

Commended Award 2005 and 2006. Established 1990. Northern gateway to World Heritage Barrington Tops. Walking distance to cafés, restaurants, shops, gallery and bushwalking on The Buckett and Mograni Mountains. Large undercover barbeque area with outdoor kitchen. Activities - bushwalking, fishing, canoeing, horse riding, scenic drives, golf, swimming, tennis. Events: Shakespeare on Avon Festival, Mountain Man Tri Challenge, rodeos, country music camps and community markets. During winter a 4 course Japanese dinner is available for only $35 per person, must pre book.

Grafton - Seelands

Seeview Farm *B&B & Homestay & Farmstay*
Mona Ibbott
440 Rogans Bridge Road
Seelands Grafton
NSW 2460
10 km N of Grafton

Tel (02) 6644 9270
or 0447 449 270
Fax (02) 6644 9270
www.bbbook.com.au/seeviewfarm.html

Double $90-$110
Single $70-$80
Children $17.50
Full breakfast
Dinner $20
1 Queen 1 Twin (2 bdrm)
Bathrooms: 1 Guest share 1 Private

   AAA Tourism ★★★☆

Seeview Farm is a pretty cattle property on the banks of the Clarence River which is noted for river boat and water skiing. Grafton is famous for its Jacaranda Festival and its historical buildings. Close to beaches and mountains. Enjoy peaceful countryside - many overseas students have visited the farm, where pets are welcome. Kangaroos and bird life to watch. Good stopover from Sydney or Brisbane. Relaxing and friendly. Children are welcome. Damper and Billy Tea on the river bank can be provided.

Gunning

Frankfield Guest House *B&B & Guest House*
Allan & Robyn Munro
1-3 Warrataw Street
Gunning
NSW 2581
45 km W of Goulburn

Tel (02) 4845 1200
or 0437 130 814
Fax (02) 4845 1490
enquiries@frankfield.com.au
www.frankfield.com.au

Double $170-$220
Full breakfast
Visa MC accepted
5 Double (5 bdrm)
Bathrooms: 2 Ensuite 3 Private

  AAA Tourism ★★★☆

Built in 1870 as the Frankfield Hotel - now a charming Guest House. Each bedroom is fitted out with antique furniture, brass and four poster beds. Relax in front of an open fire or outside in award winning gardens. $2^{1}/_{2}$ hours from Sydney, 50 minutes from Canberra, Gunning is only minutes from the new Highway. Visit cold climate vineyards and historic townships all within 30 minutes drive. Local facilities include golf, tennis and swimming.

Hawkesbury

Forming the northern border of Sydney is the majestic Hawkesbury River. From the waterfront retreat of Brooklyn to Historic towns like St Albans, Windsor, and Richmond then climbing the mountains through Kurrajong Hills to Bilpin and beyond.

This beautiful picturesque rural setting and its local community creates an atmosphere of peace and serenity. Wisemans Ferry is a serene river town set beneath towering cliffs of Hawkesbury sandstone. The ferry master still operates the punt 24 hours a day for vehicles to cross the Hawkesbury River – a time honoured tradition since 1827.

Diane and Jim Swaisland, Ossian Hall B&B

Hawkesbury - Colo

Ossian Hall *Luxury Self Contained Apartment & 3 Self Contained Cottages for couples.*

Diane & Jim Swaisland
1928 Singleton Road
Colo, NSW 2756
26 km NE of Windsor

Tel (02) 4575 5250
or 0428 640 435
Fax (02) 4575 5169
info@ossianhall.com.au
www.ossianhall.com.au

Double $215-$240
Single $215-$240
Full provisions
Dinner by arrangement
Packages available
Visa MC Amex accepted
4 Queen (4 bdrm)
Bathrooms: 4 Ensuite 1 Private
Romantic 2 person spas with quality toiletries

AAA Tourism
★★★★☆

Located in a secluded valley on the beautiful Colo River surrounded by natural bush with abundant birds. Cottages are self contained designed for a romantic escape for couples with 2 person spa, logfire, air conditioned, TV, DVD, video. Try our 4 person hot tub spa, solar pool, games room, bikes, kayaks or dinghy for exploring the pristine river. Complete privacy with beautiful outlook. Breakfast basket supplied. Picnic/BBQ, evening meals and massages also available. Ask about our Romantic Horse & Carriage packages.

Hay

Bank Bed & Breakfast *B&B*
Sally Smith
86 Lachlan Street
Hay
NSW 2711
In Hay Central

Tel (02) 6993 1730
or 0429 931 730
Fax (02) 6993 3440
ttsk@tpg.com.au
http://www1.tpg.com.au/users/ttsk

Double $120
Single $80
Full breakfast
1 King 1 Twin (2 bdrm)
Bathrooms: 1 Private

This National Trust classified mansion was built in 1891 to house the London Chartered Bank, one of the historic buildings restored to its original condition in Lachlan Street. The residence consists of a large dining room complete with period furniture and decor. The cedar staircase leads to the guest suite of two bedrooms and a fully modernised bathroom (complete with spa). The guest sitting room opens onto the balcony overlooking the main street. We look forward to you experiencing the hospitality of Hay with us.

Hunter Valley - Aberdeen - Scone

Craigmhor Mountain Retreat *Luxury B&B & Homestay & Separate Suite & Self Contained Apartment*
Gay Hoskings
Upper Rouchel Road
Upper Rouchel, NSW 2336
48 km E of Aberdeen

Tel (02) 6543 6393
Fax (02) 65436394
bnb@craigmhor.com.au
www.craigmhor.com.au

Double $135-$165 **Single** $70-$85
Children $35-$45 Full breakfast
Dinner $30-$50 served with
Upper Hunter Wines
4WD tours from $100
Visa MC accepted
3 Queen 1 Twin (4 bdrm)
Bathrooms: 2 Ensuite 1 Guest share

AAA Tourism
★★★★

Total contrast to city living - country hospitality, seclusion, splendid views, crisp mountain air in foothills of Barrington Tops. Peace and tranquillity assured - just you, your host, 1000 ha Australian bush and all its wildlife. Homestay; B&B; Self-Catered; Mix & Match to suit. Possible activities: doing absolutely nothing, picnicking by mountain streams, bush walking (50 km of forest trails), mountain biking, fishing stocked dams, Lake Glenbawn, 4-WD touring (optional extra), exploring Upper Hunter Country - magnificent horse studs, historic towns, wineries, National Parks.

The Old George and Dragon Guesthouse

Guest House
Nicolena & Martin Hurley
50 Melbourne Street
East Maitland
NSW 2323
5 km E of Maitland

Tel (02) 4934 6080 or 0412 995 639
Fax (02) 4933 6076
reservations@oldgeorgedragonguesthouse.com.au
www.oldgeorgedragonguesthouse.com.au

Double $140-$240
Single $130-$190
Full breakfast
Dinner, Bed & Breakfast package $340-$380 per couple
Visa MC Diners Amex Eftpos accepted
2 King 3 Queen (5 bdrm)
All guestrooms themed individually
Bathrooms: 5 Ensuite

Your hosts Nicolena and Martin will greet you on arrival. Our service is discreet and professional.
Formerly a coach inn in the main route north from Sydney, the guesthouse has five guestrooms with ensuites, all individually decorated with high ceilings, flat LCD Television, DVD -CD Player & wireless broadband (fees apply). A spacious layout convey a comforting sense of space and privacy. The guest lounge has an open fire place for the

winter months. The restaurant located next to the guesthouse features an extensive menu range with a remarkable aged wine list. The guesthouse is located close to Morpeth , famous wineries of Pokolbin, rugged glories of Barrington Tops and the sunny salty seduction of Port Stephens. The ideal place to stay for business or pleasure, special occasions, wedding night or group getaway.

Hunter Valley - Lochinvar

Lochinvar House *Luxury B&B & Farmstay*
Brent Winner & Kendall McGuirk
Kaludah Estate,
1204 New England Highway
Lochinvar , NSW 2321
*3 km W of Lochinvar (turn off Hwy
Kaludah Ck)*

Tel (02) 4930 7873
or 0428 864 036
Fax (02) 4930 7798
lochinvarhse@yahoo.com.au
www.geocities.com/lochinvarhse

Double $110-$165 Single $88-$143
Full breakfast
Dinner B/A
1 King/Twin 4 Queen 1 Double (6 bdrm)
2 Guest share: Homestead 1 private: Cottage

Historic Georgian-Victorian country homestead circa 1841 on Kaludah Estate, an 88 acre grazing property on the Hunter River. With grand entrance and dining room, luxuriously appointed rooms featuring 13 foot ceilings and antique furnishings, Lochinvar House overlooks beautiful Loch Katrine with views over the surrounding countryside. A large swimming pool and spa with BBQ area are available. Situated 1 km north of the New England Highway, close to restaurants, Wyndham Estate and other vineyards, equestrian centre, historic Maitland and Greta for antiques. Kennels available. Ideal for small groups and conferences.

~

Hunter Valley - Lovedale - Pokolbin

Hill Top Country Guest House *Luxury B&B & Homestay & Farmstay & Self Contained Apartment & Guest House*
Margaret Bancroft
288 Talga Road
Rothbury
NSW 2320
17 km N of Cessnock

Tel (02) 4930 7111
Fax (02) 4930 9048
stay@hilltopguesthouse.com.au
www.hilltopguesthouse.com.au

Double $90-$250
Full breakfast
Visa MC accepted
2 King/Twin1 King 3 Queen
4 Twin (6 bdrm)
Bathrooms: 4 Ensuite 2 Private spa baths

An Australian Country Experience, staying in the colonial homestead or modern Villas. Situated on the Molly Morgan Range with spectacular views of the Hunter Valley and Wine Country. Join the 4WD Night Wildlife Safari, horse riding and encounter abundant native wildlife of kangaroos, wombats, echidnas, possums roaming in their natural environment. Winery tours leave daily. The luxury guest house offers Spa Suites, wood fires, 10' billiard table, Grand Piano, delicious meals, massages, beauty treatments, sauna, pool and air-conditioning. The guest house is ideal for couples and family and friends gatherings.

Bronte Guesthouse *Guest House*
Nicolena & Martin Hurley
147 Swan Street
Morpeth
NSW 2321
10 km E of Maitland

Tel (02) 4934 6080
or 0412 995 639
Fax (02) 4933 6076
reservations@bronteguesthouse.com.au
www.bronteguesthouse.com.au

AAA Tourism
★★★★

Double $120-$200 Single $110-$195
Full breakfast
Visa MC Diners Amex Eftpos accepted
3 King 3 Queen (6 bdrm)
Contemporary style accommodation
Bathrooms: 6 Ensuite One room has a bath

Historic, charming, chic and comfortable, welcoming service with attention to detail. All rooms are themed to reflect the needs of the sophisticated traveller and offer complete luxury with ensuites, individually controlled air conditioning, LCD Flat Televisions, DVD Players, CD Players and wireless broadband (fees apply).

There are two guest lounges with open fire places for the winter months. Breakfast is served on the guesthouse's balcony overlooking the township of Morpeth and the Hunter River.

Located in the heart of Morpeth, a fascinating little village, which started life in 1821 as a river port for the Hunter River. The Hunter Wineries are a short drive away as is Port Stephens.

The ideal place to stay for business or pleasure, special occasions, wedding night or group getaway.

Hunter Valley - Morpeth

Morpeth Convent Guest House *Luxury B&B*

Loris Chahl
24 James Street
Morpeth, NSW 2321
35 km NW of Newcastle

Tel (02) 4934 4176
or 1300 855 251
Fax (02) 4934 4179
info@morpethconvent.com.au
www.morpethconvent.com.au

Double $130-$165
Children only if whole house is occupied
by the party
Full breakfast
Dinner by arrangement
Special tariffs available mid-week
Visa MC Eftpos accepted
4 Queen 1 Twin (5 bdrm) polished floors, airconditioned, TV
Bathrooms: 4 Ensuite 1 Private queen rooms have ensuite, twin room private bath

Morpeth Convent Guest House is a grand two storey building once home to nuns of a teaching order, now refurbished to cater for bed-and-breakfast style accommodation with every modern comfort. The glorious house features sprawling verandas both upstairs and down, two spacious common rooms and breakfast room with bay windows. This unique accommodation experience is nestled in the heart of Morpeth NSW Australia - a town that's steeped in history and is the perfect place to get-away with family, friends or on your own.

Hunter Valley - Pokolbin

Catersfield House *Guest House*

Rosemary & Alec Cater
96 Mistletoe Lane
Pokolbin, NSW 2320
23 km NW of Cessnock

Tel (02) 4998 7220
Fax (02) 4998 7558
catersfield@catersfield.com.au
www.catersfield.com.au

Double $160-$225
Full breakfast
Dinner $50 for 3 course $40 for 2 course
Extra Adult $35
Weekend package from $440
Visa MC Diners Amex Eftpos accepted
7 King 1 Queen 14 Twin (8 bdrm)
Bathrooms: 8 Ensuite

    AAA Tourism ★★★★

A Boutique Country Resort situated amongst the vineyards of Pokolbin with spectacular views of the Brokenback Ranges. A total of eight guestrooms comprised of five luxurious bedrooms with king-size or twin beds, two with two-person spas, a special French room with a traditional four poster bed, a separate Summerhouse also with a two person spa. Rooms have reverse cycle A/C, TVs, VCRs, fridges, tea/coffee facilities, irons/boards and hairdryers. There is a log fire in the Guests lounge, a salt-water swimming pool, petanque, fishing and BBQ facilities. A hot country breakfast is included in the tariff and Dinner is available. Guests can also enjoy gourmet coffee and fine food from Catersfield's Café Monteverdi. Catersfield House specialises in Estate Weddings.

Hunter Valley - Pokolbin

Elfin Hill *Farmstay & Separate Suite & Guest House*

Marie & Mark Blackmore
Marrowbone Road
Pokolbin, NSW 2320
5 km W of Cessnock

Tel (02) 4998 7543
or 0416 209 709
0406 531 709
Fax (02) 4998 7817
relax@elfinhill.com.au
www.elfinhill.com.au

Double $110-$250 **Single** $98-$250
Children $40
Full breakfast
Extra person $50
Visa MC Amex Eftpos accepted
7 Queen 2 Double 4 Twin 5 Single (7 bdrm)
Bathrooms: 7 Ensuite

AAA Tourism
★★★☆

Enjoy delightful country accommodation, serenely elevated with spectacular views of surrounding vineyards. Native wildlife. Rooms are comfy with everything you need to make your stay easy and enjoyable. BBQ beside the saltwater pool. Fabulous comfortable guest lounge. Easy bush walking. Close to Wine Tasting and Fantastic Cuisine, cheese, galleries etc. Excellent breakfast in your room or eat outside at one of many areas. Just completed a separate studio with mezzanine sleeping, ensuite, kitchen, amazing views, romantic and special.

Hunter Valley - Wine Country - Wollombi

Capers Guest House and Cottage *Luxury B&B & Self Contained House & Guest House*

Jane Young
2859 Wollombi Road
Wollombi
NSW 2325
29 km SW of Cessnock

Tel (02) 4998 3211
or 0409 305 285
Fax (02) 4998 3458
stay@capers.com.au
www.capers.com.au

Double $200-$380 **Single** $200-$380
Full breakfast
Dinner $55-$65
Cottage from $75 per person per night
Visa MC Diners Amex accepted
1 King 5 Queen 2 Double 1 Twin (9 bdrm)
Bathrooms: 8 Ensuite

AAA Tourism
★★★★☆

Majestic Guesthouse Retreat, set in the historic village of Wollombi. Six elegantly appointed guest rooms, reverse-cycle air-conditioning and spacious guest lounge with double sided open log fire places. Includes full country breakfast, complimentary port and chocolates. Fully licensed and dinner can be arranged. Cottage: Stay two nights in luxury three bedroom cottages which accommodates up to 7 people. Open fire or A/C in the summer, large hamper breakfast, two bathrooms one with Spa bath, gourmet kitchen, sweetest garden with BBQ, TV, CD, and DVD players.

Hunter Valley - Wollombi - Laguna

Judsons at Laguna *Luxury Separate Suite & Guest House*
Di & Adrian Judson
3868 Great North Road
Laguna
NSW 2325
8 km S of Wollombi

Tel (02) 4998 8085
Fax (02) 4998 8563
di@judsonsatlaguna.com.au
www.judsonsatlaguna.com.au

Double $180-$350
Special breakfast
Dinner $25-$75
Visa MC Amex Eftpos accepted
4 Queen (4 bdrm)
Bathrooms: 4 Ensuite
Double Spa Baths

    AAA Tourism ★★★★☆

From the moment you thread along the private drive that winds up the valley, you're in for a special experience that combines the best of country living with style and sophistication. Each suite is bright and meticulously kept, with a lounge/dining room separate from the bedroom and includes: Open wood fire, Spa baths, Free internet connection, CD/DVD players Complimentary DVD library, antipasto platter, beer and sherry on arrival, Kitchenette, r/c a/c. In-ground pool in bush setting. A variety of meals is available.

~

Jervis Bay

Experience the dramatic beauty of Jervis Bay and its pleasant coastal climate. It's an unspoilt paradise just 2½ -3 hours away from Sydney or Canberra.

Walk on the beach and look for dolphins playing in the surf, go fishing, swimming or diving, a dolphin-watch cruise (year round) or a whale-watch cruise (June-July, September-October).

Be dazzled by the whitest sand in the world. Visit Booderee National Park, where you can go walking, visit the amazing ruined lighthouse, picnic in the botanical gardens, see kangaroos and marvel at the many beautiful parrots.
Bill Rogers

Jervis Bay - Huskisson

Dolphin Sands Jervis Bay *B&B & Self Contained Cottage*
Wayne and Beatrice Whitten
6 Tomerong Street
Jervis Bay, Huskisson
NSW 2540
25 km S of Nowra

Tel (02) 4441 5511 or 0418 476 280
Fax (02) 4441 7712
info@dolphinsands.com
www.dolphinsands.com

Double $175-$295
Children welcome in S/C cottage
Full breakfast
Visa MC Amex Eftpos accepted
4 Queen 1 Twin (5 bdrm)
Bathrooms: 5 Ensuite 2 Queen Spa
Rooms, 1 queen with bath and shower

   AAA Tourism ★★★★☆

Dolphin Sands is what life by the ocean is all about. Dolphin Sands is a tranquil couples retreat, only minutes from the White Sands, Dolphins, and Clear Blue Waters of Jervis Bay. Hosts Wayne and Beatrice Whitten designed your luxury accommodations creating an intimate and relaxing atmosphere, while maintaining guest room privacy. Each room has the features expected of a luxury retreat; mini-fridge, TV, queen beds, bathrobes, tea/coffee facilities, aircon and ensuites. Also Dolphin Cottage, an original Creswell Cottage. S/C accommodation. Two queen rooms and a sleep out suitable for two young adults (children).

Jervis Bay - Vincentia

Nelson Beach Lodge *B&B*
Robyn Brown
404 Elizabeth Drive
Vincentia
NSW 2540
30 km S of Nowra

Tel (02) 4441 6006
or 0402 263 997
Fax (02) 4441 6006
rbrown303@hotmail.com
www.bbbook.com.au/nelson.html

Double $95-$130 Single $55-$95
Children half price
Special breakfast
Dinner $25
Visa MC accepted
1 King/Twin 3 Queen 2 Twin (4 bdrm)
Beds have electric blankets
Bathrooms: 1 Ensuite 1 Family share 1 Guest share 1 Private

Just two minutes walk from white sands

Enjoy a relaxing weekend or stopover at Nelson Beach Lodge. Ideally situated 2 1/2 hours from Sydney and Canberra. A cosy comfortable home, with guest lounge and balcony overlooking Jervis Bay and secluded garden. Just two minutes walk from white sands, red cliffs and crystal clear waters of Nelson Beach. Baywatch cruises see the dolphins, seals and penguins. Also diving, fishing, swimming, sailing, golf, bike riding and bush walking tracks around the waterfront and many picnic spots in local National and Marine Park, Botanic Gardens, Winery, and historic towns nearby. Aussie Host Business.

Jindabyne - Snowy Mountains

Troldhaugen Lodge *B&B & Guest House*

John & Sandra Bradshaw
13 Cobbodah Street
Jindabyne
NSW 2627
30 km W of Berridale

Tel (02) 6456 2718
or 0409 562 718
Fax (02) 6456 2718
troldhaugen@ozemail.com.au
www.troldhaugen.com.au

Double $75-$150 Single $50-$120
Children $15- $40
Continental breakfast
Cooked breakfast $7-$10
Visa MC Amex accepted
1 Queen 8 Double 1 Single (10 bdrm)
6 double rooms have extra bedding for up to 5 persons
Bathrooms: 10 Ensuite

AAA Tourism
★★★☆

Centrally located in Jindabyne within walking distance to shops, hotels, restaurants, club and lake. Troldhaugen is situated at the end of a quiet cul-de-sac. A friendly owner/operated lodge catering for the family or couples, holiday. Facilities include guest lounge with open fireplace, TV and videos. Game room with tennis & pool tables, drying room & ski racks. All rooms are centrally heated and have own ensuites. Features include mountain and lake views.

Kangaroo Valley

The Loveshack *Self Contained House*

Gabrielle Rashleigh, Mal Williams
& Chris Young
Kangaroo Valley
Contact for Details
5 km N of Kangaroo Valley

Tel (02) 9967 5900
Fax (02) 9967 5944
wines@youngandrashleigh.com
www.youngandrashleigh.com

Double $182.50-$365
Accommodation only
Foldout bed in loungeroom
Visa MC Diners Eftpos accepted
1 Queen (1 bdrm)
Beautifully decorated and furnished
Bathrooms: 1 Ensuite with Spa Bath

The Love Shack sleeps up to 4 people in a separate queen bedroom and an inner spring sofa bed in the loungeroom. A spa bathroom, fully equipped kitchen, and a deck with BBQ, also has a gas heater. There is a TV, stereo/CD player and DVD player. The polished timber floor boards blends in well with the surrounding bush and river and evokes a feeling of peace and tranquility.

Kiama

Kiama, a beautiful seaside town just 90 minutes drive south of Sydney and 2½ hours from Canberra. Famous for its blowholes, beaches, and natural beauty, the area provides visitors with a wealth of experiences. The pristine beaches contrast with the magnificent hinterland with its mosaic of rainforest and green pastures dotted with grazing dairy cattle.

The Hinterland Trail gives breathtaking views of the coast and farming valleys while taking you past historic dry stone walls to Jamberoo, Minnamurra Rainforest, and Barren Grounds Nature Reserve. Dianne Rendel, Seashells

Kiama

Kiama Bed & Breakfast *Guest House & Self-catering cottage with Kitchen*

Tony & Marian van Zanen
15 Riversdale Road
Kiama
NSW 2533
2.5 km W of Kiama

Tel (02) 4232 2844
Fax (02) 4232 2868
kiamabnb@kbb.com.au
www.kbb.com.au

Double $150-$240
Single $100-$150
Children $33
Special breakfast
Visa MC Diners Eftpos accepted
2 King 2 Queen 1 Double
4 Single (4 bdrm)
Bathrooms: 4 Ensuite

AAA Tourism
★★★★★

Take an easy drive just one and a half hours south of Sydney and you will find yourself in the green hills of Kiama and Jamberoo where you will discover the multi award-winning Kiama Bed & Breakfast and Cottage. Enjoy comfortable homestyle 5-star accommodation on landscaped rainforest garden acreage overlooking the spectacular rural scenery of Jamberoo Valley and rainforest escarpment, yet only 2km from the bustling seaside township of Kiama. Accommodation for singles, doubles, families and groups of 8 or more with your choice of breakfast style. For more information, see our website on www.kbb.com.

Kiama

Bed and Views Kiama *B&B*
Sabine & Rudi Dux
69 Riversdale Road
Kiama
NSW 2533
3 km W of Kiama

Tel (02) 4232 3662
admin@bedandviewskiama.com.au
www.bedandviewskiama.com.au

Double $140-$160
Full breakfast
Lovebird Suite from $190
Visa MC accepted
1 King/Twin2 King 1 Queen (4 bdrm)
Comfortable r/c air-con. all rooms
Bathrooms: 4 Ensuite
One with spa under a glass roof

Enjoy crystal clear waters at various beaches, see the world's famous Blow Hole, walk the nearby rainforest or find your favourite spot in the garden with unspoilt ocean and rural views. Only 2 minutes away from the seaside town Kiama this B&B offers modern king and queen-bed rooms, ensuites, one with spa, all air-conditioned (cool/heat). Welcoming European hospitality invites to a 'spoilt for choice' breakfast. Day-tour suggestions and booking assistance provided. "What a remarkable combination of stunning views, most comfortable bed, delicious breakfast and a warm and friendly welcome." L&D Wilson, Melbourne.

Kiama

Kiama Sea Mist Cottage *Self Contained House*
Marilyn Richardson
37 Tingira Crecent
Kiama
NSW 2533
1 km S of Kiama

Tel (02) 4233 2116
or 0408 332118
seamistcottage@optusnet.com.au
www.kiama.com.au/seamist

Double $175-$350
Accommodation only
Weekly rates from $850-$2350
Visa MC accepted
1 Queen 1 Double 2 Single (3 bdrm)
Bathrooms: 1 Ensuite 1 Private
Ensuite to Master bedroom

Waterfront Cottage near the Little Blowhole. Panoramic ocean views from spacious living areas. Relax and unwind on the deck or take a stroll along the Coastal Walk to the beach. Dolphin & whale watch (seasonal). Self-cater facilities.Modern kitchen, microwave, dishwasher. Internal laundry. 2 TVs/2VCR/CD/DVD/Videos. BBQ. A/C. Weekend Check-in 2.30pm Friday Check-out 2pm Sunday (if available). Sleeps 6. Sydney 90 minutes, Canberra 2.5 hours. "Medicine for the soul" NS Sydney. "The house and location were perfect" CS St. Ives.

Kiama

Seashells Kiama *Self Contained House*
Dianne Rendel
72 Bong Bong Street
Kiama
NSW 2533
0.5 km SW of Kiama P.O.

Tel (02) 4232 2504
or 0414 423 225
Fax (02) 4232 3419
dianne@seashellskiama.com.au
www.seashellskiama.com.au

Double $200-$250
Children and babies rates available
Accommodation only
2nights min booking
Peak season wkly for whole bungalow POA
1 Queen 1 Double 2 Single (3 bdrm) + 1 porta cot
Bathrooms: 3 Private includes 1 bath & 1 separate WC

Unwind . . . Relax . . . and experience the delights of Kiama from this thoughtfully renovated 1960s bungalow. The spacious living area with sweeping town and ocean views is sunroom by day and cosy living room by night. Neat as a pin and full of light this retro-styled home has all the amenities you would expect and more . . . best of all, has personality. Whether looking for a weekend away or a longer stay Seashells Kiama is ideal for a summer holiday or winter retreat - the perfect getaway for couples, families and friends. Illawarra Tourism Award Winner.

≈

Lismore

Suzanne's Hideaway *Self Contained House*
Peter & Suzanne McGuinness
20 Elliot Road,
Clunes via Lismore
NSW 2480
18 km NE of Lismore

Tel (02) 6629 1228
Fax (02) 6629 1557
suzanne@suzanneshideaway.com.au
www.suzanneshideaway.com.au

Double $150-$330 Single $150-$330
Children $10
Accommodation only
Extra adult $40
Visa MC accepted
2 King/Twin 2 King 6 Queen 4 Single
(9 bdrm) 1, 2, & 3 bedroom villas
Bathrooms: 2 Ensuite 6 Family share
6 Private villas have own large spa baths

Your own private resort. Large 1, 2, or 3 bedroom S/C villas with spa baths or S/C studio. Set in sub-tropical gardens and vast panorama. Walk to our rain forest lined river and swim or fish. Use our salt water swimming pool, floodlit synthetic grass tennis court and gym equipment. Linen included, A/C TV, DVD, CD/radio. BBQ. Laundry. Licensed general store, cafés, butcher nearby. Byron Bay/ Lismore/National Park 20 mins. Treat yourself to a luxurious quiet hideaway. Children welcome. 4 star AAA rated.

Lismore - Clunes

PJ's *B&B*
Terry & Susan Hurst
152 Johnston Road
Clunes
NSW 2480
16 km N of Lismore

Tel (02) 6629 1788
or 0412 996 243
Fax (02) 6629 1744
pjsbb@bigpond.com
www.pjsretreat.com

Double $140
Single $125
Full breakfast
Eftpos accepted
3 King (3 bdrm)
Bathrooms: 3 Ensuite

 AAA Tourism
★★★★☆

P J's looks over some of the most beautiful countryside in NSW. All guest rooms have panoramic views that are spectacular. The stylishly purpose built B&B which features three elegant and spacious bedrooms all with the usual comforts including complimentary port, chocolates and local coffee. A personalised country breakfast is served. PJ's is the ideal spot from which to experience the many wonders of the Northern Rivers. Or just simply relax by the saltwater pool or your own private courtyard and soak up the view. Quality accommodation at an affordable price.

Manilla Tamworth District

Oakhampton Homestead & Country Holidays *B&B & Farmstay, Homestead, Apartment, Cottage & Cabins*
Belinda & James Nixon
Oakhampton Road, Manilla, NSW 2346
21 km N of Manilla

Tel (02) 6785 6517 or 0429 496 936
Fax (02) 6785 6573
belinda@oakhampton.biz
www.oakhampton.biz

Double $140-$170 Single $85-$100
Children under 12 half price
Full breakfast
Dinner from $35 (2 course), $55 (3 course)
Cabins from $35pp, Cottage from $135pn,
Apartment from $220
Visa MC JCB accepted
6 Queen 10 Twin 12 Single (17 bdrm)
H/std: 3; Apt 2, Cot 3, Cabin 9
Bathrooms: 5 Ensuite 1 Guest share 2 Private

 AAA Tourism
★★★★

O akhampton is a working farm of 4000 acres, offering a variety of activities including horse riding, tennis, swimming and canoeing. The 4 star rated Homestead overlooks the large garden has 3 rooms each with ensuite bathrooms. The 4 star rated unit has 2 bedrooms, private bathroom, kitchen, dining room, sitting room, air/con, a large verandah and private entrance. The Top Spot cottage was built about 1900 and has 3 bedrooms, private bathroom, kitchen, dining room, sitting room, fireplace, wonderful views. The cabins are set in a large area for games and group activities.

Merimbula

Bella Vista *B&B*
Judy Hori
16 Main Street
Merimbula
NSW 2548
1 km N of Town Centre

Tel (02) 6495 1373
Fax (02) 6495 2344
bellavistauno@bigpond.com
www.merimbulabellavista.com.au

Double $150-$200
Full breakfast
2 King/Twin (2 bdrm)
Bathrooms: 2 Ensuite

AAA Tourism
★★★★☆

Bella Vista is an Award Winning designed boutique B&B with entrance to your private area with king size bed, bathroom, under-floor heating, tea and coffee making facilities. Private access to the lake. Enjoy a delicious breakfast while admiring the spectacular views from the large deck, watch the pelicans, swans and bird life go by. Minutes walk to shops, restaurants and clubs. Minutes drive to pristine beaches, golf clubs, whale watching and fishing. We are half way between Sydney and Melbourne with daily flights taking just over an hour. Also 2 hours to the snow fields.

~

Merimbula

Robyn's Nest Guest House *Luxury BnB and Self Contained Villas*
Robyn Britten
188 Merimbula Drive
Merimbula
NSW 2548
2 km N of Merimbula

Tel (02) 6495 4956
Fax (02) 6495 2426
enquiries@robynsnest.com.au
www.robynsnest.com.au

Double $175-$250 Single $140-$215
Children $25-$50
Full breakfast
Self Contained Villas
Visa MC Amex Eftpos accepted
5 King/Twin 10 King 11 Queen
2 Twin (28 bdrm)
Old world charm, modern comfort
Bathrooms: 28 Ensuite

    AAA Tourism
★★★★★

Robyn's Nest is a 5* multi-award winning luxury BnB set amid 100 acres of bushland with 25acres of Absolute Lake Frontage with water views from every room. Halfway between Sydney and Melbourne on the coastal route, 2hrs from Canberra and 2hrs from the snowfields. Facilities heated pool, spas, sauna, tennis court, jetty/boat and mooring into prime fish breeding grounds. 3mins from the town centre that has 20 restaurants, pristine beaches, whale watching, bushwalking, deep sea & rock fishing. Romantic Indulgence and adventure packages available.

Milton - Ulladulla

Meadowlake Lodge *Luxury B&B*
Diana & Peter Falloon
318 Wilfords Lane
Milton
NSW 2538
3 km S of Milton

Tel (02) 4455 7722
Fax (02) 4455 7733
meadowlake@bigpond.com
www.meadowlakelodge.com.au

Double $170-$230 Single $140-$190
Not suitable for children under 6
Full breakfast
Dinner B/A three courses $60pp BYO
Visa MC Amex accepted
1 King/Twin 2 Queen (3 bdrm)
Elegant and spacious
Bathrooms: 3 Ensuite Separate shower and bath

    AAA Tourism ★★★★★

I n 2004, 2005 and 2006 Meadowlake won the South Coast Tourism Award in the prestigious category of Accommodation Up to Five Stars. The luxurious Five Star country house overlooks lakes and wetlands. Only 3 hours from Sydney and 2.5 from Canberra. Close to historic Milton. Near the beaches at Mollymook and bush walks in the Budawangs. Spacious and elegant rooms have en suites with baths. Dinners by arrangement. At Meadowlake Lodge luxury is a way of life. Listen to the sounds of nature.

~

Moruya

Moruya's location on the banks of the picturesque Moruya River midway between Batemans Bay and Narooma - the ideal centre for exploring the beauties of the Eurobodalla Nature Coast, the Deua National Parks and wilderness areas.

The township maintains its country town atmosphere with heritage buildings, museum, craft and antique shops, plus the unique display of wood carvings in the main street.

Within easy travelling are Tuross, Narooma, Tilba and Bermagui to the South, with Mogo, Broulee, Batemans Bay, Nelligen and Durass to the North. By road Sydney is 5 hours away and Melbourne 9 hours, making an ideal overnight stop.
John Spencer, Bryn Glas B&B

Moruya

Bryn Glas *Luxury B&B & Self Contained Cottage*
Sandra & John Spencer
19 Valley View Lane
Moruya
NSW 2537
3 km S of Moruya PO

Tel (02) 4474 0826
info@brynglas.com.au
www.brynglas.com.au

Double $130-$170
Single $120-$140
Children in cottage only $10 per stay
Full breakfast
Visa MC accepted
2 Queen (3 bdrm) + Cottage
Bathrooms: 2 Ensuite
1 Bathroom in Cottage

AAA Tourism
★★★★☆

Four and a Half Star Quality with Rural Tranquility. Bryn Glas is situated on 15 rural acres, plus s/c cottage sleeping 4. Within a short driving distance are Batemans Bay, Mogo, Tuross and Narooma, wonderful beaches and National Parks, fishing and boating. Bryn Glas is rated 4 Star plus, has Air Conditioned ensuite bedrooms with TV, guest sitting/dining/TV room, wide verandas with magnificent mountain views and country landscape. Stroll round the property and see our young calves, chickens our developing gardens. Wireless Broadband now available.

Murwillumbah

Nestled between the NSW and Queensland Border and Byron Shire, the Tweed enchants those lucky enough to stumble upon this largely undiscovered area. Home to 5 World Heritage listed National Parks, including Mt Warning, the spot where the dawn sun first touches Australia.

Pristine beaches, untouched rainforests, world class artisans, golf, horse-riding, scenic joy flights, multi-million dollar art gallery and more. From the Tweed coastal region, dotted with small towns to the spectacular hinterland mountains and valleys, with quaint villages, sidewalk cafés, galleries, arts and crafts.

The Tweed is the Jewel in the Crown of the Northern Rivers and has something to satisfy all tastes and pockets.
Tracy and Clive Parker, Hillcrest Mountain View

Murwillumbah - Crystal Creek

Hillcrest Mountain View Retreat *Luxury B&B & Farmstay & Separate Suite*
& Air-conditioned Cottage with full kitchen
Clive & Tracy Parker
Upper Crystal Creek Road
Murwillumbah
NSW 2484
12 km NW of Murwillumbah

Tel (02) 6679 1023
romance@hillcrestbb.com
www.hillcrestbb.com/

Double $165-$350
Full breakfast
Dinner B/A from $170 per couple
Visa MC accepted
3 Queen (3 bdrm)
In-room TV, DVD, video, a/c
Bathrooms: 3 Ensuite
Two with luxury double spa baths

  AAA Tourism ★★★★★

Multi Tourism Award winning specialists in romantic getaways offering peace, privacy, spectacular views from Mt Warning to the Springbrook rainforests, solar-heated salt-water pool, luxury double spa baths, massage, wood fire, air-conditioning & jolly good food. Choose from 2 B&B suites in the main house private guest wing or 1 fully self-contained Honeymoon Spa Cottage in its own secluded garden. Centrally located to 5 World Heritage National Parks, golf, horse-riding, galleries, markets and more. Only 35 minutes from Gold Coast airport, 95 minutes from Brisbane.

Myall Lakes - Bulahdelah

Bombah Point Eco Cottages *Luxury Self Contained Cottages - Six*
Jill and Peter Madden
969 Bombah Point Road
Bulahdelah
NSW 2423
10 km SE of Bulahdelah

Tel (02) 4997 4401
or 0418 236 582
Fax (02) 4997 4465
jill@bombah.com.au
www.bombah.com.au

Double $189-$350
Breakfast by arrangement
Dinner by arrangement
Discounts 3 or more nights
Extra person $40 or quote if more than 2
Visa MC Eftpos accepted
1 Queen 1 Double 1 Single (2 bdrm)
Main bedroom and Loft bedroom
Bathrooms: 1 Private (One in each cottage)

  AAA Tourism ★★★★

Six architecturally designed, open-plan, glass and timber cottages discretely positioned in secluded woodland for sensational bush and valley views. Close to lake and beaches. Surrounded by Myall Lakes National Park each private cottage is beautifully appointed and features a full surround verandah, hammock, spa bath, TV/DVD/CD, full kitchen, stainless steel appliances, gas BBQ. On site pool, bikes, kayaks & walks. 3 hours north of Sydney and only 10kms east of Pacific Highway at Bulahdelah on boundary of Myall Lakes National Park.

Pub Hill Farm *B&B & Farmstay & Self Contained cottage*
Micki & Ian Thomlinson
566 Scenic Drive Narooma
Box 227, Narooma
NSW 2546
8 km W of Narooma

Tel (02) 4476 3177
Fax (02) 4476 3177
pubhill@activ8.net.au
www.pubhillfarm.com

Double $100-$125 Single $90-$100
Full breakfast
Karibu Cottage $150 per day
2 King/Twin 2 Queen 1 Double (5 bdrm)
Bathrooms: 5 Ensuite

Pub Hill Farm is a small farm, sitting high on a hill overlooking the beautiful Wagonga Inlet and with 2 kilometres of water frontage. The birdlife is abundant and the extreme quiet makes it an ideal place to bird watch. Small mobs of kangaroos live on the property.

All rooms have water views, private outdoor areas and private entrances, plus ensuites, microwaves, fridges, TV, and tea and coffee. We welcome guests' pets. The gardens are fully fenced for their safety. If you prefer self contained accommodation, our new Karibu Cottage is gorgeous. Just for two, with mezzanine bedroom and fabulous views over Wagonga Inlet, the Karibu sits in a secluded garden where you can enjoy water views in complete privacy. There is a cosy wood fire for winter. We have travelled extensively and lived abroad in both U K and North and East Africa and enjoy swapping travellers' tales with our guests.

"Quite the best B&B we have ever stayed at, anywhere. Superb hospitality"
J & PJ, Woodham, Surrey, England.
"Am speechless - loved every minute - your hospitality was warm and wonderful"
Mary and Bill R, Los Osos, California USA.

Narromine

Camerons Farmstay *B&B & Homestay & Farmstay & Self Contained Cottage*

Ian & Kerry Cameron
Nundoone Park,
213 Ceres Road
Narromine
NSW 2821
6 km W of Narromine

Tel (02) 6889 2978
Fax (02) 6889 5229
www.bbbook.com.au/cameronsfarmstay.html

Double $110-$130 Single $90
Children $40
Continental breakfast
Dinner B/A
Self Contained Cottage from $120
2 Queen 2 Double 1 Twin 4 Single (5 bdrm)
Bathrooms: 1 Ensuite 1 Guest share

   AAA Tourism ★★★☆

Our home, 30 minutes west of Dubbo. We offer 4 star S/C cottage and B&B. Our house is modern and spacious with reverse cycle air-conditioning with each bedroom having a fan/heater; guest lounge has television, video, books, tea/coffee making facilities, fridge etc. It is surrounded by large gardens, all weather tennis court, and pool. Ian and Kerry run a successful Border Leicester Sheep stud - see lambs, shearing, haymaking, cotton growing and harvesting (seasonal), tour cotton gin. Visit: Rose Nursery, Iris Farm, Aviation Museum and Gliding Centre. "Excellent, comfortable accommodation and great hospitality. So good to come back." P&G, Belgium.

Newcastle

Newcastle, capital of the Hunter, is thriving with its heritage as an industrial city and is a sought-after week-end getaway and holiday destination.

Newcastle impresses by its beauty, cleanliness, parks and facilities. Beautiful old buildings are a reminder of our rich architectural heritage. Beaches to die for, vibrant harbour and great restaurants are all within easy access of the centre.

Nature reserves like Blackbutt, the Wetlands and the Botanic Gardens are worth a visit as is the Art Gallery, the leading regional gallery in Australia. A stroll along the Foreshore and on the Hill gives a vivid reflection of life then and now.
Rosemary Bunker, Newcomen B&B

Newcastle

Newcomen B&B *B&B & Studio Accommodation*
Rosemary Bunker
70 Newcomen Street
Newcastle
NSW 2300
0.5 km N of Newcastle Central

Tel (02) 4929 7313
or 0412 145 104
Fax (02) 4929 7645
newcomen_bb@hotmail.com
www.newcomen-bb.com.au

Double $130-$140
Single $90-$100
Children $30
Full breakfast
Visa MC accepted
1 Queen 1 Single (1 bdrm)
Good mattress and bedding
Bathrooms: 1 Private

Be delighted by this gem of a C19 home nestling in a vibrant garden. Explore the surrounding rich heritage area, stroll by the foreshore, enjoy the beach, savour city delights, laze by the pool, relax with every comfort, including air-conditioning, in harmonious decor featuring art works. A boutique mini holiday you'll love.

Newcastle - Hamilton

Hamilton Heritage *B&B*
Laraine & Colin Bunt
178 Denison Street
Hamilton, NSW 2303
6 km N of Newcastle

Tel (02) 4961 1242
or 0414 717 688
Fax (02) 4969 4758
colaine@iprimus.com.au
www.theholidayhost.com/
hamiltonheritage

Double $120-$140 Single $90-$100
Children $10-$25 (under 3 free)
Special breakfast
Wedding night champagne $185
Visa MC Diners accepted
2 Queen 1 Double 3 Single (3 bdrm)
All bedrooms airconditioned
Bathrooms: 3 Ensuite 1 bath, 1 spa, 3 showers

Hamilton Heritage B&B, "Old World Charm", situated on Historic Cameron Hill. Close to Broadmeadow Station, Broadmeadow Race Course, Newcastle Entertainment Centre & All Major Sporting Venues. Beaumont Street the Cosmopolitan Heart of Newcastle famous for its Restaurants, Newcastle CBD, Foreshore and Beaches. Feel free to enjoy the serenity of the garden or the verandah. Breakfast of choice and time served in the Breakfast Room overlooking garden Laundry facilities available. Fax and e-mail access. We also offer a unique and memorable place to stay for newlyweds.

Newcastle - Merewether

Merewether Beach B&B *B&B & Self Contained Studio*
Jane & Alf Scott
60 Hickson Street
Merewether
NSW 2291
5 km S of Newcastle PO

Tel (02) 4963 3526
or 0407 921 670
Fax (02) 4963 7926
janescott@bigpond.com
www.merewetherbeachbandb.com

Double $130 **Single** $60-$100
Children $30 (depending on age)
Full breakfast
7th night free
Visa MC accepted
1 Queen 1 Double 3 Single (2 bdrm)
Bathrooms: 1 Ensuite 1 Guest share

W ake up to this view! Go to sleep with only the sound of waves breaking on shore. 3 minutes to beach, 5 km from CBD, 1000 km from care. Featured on "Getaway", air-conditioned, self-contained studio with kitchenette, glassed-in verandah, private entrance and garden. Children welcome. Alf's ceramics and paintings lovingly adorn the rooms. With Jane's passion for cooking, expect a breakfast extravaganza. You are our only guests. Let us spoil you! "The view is as rare as the B&B itself..." L&DF, Bowral.

Orange

Greentrees *B&B & Separate Suite & Self Contained Apartment & Guest House*
Jasmin Bond
Cnr. Pinnacle and Lysterfield Roads
Orange
NSW 2800
4.5 km SW of Orange

Tel (02) 6361 4546
Fax (02) 6361 4566
jasmin.bond@bigpond.com
www.greentreeshouse.com.au

Double $130-$250 **Single** $99-$225
Children $16-$25
Full breakfast
Dinner from $30
Visa MC Amex JCB accepted
1 King/Twin 8 Queen (9 bdrm)
Bathrooms: 9 Ensuite

  AAA Tourism ★★★★

G reentrees is a very comfortable country home with peaceful valley views. Extensive lawns and gardens combine to create a tranquil and serene atmosphere. Homemade jams and preserved fruit, and locally grown fresh fruit and vegetables in season are offered to guests. There are eight rooms and one very luxurious suite. The rooms in the new wing sleep four to six people. Some have kitchenettes. The BYO restaurant is ideal for special and family celebrations. Bookings are essential. "Finalist in the 2007 Central West Regional Tourism Awards - Hospitality and Tourism."

Pacific Palms - Coomba

Whitby on Wallis B&B *Luxury B&B & Homestay*
Lew Dodds & Annabelle Lewis
1770 Coomba Road
Coomba Bay
NSW 2428
18 km NW of Pacific Palms

Tel (02) 6554 2448
or 0419 228 089
Fax (02) 6554 2448
info@whitbyonwallis.com.au
www.whitbyonwallis.com.au

Double $135-$160 **Single** $125-$135
Full breakfast
Dinner by arrangement from $30 each
Visa MC Eftpos accepted
2 King/Twin1 King (3 bdrm)
All ensuite & outdoor area.
One with kitchenette & sofabed
Bathrooms: 3 Ensuite Bath available in separate bathroom

Luxurious, spacious lake-side accommodation with privacy and magnificent views. Each bedroom has its own outdoor area, TV, tea & coffee. Large guest areas - lounges, reading room, fireplaces, tea and plunger coffee makings, home-baked biscuits, fridge. Room to mix with friends or to find a quiet nook of your own. Swim in the wet-edge pool, fish from the jetty, explore the grounds, paddle on the lake or just laze the day away. Close to National Parks, recreational and tourist activities and Pacific Palms' pristine beaches.

∽

Parkes

Kadina B&B *B&B*
Helen and Malcolm Westcott
22 Mengarvie Road
Parkes
NSW 2870
1.5 km E of Parkes CBD

Tel (02) 6862 3995
or 0412 444 452
Fax (02) 6862 6451
kadinabb@bigpond.net.au
www.kadinabnb.com

Double $120 **Single** $90
Children B/A
Full breakfast
Dinner B/A
Visa MC Diners accepted
2 Queen 1 Single (2 bdrm)
Fold up beds available for child
Bathrooms: 2 Ensuite

Come and enjoy the tranquillity and ambience of this lovely modern spacious home. Watch TV, listen to music, play piano, read or just soak in the views. Dine in our traditionally furnished dining room, patio or secluded back garden. Mal is involved in cereal growing and merino sheep farming. Guests may visit when convenient. Come and see "The Dish". Relax in our luxurious therapeutic Hot Tub. Finalist in 2004 and 2006 Inland Tourism Awards.

Parkes

The Old Parkes Convent *B&B & Self Contained Apartment*
Judy & Colin Wilson
33 Currajong Street
Parkes
NSW 2870
0.5 km E of Post Office

Tel (02) 6862 5385
or 0428 625 385
Fax (02) 6862 5158
colinwilson@hn.ozemail.com.au
www.bbbook.com.au/
TheOldParkesConvent.html

Double $140 **Single** $120
Children $15-$30
Full breakfast
Dinner By arrangement
Visa MC accepted
2 Double (2 bdrm) Open Plan
Bathrooms: 2 Ensuite

Experience spacious living in one of our exclusive apartments. You'll enjoy your own private lounge, bathroom, kitchen, and air conditioned comfort before awaking to a full and delicious breakfast. Stay a night or a few days. Built in 1923 and set on half an acre of land in the centre of town, The Old Parkes Convent was once home to the Sisters of Mercy and girl, student boarders. The Old Parkes Convent B&B is only a short stroll to the shops, clubs, hotels, and restaurants.

Port Macquarie

Woodlands Bed & Breakfast *B&B & Separate Suite*
Ian & Gretel McGinnigle
348 Oxley Highway
Port Macquarie
NSW 2444
3 km W of town centre

Tel (02) 6581 3913
or 0412 443 277
info@woodlandsbnb.com.au
www.woodlandsbnb.com.au

Double $130-$150
Single $110-$130
Full breakfast
Visa MC accepted
1 King/Twin 4 Queen (5 bdrm)
3 suites
Bathrooms: 1 Ensuite 2 Private

  AAA Tourism ★★★★

Luxury accommodation and hospitality in a secluded setting of gardens and trees with easy access to all local attractions. Air-conditioned accommodation options include the two bedroom Frangipani Suite which is partly self contained with lounge and equipped kitchen area, the two bedroom Magnolia Suite with its magnificently large bathroom and the Verandah Room, an ensuited queen size bedroom which opens out to the verandah and landscaped front gardens. All rooms have the full complement of expected comforts. Great dinner/accommodation package deals available.

Benbellen Country Retreat

Luxury B&B & Farmstay
Sherry Stumm & Peter Wildblood
Cherry Tree Lane
Hannam Vale
NSW 2443
20 km S of Laurieton

Tel (02) 6556 7788
Fax (02) 6556 7778
info@bbfarmstay.com.au
www.bbfarmstay.com.au

Double $165-$195 Single $130-$155
Full breakfast
Dinner $40+ per person
Visa MC Diners Amex Eftpos JCB accepted
2 Queen (2 bdrm) Well appointed bedrooms are
fully ensuite with balcony
Bathrooms: 2 Ensuite

Revitalise yourself with fresh air, peace and quiet with country hospitality second to none. The large open-plan homestead, with its solar-passive design and its quietly stated elegance, is purpose built with your privacy and comfort in mind. Benbellen Country Retreat is a small working alpaca farm tucked away in a lush green hidden valley at Hannam Vale, just 40 minutes from Port Macquarie, 15 minutes from Laurieton and 30 minutes from Taree. You will fall in love with the farm itself with its magical landscape of rolling hills and lotus strewn vistas in an English-style countryside. Choose our luxury ensuite rooms and our country hospitality, not to mention locally grown produce, fresh (to die for) eggs from the farm, home-baked breads and homemade jams. Environmentally friendly. Whether on a short break escape or just "passing through", we know you will be back . . .

Port Macquarie - Camden Haven

Penlan Cottage *Luxury B&B & Farmstay & Self Contained House*

Sherry Stumm & Peter Wildblood
Hannam Vale Road
Hannam Vale
NSW 2443
20 km S of Laurieton

Tel (02) 6556 7788
Fax (02) 6556 7778
info@bbfarmstay.com.au
www.bbfarmstay.com.au

Double $155-$195 Single $155-$195
Children $10-$40
Full provisions
Dinner $40+
Visa MC Diners Amex Eftpos JCB
accepted
1 Queen 1 Double 2 Single (2 bdrm)
Spacious well-designed bedrooms with quality fittings
Bathrooms: 1 Private

This charming holiday hideaway, with its uninterrupted valley views and set in its own garden of an acre and a half, is ideal for couples and families of up to six looking for a truly country experience. The main bedroom has a queen sized bed with French doors opening to the large veranda. The spacious combined living and dining area is tastefully furnished and the fully equipped kitchen/pantry has a good selection of "basic" supplies including home made jams and home baked bread. Environmentally friendly.

Port Macquarie - Camden Haven

Cherry Tree Cottage *Luxury B&B & Farmstay & Self Contained House*

Sherry Stumm & Peter Wildblood
Cherry Tree Lane
Hannam Vale
NSW 2443
20 km S of Laurieton

Tel (02) 6556 7788
Fax (02) 6556 7778
info@bbfarmstay.com.au
www.bbfarmstay.com.au

Double $155-$195
Single $155-$195
Children $10-$40
Full provisions
Dinner $40+ per person
Visa MC Diners Amex Eftpos
JCB accepted
1 Queen 3 Single (2 bdrm)
Bathrooms: 1 Private

AAA Tourism
★★★★

High overlooking the rich green paddocks and expansive dams of Benbellen Alpaca Farm, Cherry Tree Cottage is a rural hideaway ideal for couples or families of up to five. The main bedroom has a queen bed and French doors onto the expansive balcony with breathtaking views looking down Hannam Vale to South Brother Mountain. The spacious veranda provides ample room for outdoor entertaining and relaxation while soaking up the views and watching local bird life and listening to the "sounds of nature". Environmentally friendly.

Port Stephens - Shoal Bay

Located on the southern headland of Port Stephens is picturesque Shoal Bay, surrounded by Tomaree National Park, ocean and harbour beaches. This coastal area is rightly known as the "Blue Water Paradise" of the North Coast of New South Wales.

Experience one of the top 10 panoramic views in the world from the summit of Tomaree Head. Take in the magnificent harbour with a dolphin cruise (all year round) or whale watch cruise (June-October). Experience the ever-changing sand dunes of nearby Stockton Beach with a 4WD trip. Port Stephens is about 2½ hours drive from Sydney and 40 minutes from Newcastle.

Philip & Christina Latham, Shoal Bay B&B

Port Stephens - Shoal Bay

Shoal Bay Bed & Breakfast *B&B & Homestay*
Philip & Christina Latham
15 Shoal Bay Avenue
Shoal Bay
NSW 2315
3 km E of Nelson Bay

Tel (02) 4984 9183
or 0413 995 600
0421 880 344
info@shoalbaybb.com.au
www.shoalbaybb.com.au

Double $135-$165 Single $105-$135
Full breakfast
2 bedroom unit, S/C self catering, same
street, from $120 per night
Visa MC accepted
2 Queen (2 bdrm)
Spacious, luxurious rooms on first floor Large balcony
Bathrooms: 1 Ensuite 1 Private
Sunrise suite - ensuite Sunset suite - private

Enjoy "the rest of your life", escape to Shoal Bay in our quiet, spacious and modern B&B. First floor accommodation, comfortable queen beds, ducted air, ceiling fans, televisions, DVD player in rooms. Enjoy views of Tomaree, Stephens Peak and the bay from the balcony. Guest lounge with Foxtel Platinum. A recreation room with pool table, fridge, microwave, tea and coffee making facilities. Quiet cul-de-sac, 100m walk to beach, cafés and restaurants. Off street parking. Share our home with us and our cat "Watson".

Southern Highlands - Bowral

Chorleywood B&B *B&B & Self Contained Cottage*
Sue Hawick
86 Burradoo Road
Burradoo
NSW 2576
2 km S of Bowral

Tel (02) 4861 3617
Fax (02) 4861 3617
shawick@hinet.net.au
www.highlandsnsw.com.au

Double $120 **Single** $75
Baby in own cot only
Full provisions
Discount 3 nights or more
Visa MC Eftpos accepted
2 Double (1 bdrm)
Bathrooms: 1 Ensuite

W elcome to Chorleywood B&B. You will have a self-contained room, double or twin-share, with ensuite bathroom, kitchenette, ingredients for a full breakfast, TV, radio, good heating. The B&B is set in an acre of private garden with a sunny terrace. The resident Cocker Spaniel is called Hamish. Local attractions include bookshops, antiques shops, Bradman Museum, wineries, restaurants and excellent walks. Canberra, Sydney and the South Coast are all less than two hours away.

~
Southern Highlands - Moss Vale

Heronswood House *B&B*
Brian & Tina Davis
165 Argyle Street
Moss Vale
NSW 2577
1 km N of Moss Vale

Tel (02) 4869 1477
Fax (02) 4869 4079
heron@acenet.com.au
www.heronswood.com.au

Double $150-$198 **Single** $80-$180
Full breakfast
Visa MC accepted
2 King/Twin 3 Queen 1 Single (5 bdrm)
Bathrooms: 4 Ensuite 1 Private

   AAA Tourism ★★★★

T his beautiful 19th century home, in the "hub of the Highlands", offers you friendly, comfortable accommodation. The bedrooms are tastefully decorated, one adapted for the disabled. The lounge, sunroom and kitchenette are available to guests. Greeted with afternoon tea on arrival. Breakfast each morning is varied and generous, ranging from traditional to house specials . Wide verandahs and one acre of grounds encourage you to relax. Close to all local attractions plus golf, wineries and great restaurants "Arrive as a visitor, leave as a friend."

Sydney Harbour Dreaming

Discover Sydney Harbour and its Indigenous Culture all onboard one of our fantastic lunch cruises. Sit back and relax as our friendly captain and crew retell the history of Sydney Harbour including Indigenous Culture and early European settlement.

Included in your package:
- Award winning Indigenous dance group
- Gourmet BBQ Buffet including traditional "Bush-Tucker" and Modern Australian Cuisine
- Gifts and Artifacts available onboard
- Photo opportunity with Indigenous performers
- Quality vessel and superb service
- 1.5 hr cruise

Times
Depart:
11:45am Wharf No 6 Circular Quay
Depart:
12.15pm King Street Wharf 9
Return:
1:15pm Wharf No 6 Circular Quay
Return:
1.45pm King Street Wharf 9

Cost
$77.00 per adult
$39.00 per child
Family $212.00 (2 Adults, 2 Children)

Sydney Princess Cruises
P: 02 9518 7813
F: 02 9518 8757
info@sydneyprincesscruises.com.au
www.sydneyprincesscruises.com.au

Fantastic Offer!
15% off to all B&B guests when they mention this ad.

Sydney

Guests, David Lucas and Pat Woodley

Bed & Breakfast Sydney Central

Luxury B&B & Homestay
Julie Stevenson
139 Commonwealth Street
Surry Hills
NSW 2010
1 km N of Sydney Central

Tel (02) 9211 9920
or 0419 202 779
Fax (02) 9212 2450
jas@bedandbreakfastsydney.com.au
www.bedandbreakfastsydney.com.au

Double $130-$160
Continental breakfast
3 King/Twin (3 bdrm)
Air-conditioned and TV
Two bedroom suite available
Bathrooms: 1 Guest share 2 Private

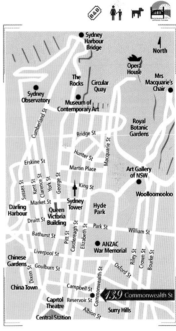

An elegant Terrace house set in the heart of the best Sydney has to offer. Relax in the tranquillity and comfort of your 'home away from home'. A short walk to The Capitol Theatre, Imax and all Theatres, Chinatown, Darling Harbour, Aquarium, Paddys and Fish Markets, Star City Casino, Chinese Garden of Friendship, Centrepoint Tower, Queen Victoria Building, Art Gallery of NSW, Museums, Law Courts, Hyde Park, Oxford Street, The Rocks, Circular Quay, the Opera House, the exciting harbour BridgeClimb. Board ferry to Manly, Zoo, Parramatta and Darling Harbour. Walk or drive to Fox Studios, the Sydney Cricket Ground, Universities, Cathedrals, Race Courses, Centennial Park, Beaches. Major attractions are Elizabeth Bay and Vaucluse House, Watsons Bay Beach 'Doyles' famous seafood restaurants. 3 Bedrooms, two with balconies, TV, Air-Conditioned. A pretty patio garden off the breakfast room. One resident cat. Not suitable for young children. KST Sydney Airporter door to door. Walk everywhere in the city from B&B.

Sydney

Y Hotel Hyde Park *Hotel*
The Manager
5-11 Wentworth Avenue
Sydney
NSW 2000
1 km W of CBD

Tel (02) 9264 2451
Fax (02) 9285 6288
res@yhotel.com.au
www.yhotel.com.au

Traditional Twin $50 per person
Studio Twin $71 per person
Continental breakfast
Visa MC Amex Eftpos accepted
(121 bdrm)
Single, twin, double and triple rooms
Bathrooms: 56 Ensuite

AAA Tourism
★★★☆

Excellent budget bed and breakfast hotel with comfy beds, warm and stylish interiors, friendly atmosphere and perfect park side location. There are backpacker, studio, deluxe and traditional rooms to choose from. City attractions are on your doorstep. Facilities include funky café with internet kiosk, guest kitchen and laundry.

Sydney

Y Hotel City South *Hotel*
The Manager
179 Cleveland Street
Chippendale
NSW 2008
4 km S of Sydney CBD

Tel (02) 8303 1303
Fax (02) 8303 1300
citysouth@yhotel.com.au
www.yhotel.com.au

Double $59pp, Single $100
Family $155 (sleeps 4)
2 B/R Apt $220 (sleeps up to 5)
Continental breakfast
Visa MC Amex Eftpos accepted
(63 bdrm) Single, double, twin, triple
and family rooms
Bathrooms: 63 Ensuite

AAA Tourism
★★★

This great value boutique bed and breakfast is surrounded by parks and the major Universities and is an ideal base to explore the inner city including Newtown, Glebe and Surry Hills. Walk to central station, Broadway and China Town. All the rooms have been designed for comfort and feature the latest interiors. Facilities include a modern gymnasium, a roof top garden with views, café with outdoor terrace, secure parking, broadband in rooms, internet kiosk, guest kitchen and laundry.

Sydney - Balmain

The Grange B&B *B&B*

Jennifer Burton
7 Vincent Street
Balmain
NSW 2041
0.2 km W of East Balmain Ferry

Tel (02) 9818 1346
or 0402 703 358
Fax (02) 9818 5694
jennifer_burton@hotmail.com
www.bbbook.com.au/TheGrangeBB.html

Double $135-$185 **Single** $100-$150
Children from 10 years Special breakfast
Visa MC Eftpos accepted
1 Queen 1 Twin (2 bdrm) Light, attractive,
antique quilts, books, airconditioned
Bathrooms: 1 Private or 1 Guest share
Full bath, separate shower, large vanity

One of Balmain's original large houses, a Georgian Sandstone home listed with National Trust. On a quiet street adjacent to waterfront parks yet only minutes from the popular Balmain Café society. Minutes from Ferry and buses to City, which is only 15-20 minutes away. The bedrooms have air conditioning, electric blankets, TV, a desk, tea/coffee making with homemade biscuits. All you can eat breakfasts including fruits, juices, cereals, yoghurts, croissants, breads, brewed coffee etc. Jennifer is well travelled and knows what guests need and enjoy.

Sydney - Chatswood

The Charrington of Chatswood *B&B & Hotel*

Robert Davies
22 Centennial Avenue
Chatswood
NSW 2067
10 km N of Sydney GPO

Tel (02) 9419 8461
Fax (02) 9419 8864
charrington_hotel@hotmail.com
www.charringtonhotel.com

Double $109-$119 **Single** $109-$119
Children free under 12 years
Breakfast by arrangement
Continental breakfast $8pp
Visa MC Eftpos accepted
12 Double 4 Twin (16 bdrm)
Some rooms have an additional single bed
Bathrooms: 16 Ensuite

Recently renovated Victorian style boutique hotel with leadlight windows and tesselated tile foyer. All rooms have a bar fridge, microwave oven, tea and coffee making facilities, IDD, ceiling fans, free wireless internet access, phone, TV, bathroom and their own balcony. There is a guest kitchen, computer room and coin operated laundry.

Sydney - Clovelly

Clovelly Bed & Breakfast *B&B & Homestay*
Tony & Shirley Murray
2 Pacific Street
Clovelly
NSW 2031
6 km SE of Sydney

Tel (02) 9665 0009
or 0419 609 276
clovellybandb@yahoo.com
www.bbbook.com.au/hosts/clovelly01.html

Double $130-$170 Single $100-$130
Full breakfast
Visa MC Diners accepted
1 Queen 1 Double 2 Twin (2 bdrm)
TV/DVD, hairdryer, robes,
electric blankets, doonas
Bathrooms: 1 Ensuite 1 Private
Bathroom linen changed daily

AAA Tourism ★★★★

Clovelly, Coogee and Bronte beaches and cafés are within walking distance. Transport to Sydney's tourist attractions is nearby. Afternoon tea will be served on arrival. Tea and coffee available all day. Breakfast includes fresh fruit, juices, home made bread and a hot dish. The air conditioned bedrooms are upstairs and each has a television, hairdryer and bathrobes. Rooms are serviced daily. Guests have a separate sitting room. "Thank you for a delightful, memorable visit...so clean and personal...look forward to coming again" Robert.

Sydney - Drummoyne

Eboracum *B&B & Homestay*
Jeannette & Michael York
18A Drummoyne Avenue
Drummoyne
NSW 2047
5 km W of Sydney

Tel (02) 9181 3541
or 0414 920 975
mjyork@bigpond.com
www.bbbook.com.au/eboracum.html

Double $130
Single $100
Full breakfast
Dinner B/A
1 King/Twin 1 Double (2 bdrm)
Bathrooms: 1 Family share 1 Private

Charming water frontage home by the Parramatta River, amid beautiful trees, with glorious views. Boatshed and wharf at waters edge. Handy to transport, short stroll to the bus or Rivercat ferry wharf, off street under cover parking. Ideal central location for business or pleasure, 5km to Sydney CBD, Darling Harbour, Opera House, museums, theatres and sporting venues. Many restaurants and clubs, nearby... Enjoy the hospitality of Jeannette and Michael, with their two cats and the ambience of their comfortable home.

Sydney - Engadine

Engadine Bed & Breakfast *Luxury B&B & Family Suites, S/C Apartments*

Pamela & Philip Pearse
33 Jerrara Street
Engadine, NSW 2233
28 km S of Sydney

Tel (02) 9520 7009
or 0412 950 606
0419 950 606
Fax (02) 9520 7009
relax@jerrara.com.au
www.engadinebnb.com

Double $125-$200
Children under 5 $10, 5-12 $25
Teenager & Extra Adult $50
Full breakfast   Dinner B/A
Family Apartment from $920 weekly
Visa MC Eftpos accepted
1 King 1 Queen 1 Double 2 Single (3 bdrm)
Bathrooms: 2 Ensuite 1 Guest share 2 Private
Double bathrooms & ensuite facility

Peace, quiet & privacy Adult & Family Stay. Elegant Private Suites. Close to Sydney's Royal National Park. Nestled amidst trees in leafy Sutherland Shire, 35 minutes from southern Sydney CBD & Kingsford-Smith Airport. Romantic couples getaway secluded private retreat. As well as, self catering, spacious welcoming 1 & 2 bedroom private en-suite apartments. Kitchenettes, tv, dvd, cd, barbeque, covered courtyard & hydrotherapy hot spa. Guests areas have magnificent views, valley bushland, mountain vistas, & city lights. U/C Parking.

Sydney - Glebe

Bellevue Terrace *Homestay*

Jan
19 Bellevue Street
Glebe
NSW 2037
3 km W of Sydney Central

Tel (02) 9660 6096
Fax (02) 9660 6096
bellevuebnb@pocketmail.com.au
www.babs.com.au/bellevue

Double $110
Single $80
Full breakfast
1 Queen 1 Double 2 Single (3 bdrm)
Bathrooms: 2 Guest share

My spacious, elegant townhouse is situated on a quiet residential street in the inner city suburb of Glebe, where you will find a variety of restaurants, boutiques, galleries & pubs. Close to Sydney University, UTS & UNSW campuses. Walk to Darling Harbour, Chinatown, Paddy's Market and the Powerhouse Museum, or take a bus to the City centre, just 3 kms away. We can supply maps, brochures and lots of ideas for things to see and do in Sydney.

Sydney - Glebe
Cathie Lesslie Bed & Breakfast *Homestay*

Cathie Lesslie
18 Boyce Street
Glebe
NSW 2037
3 km SW of Sydney

Tel (02) 9692 0548
cathielesslie@gmail.com
cathielesslie.net

Double $110
Single $80
Children $15
Full breakfast
Visa MC accepted
3 Double 2 Single (4 bdrm)
Bathrooms: 1 Family share 1 Guest share

Quiet leafy inner city, close to transport, cafés, cinemas, universities and Darling Harbour. Large comfortable room with cable TV, fridge and tea and coffee facilities. Hot "bacon and eggs" breakfast, your choice including fruit, juiced oranges and freshly baked croissants. We want you to feel welcome and at ease. Please phone first for bookings.

Sydney - Glebe
Harolden *Homestay*

Leonie Dawes
Please Phone (02) 9660 5881
3 km W of Sydney Central

Tel (02) 9660 5881
or 0414 481 881
harolden@senet.com.au
www.bbbook.com.au/harolden.html

Double $110
Single $70-$80
Full breakfast
1 Double 1 Single (2 bdrm)
Bathrooms: 1 Guest share

Experience warm hospitality in historic suburb of Glebe, the heart of a vibrant café/restaurant area & close to city centre. City buses outside the door to The Rocks, Circular Quay, Opera House and also seasonal events at Olympic Stadium and Sydney Showground. Walking distance to Sydney University, Prince Alfred Hospital and Light Rail to Darling Harbour and Central Station. Your host, a descendant from the First Fleet to arrive in Sydney Cove in 1788, has travelled widely in Australia and overseas.

Sydney - Glebe

Tricketts *B&B & Guest House*

Elizabeth Trickett
270 Glebe Point Road
Glebe
NSW 2037
2.5 km W of Sydney Central

Tel (02) 9552 1141
Fax (02) 9692 9462
trickettsbandb@hotmail.com
www.tricketts.com.au

Double $198 Single $176
Special breakfast
Visa MC Diners Amex Eftpos accepted
1 King 6 Queen 1 Twin (7 bdrm)
Bathrooms: 7 Ensuite

AAA Tourism
★★★★☆

Tricketts is a lovely Victorian mansion whose magnificent ballroom was once used as the Children's Court. Today this historic building has been fully restored to its original splendour. Large bedrooms with high ceilings, all beautifully decorated, all with ensuite, have top range Sealy beds. Breakfast is served in the conservatory and in summer out on the secluded deck overlooking the garden with bottle brush trees providing a wonderful splash of colour. The tranquillity makes one forget the city is a short 431 bus ride away and Darling Harbour, Fish Markets, Power House Museum, the Chinese Temple and Sydney University are close by. Glebe is an historic suburb full of interesting old homes that have been lovingly restored; and old fashioned gardens giving strong overtones of a bygone era. We are at the quieter "waterend" of Glebe Point Road, and a little further up lies the restaurant heart of Glebe, well known all over Sydney.

Off street parking is available. We enjoy providing a luxury homestay for travellers and business people. Also at Tricketts, the resident cat is Bandit, who ignores us all. Children over 12 in B&B. Tricketts is fully centrally heated and air-conditioned. We ask guests to smoke outside on verandahs.

Sydney - Greenwich

Greenwich B&B *B&B & Homestay & Self Contained Apartment*
Jeanette & David Lloyd
15 Hinkler Street
Greenwich
NSW 2065
5 km N of Sydney

Tel (02) 9438 1204
or 0411 409 716
Fax (02) 9438 1484
info@greenwichbandb.com.au
www.greenwichbandb.com.au

Double $99-$145
Single $77-$125
Continental provisions
Visa MC Amex accepted
1 King/Twin 1 Queen 1 Double (3 bdrm)
Bathrooms: 1 Ensuite 2 Private

Relaxed and friendly hosted accommodation in leafy Greenwich just 5km from the Sydney CBD. Enjoy spacious and private guests air-conditioned lounge/dining areas in a classic Australian Federation home. Kitchenette & laundry facility is available. Two resident dogs offer a friendly welcome. Internet and E-mail access is available. Ample off street parking. Greenwich B&B is ideal for business or leisure stays and is conveniently located to public transport (Bus, Train, Ferry) shopping, entertainment and restaurants. Transport to St Leonard's station can be arranged. Airport shuttle is available.

～

Brundah
Ballina
"The attention to detail at Brundah is exceptional – beautiful linen, lively trinkets, delicious breakfast."
Sonia Casanova, Griffith, NSW

PJ's Byron Bay
Byron Bay
"Delightful. This sums up the accommodation, surrounds, little homely touches, hostess and her dog Nikki. And close to all the attractions."
Ric and Ailsa Maxwell, Eaton, WA.
～

Sydney - Hunters Hill

Magnolia House Bed & Breakfast *B&B & Homestay*

Fofie Lau
20 John Street
Hunters Hill
NSW 2110
7 km NW of Sydney

Tel (02) 9879 7078
or 0418 999 553
Fax (02) 9817 3705
fofie@magnoliahouse.com.au
www.magnoliahouse.com.au

Double $150-$220
Full breakfast
Dinner B/A
Visa MC Diners accepted
1 King/Twin 1 Queen (2 bdrm)
Bathrooms: 2 Ensuite

Magnolia House is conveniently located only 7 km from the heart of Sydney and is placed within easy reach of transport that takes you directly to the city centre. Bus or ferry transport is close by.

Sydney Airport, The Sydney Opera House, Sydney Harbour and The Harbour Bridge, the CBD, galleries, museums, are all within easy reach.

Taking the ferry to Sydney Harbour and The Opera House is a memorable trip. Hunters Hill is one of Australia's oldest residential areas. Located on a peninsula between the Lane Cove and Parramatta Rivers, much of the suburb enjoys spectacular views over Sydney Harbour. Transfers from the airport can be easily arranged.

Sydney - Manly - Balgowlah Heights

LillyPilly Cottage *Self Contained Studio*
Hans & Tricia Oechslin
72 Woodland Street
Balgowlah Heights
NSW 2093
3 km W of Manly

Tel (02) 9949 7090
Fax (02) 9949 4094
info@lillypillycottage.com.au
www.lillypillycottage.com.au

Double $115-$150
Single $115-$150
Continental provisions
Tariff is seasonal
1 Queen (1 bdrm)
Bathrooms: 1 Ensuite

This cosy garden studio for two is self-contained with a private entrance from your garden patio. Offering peace and privacy, a few minutes drive from lively Manly, the Studio features every amenity, including Queen bed, en-suite bathroom and well equipped kitchenette. Also CD/TV/DVD, fan, heater, WiFi and BBQ. Shops, restaurants, bus and beautiful harbour walkways are nearby. Generous continental breakfast hamper or self-catering rate for longer stays. We will ensure your visit is enjoyable. Sebastian cat may visit. "Location:10/10, Facilities:10/10, Hospitality:12/10! Well done!" K.D. Johannesburg

Sydney - Newtown

Chloe's Bed & Breakfast *B&B & Self Contained House*
Fiona McNulty
15 Campbell Street
Newtown
NSW 2042
4 km SW of Sydney CBD

Tel 0411 828 144
or (02) 9517 3715
Fax (02) 9517 3714
chloesbandb@bigpond.com
www.chloesbedandbreakfast.com

Double $200-$500
Full provisions
Visa MC Eftpos accepted
1 King/Twin 1 Queen (2 bdrm)
1 sofa bed
Bathrooms: 1 Guest share
One guest/group/family at one time - no stranger share

Chloe's is your home in Sydney. Conveniently located in Newtown between Sydney Airport and the heart of Sydney's CBD. Sensational shopping, dining and cafés are at your doorstep. This private, two storey terrace has historical charm and the layout ensures complete privacy. Fully self-contained and equipped with everything you need for a relaxing and enjoyable stay. Complete with two bedrooms upstairs and open-plan living and dining downstairs with full kitchen and bathroom. The house is the perfect size for 5-6 people.

Sydney - Northern Beaches Peninsula

The Pittwater Bed & Breakfast *B&B*

Colette & James Campbell
15 Farview Road
Bilgola Plateau
NSW 2106
1 km N of Newport Beach

Tel (02) 9918 6932
or 0418 407 228
Fax (02) 9918 6485
colette@thepittwater.com.au
www.thepittwater.com.au

Double $165-$180
Single $165-$180
Special breakfast
Dinner $55 per person
Visa MC Amex JCB accepted
2 King/Twin 2 Queen (2 bdrm)
Bathrooms: 2 Ensuite

Comfortable beds, ensuite bathrooms, full gourmet breakfast, peace, quiet and privacy. Close to Sydney's famous Palm Beach and great local restaurants, Colette and James would be delighted to welcome you to The Pittwater. Our family home is situated on the high plateau above Newport Beach. The guest areas have spectacular panoramic views of the ocean and coastline, including an attractive garden and large solar heated swimming pool. The Pittwater offers a range of complimentary services and may include airport pickup after a long-haul flight.

Kadina
Parkes
"Our hockey team was jealous of where we stayed. Helen and Mal's hospitality and breakfast is unsurpassed by most other places I have stayed."
M Chidzey, Yowie Bay, NSW

Shoal Bay Bed & Breakfast
Port Stephens - Shoal Bay
"Thankyou for a lovely stay and we have great memories of your lovely home and great generosity. We had a great time on the rest of our Aussie trip too."
Marylyn & Wes Palmer, Wanganui, New Zealand

Sydney - Paddington

Harts *Homestay*
Katherine Hart
91 Stewart Street, nearest cross street - Gordon
Paddington 2021
NSW 2021
2.8 km E of Sydney Central

Tel (02) 9380 5516
paddington91@bigpond.com
www.bbbook.com.au/new_south_wales/results/
listing_

Double $125-$150
Single $85-$115
Special breakfast
High season rates apply
1 Queen 1 Twin 1 Single (3 bdrm)
Bathrooms: 1 Ensuite 1 Guest share 1 Private

Conveniently located 19th Century Cottage in Sydney's Historic Paddington, courtyard garden, two minutes from Oxford Street and the bus service to the CBD, Sydney Harbour, Circular Quay, The Rocks, The Opera House, Botanical Gardens, Sydney Casino, Chinatown, and Bondi Beach. Nearby Centennial Park, Fox Studios, Aussie Stadium, Sydney Cricket Ground, Art Galleries, Antique Shops, Pubs, Restaurants, Fashion Boutiques, Cinemas, Paddington Markets.

All rooms with T.V, clock radios, electric blankets and feather quilts. Ironing facilities, varied breakfasts, fruit platters. One resident Abyssinian cat.

"Dear Katherine, I remember you with a great pleasure. You are so kind and your breakfasts so good. My stay in your home was a great happiness." Michel, France. *"I'm missing your magnificent breakfasts which will stand out in my memory. Thank you for all your care of us."* Jeanne, UK.
Mentioned in Lonely Planet Guide to Sydney

Sydney - Parramatta
Harborne Bed & Breakfast *B&B*

Josephine Assaf
21 Boundary Street
Parramatta
NSW 2150
2 km S of Parramatta

Tel (02) 9687 8988
Fax (02) 9687 8998
www.bbbook.com.au/harborne.html

Double $105-$140
Single $95-$130
Continental provisions
Dinner from $20
Family suite for up to 7 adults
Extra person $10
Visa MC Diners Amex Eftpos accepted
7 Queen 1 Single (8 bdrm)
Bathrooms: 3 Ensuite 1 Guest share 1 Private

 AAA Tourism ★★★★

Harborne is a magnificent 1858 Georgian sandstone mansion. Harborne has recently been restored as a charming 8 room B&B. The beautiful home and the lush gardens have been classified by the National Trust. A glazed breakfast atrium with tea & coffee facilities is available. Harborne is ideal for a relaxed stay or business or team stay. Harborne, Your Home Away From Home.

Sydney - Potts Point
Simpsons of Potts Point Boutique Hotel *B&B & Guest House*

Keith Wherry
8 Challis Avenue
Potts Point, Sydney, NSW 2011
2 km E of Sydney City

Tel (02) 9356 2199
or 0408 282 802
0402 765 507
0408 292 802
Fax (02) 9356 4476
info@simpsonshotel.com
www.simpsonshotel.com

Double $215-$285 Single $175-$215
Continental breakfast
Visa MC Diners Amex accepted
3 King/Twin 2 King 7 Queen 2 Twin
2 Single (12 bdrm) All individually decorated with modern convieniences
Bathrooms: 12 Ensuite 3 King-bed rooms also have bath-tub

An historic 1892 mansion, the bedrooms have private bathrooms, air-conditioning and all modern conveniences. The building itself has high ceilings, spacious rooms, stained glass windows and grand hallways. Located in quiet, exclusive tree-lined Potts Point, less than one mile (leisurely 15min. stroll along the water) from the heart of Sydney or through the beautiful Botanical Gardens to The Opera House, Circular Quay Harbour Ferries or the historic Rocks area. It's within walking distance of some of the city's finest restaurants as well as the Oxford Street bars, clubs and night life.

Sydney - Potts Point

Victoria Court Sydney *B&B*
Manager
122 Victoria Street
Sydney, Potts Point
NSW 2011
1.5 km E of Sydney CBD

Tel (02) 9357 3200
or 1800 63 05 05
Fax (02) 9357 7606
info@VictoriaCourt.com.au
www.VictoriaCourt.com.au

Double $99-$330
Single $80-$330
Full breakfast
Visa MC Diners Amex accepted
22 King/Twin 3 Single (25 bdrm)
Bathrooms: 25 Ensuite

AAA Tourism

Victoria Court, whose charming terrace house dates from 1881, is centrally located on quiet, leafy Victoria Street in Sydney's elegant Potts Point; the ideal base from which to explore Sydney.

It is within minutes of the Opera House, the Central Business District and Beaches. Friendly and personalised service is offered in an informal atmosphere and amidst Victorian charm. No two rooms are alike; most have marble fireplaces, some have four-poster beds and others feature balconies with views over National Trust classified Victoria Street.

All rooms have ensuite bathrooms, hairdryers, air-conditioning, colour television, a safe, radio-clock, coffee/tea making facilities and direct dial telephones. In the immediate vicinity are some of Sydney's most renowned restaurants and countless cafés with menus priced to suit all budgets. Public transport, car rental, travel agencies and banks are nearby. An airport shuttle bus operates to and from Victoria Court and security parking is available.

Sydney - Rose Bay

Syl's Sydney Homestay *Homestay & Self Contained Apartment*

AAA Tourism
★★★☆

Sylvia & Paul Ure
75 Beresford Road
Rose Bay
NSW 2029
6 km E of Sydney

Tel (02) 9327 7079
or 0411 350 010
Fax (02) 9362 9292
homestay@infolearn.com.au
www.sylssydneyhomestay.com.au

Double $120-$150 Single $85-$95
Continental breakfast
Double in Self Contained Apartment $180
Extra person $40
Visa MC accepted
1 Queen 1 Double 4 Single (2 bdrm)
Bathrooms: 1 Guest share 1 Private

Rose Bay is one of Sydney's most beautiful harbourside suburbs and hospitality and friendliness are the essence of our modern, spacious family B&B with bush and harbour views, pet dog and that real home away from home atmosphere.

We are just a short stroll from cafés, restaurants, tennis, golf, sailing and the most beautiful harbour in the world and on excellent bus and ferry routes to the City and Opera House, Bondi Beach, train stations and shopping centres. Our B&B was featured on British TV in 1991 and we were one of Sydney's first B & Bs operating since 1980. Syl and Paul are well travelled and always ready to share their local knowledge and hospitality in a relaxed informal setting to help travellers enjoy our wonderful city. So if formality is what you seek, then Syl's is not for you! All rooms have TV and the self contained garden apartment is ideal for families. Resident gentle Pet dog. Guests are requested not to smoke inside the house.

New South Wales

Sydney - Scotland Island

Scotland Island Lodge *B&B*
Rosemary and Colin Haskell
2 Kevin Avenue
Scotland Island
NSW 2105

Tel (02) 9979 3301
Fax (02) 9979 3301
rhaskell@bigpond.net.au
scotlandislandlodge.com.au

Double $150-$180
Single $100-$120
Full breakfast
Dinner $40 per person
Visa MC accepted
1 King 2 Queen 1 Twin (3 bdrm)
Bathrooms: 2 Ensuite 1 Private

Unique exclusive Bed & Breakfast on beautiful Scotland Island. Ideal for couples and small groups. Kayak to Salvation Creek and experience the wonder of Pittwater. 'Too often, the breakfast part of B&B's falls by the wayside, but Rosemary is passionate about cooking and her big English breakfasts are out of this world.' 'The Beds. Perfect for a deep sleep before being woken by the birds.' Extracts from an article in the Sun Herald Travel Section by Kate Cox leading travel writer.

Sydney Harbour - Balmain

An Oasis In The City *Neil Duncan*
20 Colgate Avenue
Balmain
NSW 2041
2 km W of Sydney

Tel (02) 9810 3487
or 0408 476 421
Fax (02) 9810 3487
anoasis@optusnet.com.au
www.bbbook.com.au/oasis.html

Double $160-$180
Single $150-$170
Full breakfast
2 night minimum
1 Queen (1 bdrm)
Large cathedral room with harbour view
Bathrooms: 1 Ensuite

Located in one of Sydney's most historic and charming inner suburbs, Balmain Village, An Oasis offers a very large, sun-filled room with views over Sydney Harbour. The suite is completely private, with own bathroom and entrance. We offer a substantial Continental breakfast. Included in the room are a fridge, electric kettle, toaster and hairdryer, television and DVD playerand reverse cycle air-conditioner. There is a hot outdoor spa available to our guests with complimentary spa towels. An Oasis is a walk away from restaurants, cafes, pubs and bars. Public transport is also minutes away and include ferries and buses into Sydney. Dog friendly parks are also close by.

Tamworth

Jacaranda Cottage Bed & Breakfast *Luxury B&B*

Helen Hinwood
105 Carthage Street
Tamworth
NSW 2340
0.4 km E of Tamworth

Tel (02) 6766 4281
or 0438 618 263
Fax (02) 6766 1886
rest@jacarandacottagebedandbreakfast.com.au
www.jacarandacottagebedandbreakfast.com.au

Double $110-$165
Single $90-$135
Children $20
Full breakfast
Visa MC Amex Eftpos JCB accepted
3 Queen (3 bdrm) large & comfortable
Bathrooms: 1 Ensuite 1 Guest share

Located in the heart of leafy East Tamworth, only a short stroll from the CBD, Jacaranda Cottage offers large comfortable bedrooms with queen sized beds, lead light windows, reverse cycle air-conditioning. There is a separate guest lounge to relax in with TV, fridge and coffee making facilities. Delicious home cooked breakfasts are served in the family dining room or on the leafy verandah. At the bottom of the cottage garden is the private studio loft, well suited for either your business needs or romantic getaways.

Taree

Tallowood Ridge *B&B & Farmstay & Self Contained Cabin*

Shirley Smith
79 Mooral Creek Road
Cedar Party via Wingham
NSW 2429
8 km NW of Wingham

Tel (02) 6557 0438
or 0411 035 945
Fax (02) 6557 0438
twr@ceinternet.com.au
www.bbbook.com.au/tallowoodridge.html

Double $90-$100
Single $60-$70
Children $20
Continental breakfast
2 Double 4 Single (3 bdrm)
Bathrooms: 1 Ensuite 1 Private

Come and share the country lifestyle. Enjoy the comforts of an a/c modern home set on 33 hectares of undulating hills, magnificent views, colourful birds, friendly cows and Jessie the dog. There is also a fully equipped a/c, s/c cabin acc. 4. No smoking inside please. Relax by the pool or visit the many attractions in the area, historic buildings, a museum of past history, picturesque rainforest area alongside the Manning River or visit Ellenborough Falls. Clubs, pubs and restaurants in town.

Thredbo

Alpenhorn *B&B Lodge*
Rob & Kim
6 Buckwong Place
Thredbo, NSW 2625
33 km SW of Jindabyne

Tel (02) 6457 6223
Fax (02) 6457 6153
info@alphorn.com.au
www.alphorn.com.au

Double $120-$420 Single $100-$345
Family rates available on our website:
www.alphorn.com.au
Continental breakfast
Hot Breakfast & restaurant winter only
Visa MC accepted
All Summer/Winter tariffs available on website
4 Queen 4 Double 4 Twin 4 Single (21 bdrm)
4Queen Twin, 4 Double, 3 Triple, 8 Quad Family and 2 Bunk rooms available
Bathrooms: 21 Ensuite

AAA Tourism
★★★☆

A t Alpenhorn our friendly staff set the scene for an enjoyable, affordable holiday staying in the heart of Thredbo. We happily cater for the solo traveller, couple, family or group. Our guest lounges, balcony and sun filled courtyard with BBQ facilities offer great places for relaxing. All rooms offer ensuites, clock radios, TV, bar fridge, tea and coffee making facilities and hair dryers. Continental breakfast is provided all year with hot breakfast during winter periods. Our licensed Thai Restaurant is open winter only.

Thredbo - Jindabyne - Snowy Mountains

Bimblegumbie *B&B & Separate Suite & Guest House & Self Contained Cottages*
Prudence Parker
942 Alpine Way, Crackenback
Thredbo Valley
NSW 2627
9 km SW of Jindabyne

Tel (02) 6456 2185
Fax (02) 6456 2060
holiday@bimblegumbie.com.au
www.bimblegumbie.com.au

Double $148-$240 Single $80-$160
Children $5 to half price depending on age
Accommodation only
Dinner $42.50 for 3-course
Breakfast $17.50
Visa MC Amex Eftpos accepted
2 King 5 Queen 3 Twin (10 bdrm)
Bathrooms: 2 Ensuite 2 Guest share
3 Private 1 has bath

    AAA Tourism
★★★☆

B B, Room only & Self Contained Cottages. Pet friendly. Peaceful, private & relaxing, award winning wonderful gardens, colourful birdlife and wildlife. Delicious homemade yummy breakfasts & dinners, jams, sauces & specialities. Interesting eclectic artistic decor. A collector's delight. Resident very friendly dogs. Return guests pay 10% less. 150 acres mountain virgin bush walks, close to ski fields, horse riding, trout fishing, Lake Jindabyne. Relax, recuperate, rejuvenate, reflect, respond, remember, return.

Tilba

Tolkienesque rocky outcrops among rolling green hills entice visitors to the National Trust villages of Central Tilba and Tilba Tilba. Set in the Tilba Valley with the majesty of Gulaga (Mt Dromedary) as a backdrop, the area is well known for its cheese, gold mining past, gardens and more recently art, craft, heritage and indigenous culture.

Within easy driving distance from Narooma and Bermagui the area has access to a pristine coastline with many secluded beaches. The temperate climate – the area's best kept secret – means that visitors can discover, explore and enjoy what's on offer all year round.
Stuart Absalom, Green Gables

Tilba Tilba - Narooma

Green Gables *B&B*
Stuart Absalom & Philip Mawer
269 Corkhill Drive
Tilba Tilba
NSW 2546
16 km S of Narooma

Tel (02) 4473 7435
or 0419 589 404
Fax (02) 4473 7835
relax@greengables.com.au
www.greengables.com.au

Double $140-$170
Single $90-$110
Children $20-$40
Full breakfast
Dinner $30-$40 B/A
Visa MC Diners Amex accepted
3 Queen 1 Twin (3 bdrm)
Bathrooms: 2 Ensuite 1 Private

  AAA Tourism ★★★★

Mesmerising views, stylish accommodation, generous hospitality, fine food, endless relaxation at any time of the year, close to all the Tilba area has to offer. Set in lush gardens there are three large bedrooms with ensuite/private bathrooms and an inviting guest sitting room. Dinner is available by arrangement either served on the verandah or in the private dining room. What better way to experience the natural beauty of the unique Tilba area with its irresistible combination of mountains and unspoilt ocean beaches.

Ulladulla

Ulladulla Guest House

B&B & Self Contained Apartment & Guest House

39 Burrill Street
Ulladulla
NSW 2539
0.1 km S of Ulladulla

Tel (02) 4455 1796
or 1800 700 905
ugh@guesthouse.com.au
www.guesthouse.com.au

Double $158-$318 **Single** $100-$248
Children $50
Full breakfast
Dinner $40-$90
Visa MC Diners Amex Eftpos accepted
1 King/Twin 2 King 6 Queen 1 Double 3 Single (10 bdrm)
Bathrooms: 10 Ensuite

Located only 100 metres south of the picturesque harbour on the beautiful South Coast.

Accommodation: All rooms with ensuites, queen bed, custom-designed furniture and original artwork. Executive suites have marble bathroom with private spa and king size bed. Two self-contained units have private entrances and cooking facilities.

Restaurant: Elizans French Restaurant is 2007 Winner Best Restaurant South Coast. Our executive chef applies French cooking techniques to fresh local produce, Elizans is fully licensed with an award winning wine list.

Art Gallery: With permanent exhibiting Artists David Benson, Dianne Gee, Tracey Creighton and Judy Trick.

Features: Excellent recreational facilities include heated salt-water pool, internal and external spas, sauna, in-room massage and gym. Ulladulla Guest House is recommended by number of reputable guides Frommers (US), Rough (UK), Time-Out (London), Johansens.

Wellington

Carinya B&B *B&B*
Miceal & Helen O'Brien
111 Arthur Street (Mitchell Highway)
Wellington
NSW 2820
0.5 km S of Wellington

Tel (02) 6845 4320
or 0427 459 794
Fax (02) 6845 3089
carinya@well-com.net.au
www.bbbook.com.au/carinyabb.html

Double $89-$99 **Single** $80-$85
Children $12 - $15
Full breakfast
Visa MC accepted
1 King/Twin 2 Queen 2 Single (3 bdrm)
1 Family, 1 Queen, 1 King
Bathrooms: 2 Guest share

  AAA Tourism ★★★☆

Carinya is an old homestead in a lovely garden setting. Pool and tennis court available. Off street parking a plus. Situated Sydney side of Wellington, on the Mitchell Highway. Family friendly. Billiard table is always popular. Close to everything, especially Wellington Caves and Japanese Garden. Walk Mt Arthur or inspect significant historic buildings and acclaimed Cameron Park. Drives to Burrendong Botanic Garden & Arboretum and Burrendong Dam make Wellington a pleasant stopover. Other attractions; Dubbo Zoo, Mudgee and Parkes are ideal for short excursions.

~

Wollongong - Mount Pleasant - South Coast

Above Wollongong at Pleasant Heights B&B *Luxury B&B & spa suites with kitchenette*
John & Tracey Groeneveld
77 New Mt Pleasant Road
Wollongong, NSW 2519
5 km NW of Wollongong

Tel (02) 4283 3355
or 0415 428 950
Fax (02) 4283 1655
info@pleasantheights.com.au
www.pleasantheights.com.au

Double $185-$420
Children by arrangement
Full provisions
Dinner by arrangement
Midweek specials available
Visa MC Diners Amex accepted
1 King/Twin 2 Queen (3 bdrm)
Bathrooms: 1 Ensuite 2 spa suites

Above Wollongong at Pleasant Heights provides exquisite accommodation which opens into a lush, bushland setting, complete with sweeping coastal views. Guests choose between an eclectic trio of suites: two stylish spa suites in exotic, modern themes, and our chic, adorable studio with The View......serenity - harmony - solitude. Each suite has its own entrance with either a courtyard, terrace or balcony and also offers a range of indulgences, including aromatherapy massage. And of course, a lavish breakfast hamper is provided for each stay.

Yass

Kerrowgair *B&B*
Judy & John Heggart
24 Grampian Street
Yass
NSW 2582
1.5 km N of Yass

Tel (02) 6226 4932
or 0417 259 982
info@kerrowgair.com.au
www.kerrowgair.com.au

Double $130-$150
Full breakfast
Visa MC Diners Eftpos accepted
3 Queen 1 Twin (4 bdrm)
Bathrooms: 4 Ensuite

    AAA Tourism ★★★★☆

Kerrowgair - A beautifully restored Georgian house (C.1853), in historic Yass, one hour from the Nation's capital. This outstanding heritage house has large bedrooms, all with ensuites, and gracious sitting and dining rooms, with open fires, for the use of guests. It is complimented by the shady verandahs and covered terrace. Set in over an acre of beautiful gardens, guests can enjoy the peace and tranquillity of the ancient trees, rose gardens and pond. Kerrowgair has become renowned for it's warm hospitality and superb breakfasts.

Yass - Rye Park

The Old School *B&B & Country House (self-contained)*
Margaret Emery
Yass Street
Rye Park
NSW 2586
20 km SE of Boorowa, 40 km N of Yass

Tel (02) 4845 1230
or 0418 483 613
(02) 6227 2243
Fax (02) 4845 1260
theoldschool@bigpond.com
www.theoldschool.com.au

Double $130-$160 **Single** $100-$120
Children $25
Special breakfast
Dinner $60
Country House $1,500 per week
Visa MC Diners Amex accepted
1 King 2 Queen 1 Double 1 Twin 2 Single (5 bdrm) 2 suites, 3 rooms each, ensuite,
Bathrooms: 2 Ensuite 1 Family share 1 Private Orchard Wing suite has a bath

Fine food, warm fires, good books and a piano make this retreat a return to life's simple pleasures. Set on four acres amidst trees, roses, gardens and ponds an atmosphere is created that encourages relaxation. Margaret has built a reputation for her food and offers a seasonal menu, with influences from Belgium, the Mediterranean and Asia. The Old School won an Award of Distinction in the 2000 Capital Country Awards for Excellence in Tourism. Rye Park is half an hour north of Yass.

Young - Cootamundra

Old Nubba Schoolhouse *Self Contained House & Self-Contained Farm Cottages*

Fred & Genine Clark
Old Nubba
Wallendbeen
NSW 2588
3 km N of Wallendbeen

Tel (02) 6943 2513
or 0438 432 513
Fax (02) 6943 2590
oldnubba@bigpond.com
www.bbbook.com.au/
oldnubbaschoolhouse.html

Double $95-$120
Single $75-$95
Children $10-$20
Full provisions
2 Queen 2 Double 8 Single (7 bdrm)
Bathrooms: 3 Private

Old Nubba is a sheep/grain farm between Cootamumdra and Young, 3 ½ hours Sydney, 1 ½ hours Canberra. The Schoolhouse, Killarney Cottage and Peppertree Cottage are all fully self-contained and have slow-combustion heating, reverse cycle air-conditioning, electric blankets and linen/towels provided. They sleep 4-8 and are set in their own gardens thru the trees from the homestead. Farm attractions include peace and quiet, bush walks, birdlife, bike riding, fishing and olive picking. Well behaved doggies and cats welcome. Many local tourist attractions nearby.

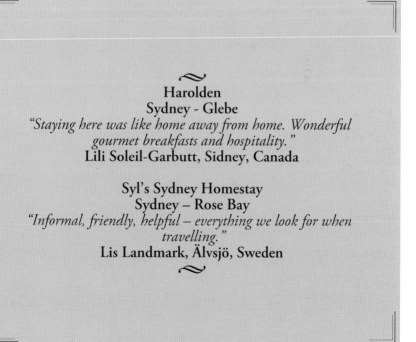

~

Harolden
Sydney - Glebe
"Staying here was like home away from home. Wonderful gourmet breakfasts and hospitality."
Lili Soleil-Garbutt, Sidney, Canada

Syl's Sydney Homestay
Sydney – Rose Bay
"Informal, friendly, helpful – everything we look for when travelling."
Lis Landmark, Älvsjö, Sweden

~

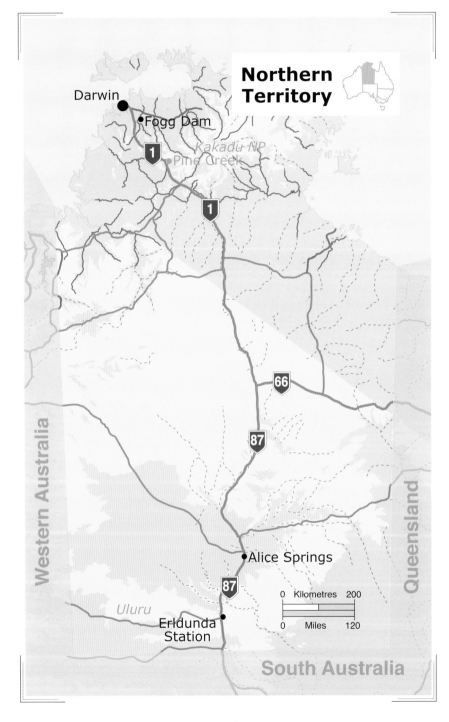

Alice Springs

The Centre is full of diversity, in its natural forms, in the unique wildlife which thrives in this arid area, and the natural beauty in this vast dry land. Beautiful scenery, with clear blue skies during the day, with the sun shining, whether it's 40C or 10C. And clear evening skies with millions of stars to gaze at from your swag, and find the satellites moving across the night sky.

Alice Springs is a modern town providing modern amenities to match any city.

Alice has a strong link with the past, both European settlement and the Aboriginal and their culture, with plenty of attractions in the Town area to visit, taking at least two days to enjoy, before heading south to Kings Canyon and Ayers Rock.
Kathy Fritz, Kathy's Place B&B

Alice Springs
Nthaba Cottage B&B *B&B*
Anne & Will Cormack & Pets
83 Cromwell Drive
Alice Springs
NT 0870
2.5 km N of Town Centre

Tel (08) 8952 9003
or 0407 721 048
Fax (08) 8953 3295
nthaba@nthabacottage.com.au
www.nthabacottage.com.au

Double $125-$155
Single $100-$125
Full breakfast
Visa MC accepted
1 King/Twin 1 Double (2 bdrm)
Bathrooms: 1 Ensuite 1 Private

 AAA Tourism
★★★★

Surrounded by the spectacular MacDonnell Ranges, Nthaba features a quality cottage separate from the main house plus a private suite under the main roof. The cottage has one kingsize or two single beds and the cosy sitting-room with television has Edwardian chairs and other favourite pieces. The suite has a double bed, ensuite bathroom and private entrance. Both open onto a lovely private garden. Nthaba is convenient to the new convention centre, casino and golf course. Your host, Will, is keen to share his local bird knowledge with you. Resident friendly cat and dog.

Alice Springs

Kathy's Place Bed & Breakfast *B&B & Homestay*
Kathy & Karl Fritz
4 Cassia Court
Alice Springs
NT 0870
3 km E of Alice Springs

Tel (08) 8952 9791
or 0407 529 791
Fax (08) 8952 0052
kathy@kathysplace.com.au
www.kathysplace.com.au

Double $140 Single $80
Children $10 each
Full breakfast
Additional person in same room $30
Visa MC accepted
2 Queen 1 Single (2 bdrm)
Bathrooms: 1 Guest share Separate toilet

Friendly Australian home, courtesy arrival transfers, tours arranged and help provided so you can enjoy the treasures the "Alice" has to offer, taking at least two days to enjoy. Air conditioning, swimming pool and garden outdoor area with native birds that come in. Combustion heating in the cooler months providing a cosy atmosphere to chat, read, watch TV.

Alice Springs

The Hideaway *B&B & Self Contained Apartment*
John & Pauline Haden
18 Lewis Street
Alice Springs
NT 0871
500 km NE of Ayers Rock

Tel (08) 8953 1204
or 0428 531 204
Fax (08) 8953 1204
info@hideawayinalice.com
www.hideawayinalice.com

Double $120
Full provisions
Family $180
1 Queen 2 Single (2 bdrm)
Bathrooms: 1 Private

Bassa and Cocoa the resident cats will be there to add to the welcome. All rooms have fans, electric blankets and the apartment has ducted air-conditioning, a gas heater is available in winter in the separate lounge/dining area. Your hosts John and Pauline have a combined 80 years of personal local experience, we look forward to sharing this knowledge with you. We are within 5 minutes walk from the famous Cultural Precinct and a 5 minute drive from the World acclaimed Desert Park.

Darwin

Worth visiting on the way to Kakadu is Fogg Dam Conservation Reserve, created in 1956 in a project to grow and export rice to Asia: the Humpty Doo Rice Project. The project left as a heritage two moderate sized dams (Fogg Dam and Harrison Dam) which provide habitat for numerous species of animals and Australian and migratory birds.

The reserve, lies within the Adelaide River wetlands and is known internationally to biologists, birdwatchers and photographers for its rich biodiversity. It's the only Top End wetland accessible throughout the year.

Heather Boulden & Jeremy Hemphill, Eden at Fogg Dam, B&B and Certified Organic Tropical Fruit Farm

Northern Territory

~

Darwin - Fogg Dam - Humpty Doo

Eden at Fogg Dam *B&B & Self Contained Apartment*
Heather Boulden & Jeremy Hemphill
530 Anzac Parade
Middle Point
NT 0836
25 km E of Humpty Doo

Tel (08) 8988 5599
Fax (08) 8988 5582
eden@foggdam.com.au
www.foggdam.com.au

Double $130-$170
Single $110-$150
Full breakfast
Dinner $30 per person, bookings required
Special diets accommodated
Visa MC accepted
2 Queen 1 Double 2 Single (3 bdrm)
Cross breeze, overhead fans, a/c
Bathrooms: 2 Private upstairs, spa bath with shower

Come and enjoy the bush in comfort on an organic tropical fruit farm registered for Land for Wildlife. We're on the doorstep of internationally renowned Fogg Dam, which has boardwalks and viewing platforms. A popular breakfast option is to take a picnic to the dam for a spectacular sunrise accompanied by a dawn chorus of birds. We're close to a number of other tourist attractions and en route to Kakadu National Park. A unique location just 65km (40 miles) from Darwin.

Darwin - Malak

Beale's Bedfish & Breakfast *B&B & Lodge*

Heather & Allan Beale
2 Todd Crescent
Malak
NT 0812
5 km N of Airport

Tel (08) 8945 0376
Fax (08) 8945 0379
bealesbedfish@aapt.net.au
www.bealesbedfish.com.au

01/11-28/03 $80-$120 per room
01/03-31/10 $150-$200 per room
Continental breakfast
Visa MC accepted
3 Queen 8 Single (3 bdrm)
Bathrooms: 3 Ensuite

Beale's Bedfish & Breakfast is a dual purpose built establishment. Designed to cater for the B&B traveller and also to the Individuals, Families and Groups that also wish to partake in the adrenalin packed adventure of Barra or Bluewater Fishing in the Northern Territory. It is the home of Darwin's Barra Base Fishing Safaris, which can cater for all types of fishing, from Barramundi & Bluewater fishing in coastal reefs, rivers and sheltered waters to being able to fish 30 nautical miles to sea to complete adrenalin packed pelagic and deep sea fishing.

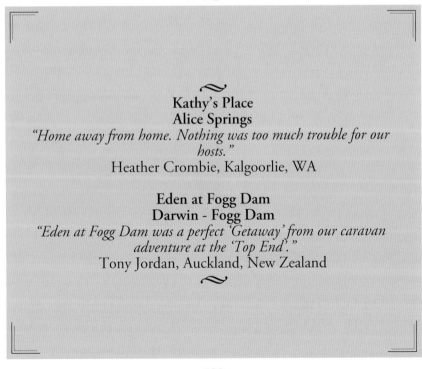

Kathy's Place
Alice Springs
"Home away from home. Nothing was too much trouble for our hosts."
Heather Crombie, Kalgoorlie, WA

Eden at Fogg Dam
Darwin - Fogg Dam
"Eden at Fogg Dam was a perfect 'Getaway' from our caravan adventure at the 'Top End'."
Tony Jordan, Auckland, New Zealand

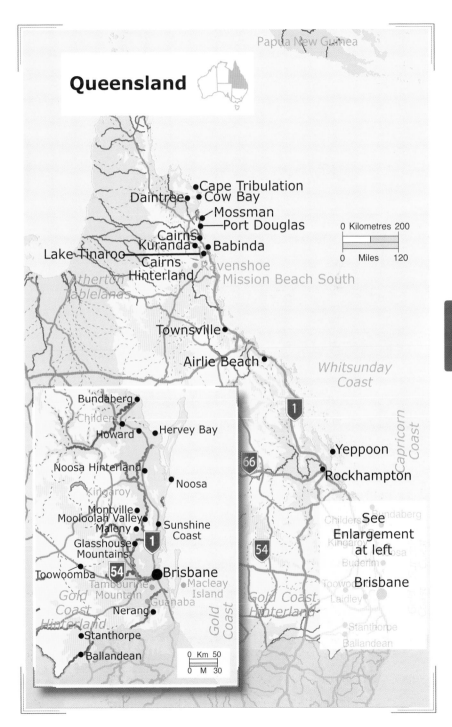

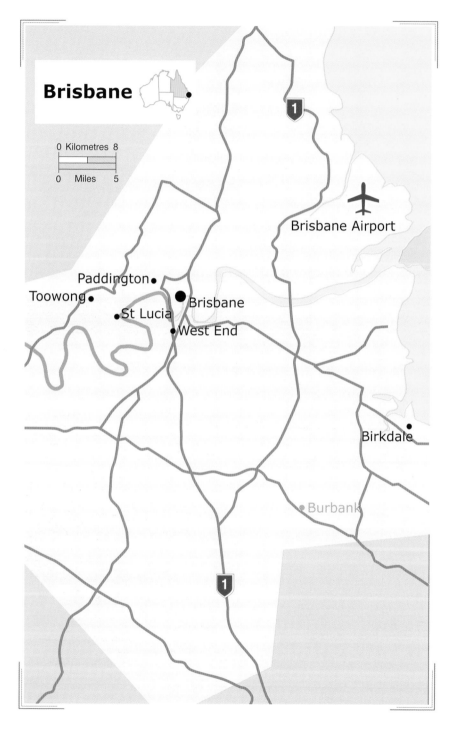

Airlie Beach - Whitsunday

Whitsunday Moorings B&B *B&B*

Peter Brooks
37 Airlie Crescent
Airlie Beach
Qld 4802
0.3 km SW of Airlie Beach

Tel (07) 4946 4692
Fax (07) 4946 4692
info@whitsundaymooringsbb.com.au
www.whitsundaymooringsbb.com.au

Double $175 **Single** $155
Children $30
Full breakfast
Extra person above two $35
Visa MC Diners Amex Eftpos accepted
2 Queen (2 bdrm)
Bathrooms: 2 Ensuite

AAA Tourism
★★★★☆

Studio apartments, private terrace, swimming pool, overhanging Abel Point Marina and Coral Sea. Spectacular views. Traditional 'a la carte' English breakfast, squeezed juice, tropical seasonal fruit, cereals, choice cooked mains, homemade jams, teas, coffee. Apartments feature crisp starched linen, daily servicing, air-conditioning, ceiling fans, 80ch satellite TV, ensuite with shower, hairdryer, 'Gilchrist & Soames' toiletries, kitchen, refrigerator, microwave, equipped light meals, clock radio, laundry facilities. Relax in the pool, a cool drink, watching the sun setting on boats returning to Abel Marina below.

Brisbane - Birkdale

Birkdale Bed & Breakfast *B&B*

Geoff & Margaret Finegan
3 Whitehall Avenue
Birkdale, Brisbane
Qld 4159
17 km E of Brisbane CBD

Tel (07) 3207 4442
glentrace@bigpond.com
www.bbbook.com.au/birkdalebb.html

Double $100-$110
Single $70-$80
Children $20
Full breakfast
Dinner $15-30
Visa MC Diners Amex accepted
2 Queen 1 Double 2 Single (3 bdrm)
Bathrooms: 2 Ensuite 1 Private

Only 20 minutes from Brisbane CBD and airport, but with a lovely country atmosphere. Set in half an acre of beautifully landscaped gardens, Birkdale B&B is a modern English style country home, with a new luxurious motel style guest wing and separate entrance. All bedrooms have private facilities and reverse cycle air conditioning for your comfort. Minibar. Off street parking. Enjoy feeding the birds, go whale watching in nearby Moreton Bay or meet the local koalas. Qualified Aussie Hosts. Dual Tourism Award Winner. Corporate and weekly rates.

Brisbane - Paddington - Rosalie

Fern Cottage B&B *B&B*
Mary & Geoff
89 Fernberg Road
Paddington - Rosalie
Qld 4064
2.5 km W of Brisbane

Tel (07) 3511 6685 or 0423 096 254
Fax (07) 3511 6685
info@ferncottage.net
www.ferncottage.net

Double $135-$145 Single $110-$120
Children under ten $15
Continental breakfast
Extra person $35
Weekly Rates $595 to $770
Visa MC Eftpos accepted
3 Queen 1 Single (3 bdrm)
Bathrooms: 3 Ensuite

Fern Cottage is a charmingly refurbished 1930s 'Queenslander' located in trendy Paddington/Rosalie . . . a village, only 2.5km west of downtown Brisbane . . . Enjoy modern conveniences and comforts of home in our 3 fabulously decorated, air conditioned ensuited bedrooms. Kitchenette, dining and lounge rooms and individual patios assures your privacy. Sidewalk cafés, fine restaurants, boutiques, antique shops and galleries are within walking distance. A generous continental breakfast starts your day . . . in the tropical garden courtyard. One resident pet.

Brisbane - St Lucia - Toowong

Kensington *Luxury B&B & Self Contained Apartment & 1 pet friendly apartment*
Michelle Bugler
23 Curlew Street
Toowong
Qld 4066
5 km W of Brisbane

Tel (07) 3371 3272 or 0407 016 669
kensbandb@iprimus.com.au
www.babs.com.au/kensington

Double $150-$180 Single $120
Children $25, 4-14 only
Special breakfast
Dinner $35, 2 courses B/A
Weekly Self Catering $560
Visa MC accepted
1 King/Twin 3 Queen (3 bdrm)
Spacious, arm chairs, desk, fridge, tea making facilities
Bathrooms: 3 Ensuite 2 with bath

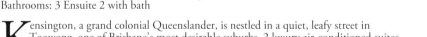

Kensington, a grand colonial Queenslander, is nestled in a quiet, leafy street in Toowong, one of Brisbane's most desirable suburbs. 2 luxury air-conditioned suites with own entrance and verandah. Ensuite bathrooms, shower, full size bath, marble fire places, polished floors with Belgian rugs, under cover parking, excellent public transport, traditional furnishing throughout. Afternoon tea or drinks with canapés on arrival, breakfast served in dining room, verandah, or in your suite. Walk to Toowong Village and David Jones. Easy access to city or university of Queensland.

Brisbane - West End

Eskdale Bed & Breakfast *B&B & Homestay*
Paul Kennedy
141 Vulture Street
West End
Qld 4101
2 km SW of Brisbane

Tel (07) 3255 2519
eskdale_brisbane@yahoo.com.au
http://eskdale.homestead.com

Double $110 **Single** $70
Children ¹/₂ price
Continental breakfast
Every 5th night free
Visa MC accepted
1 King 1 Queen 1 Double
2 Single (4 bdrm)
Bathrooms: 1 Family share 1 Guest share

Eskdale Bed & Breakfast is a typical turn-of-the century Queensland house close to the restaurant district of West End. It's 2km to the city centre across the Victoria Bridge, and just 1km from the Southbank Parklands and the Brisbane Convention and Exhibition Centre, the Queensland Performing Arts Centre, Museum and Art Gallery. You'll be close to all the action and still be able to relax on the back deck and watch the birds feeding on the Australian native plants in the garden.

~

Brisbane Central

La Torretta Bed & Breakfast *B&B & Self Contained Apartment*
Charles and Dorothy Colman
8 Brereton Street
South Brisbane
Qld 4101
1 km S of Brisbane

Tel (07) 3846 0846
or 0414 465 387
Fax (07) 3342 7863
latorretta@optusnet.com.au
www.latorretta.com.au

Double $85-$110 **Single** $65-$90
Continental breakfast
7 night minimum, shorter stays negotiable
depending on availability
Visa MC Eftpos accepted
1 Queen 1 Twin (2 bdrm) Self-Contained or B&B
Bathrooms: 2 Private

Ten minutes walk to the Convention Centre, Cultural Complex and beautiful Southbank Gardens, La Torretta is a traditional Queenslander with modern, comfortable, ground-floor guest accommodation. Our guests enjoy our friendly hospitality with attention to detail. Self-serve breakfast is provided - homemade bread, jams, juice, yoghurt and freshly ground coffee or real tea. Spacious guest-lounge/dining room with internet access (fee) and cable TV. There is a well-equipped kitchenette. West End's convivial cafés are around the corner. "A great find - excellent and friendly service!" CT, UK.

Queensland

Bundaberg

Inglebrae *B&B*
Christina & John McDonald
17 Branyan Street
Bundaberg
Qld 4670
1 km W of Bundaberg

Tel (07) 4154 4003
or 0418 889 971
Fax (07) 4154 2503
inglebrae@interworx.com.au
www.inglebrae.com

Double $130-$150
Single $100-$120
Full breakfast
Visa MC Eftpos accepted
2 Queen 1 Twin (3 bdrm)
Bathrooms: 2 Ensuite 1 Private

Inglebrae is a restored Queenslander circa 1910 with beautifully appointed air-conditioned rooms and ensuites. Take a leisurely stroll to the city centre where you will find great shopping and many fine restaurants in which to dine. Bundaberg is situated at the Southern tip of the Great Barrier Reef and is the departure point for Lady Elliott Island. Enjoy a sumptuously cooked breakfast on the verandah overlooking beautiful gardens.

Cairns

Warm, sunny tropical days tempered by cooling onshore breezes. The days are warm, the nights balmy. Cairns is the ideal base to explore and experience the many attractions of Tropical North Queensland.

Visit the Great Barrier Reef, the largest reef in the world extending over 2300 km along the Australian coast. Take a guided tour or a self drive trip to our rainforest.

Around 17,000 hectares between Daintree River & Cape Tribulation is declared National Park and much of this area is also World Heritage listed to ensure the protection of the rainforest which has been evolving for 120 million years.
Vicky Riddle

Cairns - Brinsmead

Jenny's Homestay *B&B & Homestay & Self Contained Apartment & Queen with ensuite*

Jenny & Lex Macfarlane
12 Leon Close
Brinsmead
Qld 4870
10 km W of Cairns

Tel (07) 4055 1639
or 0428 551 639
jennysbb@jennysbandb.com
www.jennysbandb.com

Double $100-$120
Single $70-$80
Special breakfast
$85-$100
1 King 2 Queen 1 Twin (4 bdrm)
Bathrooms: 2 Ensuite 1 Guest share
1 Private

Jenny and Lex invite you to our home in Cairns. Wake to the sound of birds and our beautiful rainforest garden. A continental breakfast is served in the sunroom or around the pool. My husband and I are Photographers and enjoy outdoor activities. Only a short distance to tropical beaches, great restaurants, golf courses and the famous Kuranda Train and Skyrail. We are booking agents for all tours and rental cars. A complimentary pick up on arrival. "This was our 4th stay and we enjoy it more each stay" Gary & Helen Young, Seattle Washington, USA."

Cairns - Edge Hill

Galvin's Edge Hill Bed and Breakfast *Luxury B&B & Self Contained Apartment*

Julie and Jesse Low
61 Walsh Street
Cairns
Qld 4870
0.2 km N of Edge Hill Post Office

Tel (07) 4032 1308
or 0409 345 726
Fax (07) 4032 5968
jessup@ozemail.com.au
www.cairns.aust.com/galvins

Double $125-$140 Single $95
Family rates available
Special breakfast
1 Queen 2 Single (2 bdrm)
1 with Queen and 1 with 2 single
Bathrooms: 1 Family share

   AAA Tourism ★★★★

One of Cairns' oldest & finest Queenslanders, located in quiet, leafy Edge Hill, we are one of the most conveniently located B&B's in Cairns - five minutes drive from downtown and 5 minutes from the airport. Relax in your own private two-bedroom apartment (we only take one booking at a time so there's no need to share). Enjoy our magnificent swimming pool and gardens. Three minutes walk and you're in the village of Edge Hill with restaurants, local shops, the Botanic Gardens, rainforest walks, Royal Flying Doctors HQ (museum) and more.

Cairns - Holloways Beach

Billabong B&B *B&B*
Vicky & Ted Riddle
30 Caribbean Street
Holloways Beach, Cairns
Qld 4878
10 km N of downtown Cairns

Tel (07) 4037 0162
or 0427 370 044
Fax (07) 4037 0162
info@cairnsbb.com
www.cairnsbb.com

Double $145-$165
Single $118-$125
Full breakfast
Visa MC accepted
2 Queen 1 Single (2 bdrm)
Bathrooms: 2 Ensuite

Billabong is your perfect accommodation in Cairns located on an island in the heart of a large lily-covered Billabong, close to downtown Cairns and the airport. Two queen guest suites with contemporary décor include ensuite bathrooms, air conditioning and ceiling fans. Your facilities include television, fridge, tea/coffee making and separate entrance. Large French doors open onto a private deck overlooking the Billabong featuring spectacular bird life. A short walk to the beach and restaurants. Recommended for a "Fodor's choice icon" in the 2005 Fodor's Guidebook.

Cairns - Lake Tinaroo

Tinaroo Haven Holiday Lodge *Luxury B&B & Self Contained Pole House*
Michael and Tania Taylor
Lot 42 Wavel Drive
Tinaroo Waters (via Kairi), Qld 4872
5 km S of Kairi

Tel (07) 4095 8686 or 0437 344 973
Fax (07) 3319 7232
tinlodge@fire-break.com
www.fire-break.com

Double $135-$185
Children $16 per child
No charge for children under 2
Continental provisions
Visa MC Eftpos accepted
1 Queen 1 Double (2 bdrm) 2 double sofa
beds, 1 bedroom upstairs and 1 downstairs
Bathrooms: 2 Private 1 bathroom on each level

Tinaroo Haven Holiday Lodge is centrally located within the Atherton Tablelands. It is a pole house constructed of local timbers and designed to provide views of the surrounding mountains while hidden in the tree tops on 2.5 acres of bushland. It is 200m away from Lake Tinaroo and is fully self-contained with all amenities, which includes Austar with National Geographic, Discovery, News, Sports and Movie Channels and Cartoon Network, and a DVD Player with a large selection of DVDs to choose from as well as a selection of games. There is also a laundry. The top floor includes dining area and log fireplace. The balcony provides an outdoor dining area equipped with a BBQ.

Cairns - Stratford

Lilybank *B&B*
Mike & Pat Woolford
75 Kamerunga Road
Stratford Cairns
Qld 4870
8 km N of Cairns

Tel (07) 4055 1123
Fax (07) 4058 1990
lilybank@bigpond.net.au
www.lilybank.com.au

Double $99-$121 Single $88
Special breakfast
Extra person in room $33
Visa MC Amex Eftpos JCB accepted
1 King/Twin1 King 4 Queen 4 Twin
5 Single (5 bdrm)
Bathrooms: 5 Ensuite

Lilybank - a fine example of traditional 'Queenslander' architecture. 'Lilybank' owes its success to the happy blend of hospitality and privacy offered to our guests. Bedrooms are air-conditioned, there's a guests' lounge with TV, video, salt-water pool, laundry, BBQ and off-street parking. We'll serve a wonderful breakfast and help you choose and book tours which are right for you. Our excellent local restaurants are within walking distance. Two spoodles and a galah live in our part of house. There's a beautiful tropical garden and guests are welcome to pick their own fruit in season.

Cairns - Yorkeys Knob

A Villa Gail *B&B & Self Contained Apartment*
Gail Simpson
36 Janett Street
Yorkeys Knob Cairns
Qld 4878
17 km N of Cairns

Tel (07) 4055 8178
or 0417 079 575
Fax (07) 4055 8178
gail@avillagail.com
www.avillagail.com

Double $110-$180
Single $75-$120
Special breakfast
Self Contained Apartment $180-$200
1 King 1 Queen 1 Double
1 Twin (3 bdrm)
Bathrooms: 2 Ensuite

Villa Gail on Millionaires Row was designed to make the most of our unique elevated location at Yorkey's Knob. Our cool Mediterranean-style house is set within lush tropical gardens overlooking the beach with breathtaking views across the Coral Sea. From the delightful in-ground swimming pool spacious guest's verandah or your own large room, you can relax and enjoy our tropical lifestyle. Villa Gail is only 15 minutes from Cairns, near to the Skyrail, golf course, tours to the World Heritage Wet Tropics Rainforest, the Outback and the Great Barrier Reef. All pick ups from our door.

Cairns Hinterland - Kuranda

Cadaghi Cottage *Luxury B&B & Self Contained Cottage*
Sandra & Graham Mengersen
135 Stoney Creek Road
Kuranda
Qld 4881
10 km S of Kuranda

Tel (07) 4093 0352
Fax (07) 4093 0352
info@cadaghicottage.com.au
www.cadaghicottage.com.au

Double $150-$180
Full provisions
Visa MC Eftpos accepted
1 Queen (1 bdrm)
Cosy wood fire
Bathrooms: 1 Ensuite
Double spa bath

AAA Tourism
★★★★★

Cadaghi Cottage is located adjacent to the start of the walking tracks of the World Heritage listed Rainforest, yet only minutes from the village of Kuranda. Nestled in a bush setting, offering tranquil surroundings and five star luxury, the cottage offers the discerning traveller a unique opportunity to experience Australia's natural beauty. The cottage is fully equipped with entertainment, dining and catering essentials with daily gourmet breakfast provisions and complimentary port. Start your stay with a welcoming bottle of Australian Brut Cuvee and homemade chocolates.

≈

Daintree

Explore the world's oldest living rainforest, picturesque rivers and surrounding mangrove habitats, home to a diverse array of flora and fauna with abundant bird and wildlife, butterflies and the prehistoric crocodile.

River cruises, bird watching, rainforest tours, fishing, health spas, outdoor theatre, horse riding, tropical exotic nurseries, wildlife sanctuaries, aboriginal culture, timber gallery and museum, photographic tours, scenic golf course.

Glimpse into Australia's colourful past at Daintree Village, forged from the spirits of gold rush pioneers, cedar timber getters and farmers. Only 60 minutes north of Cairns and 20 minutes north of Port Douglas.
Daintree Village Tourist Association.

Daintree - Cape Tribulation

Cape Trib Exotic Fruit Farm *B&B & Cottage, no kitchen*

Digby and Alison Gotts
Lot 5 Nicole Drive
Cape Tribulation, Qld 4873
80 km N of Mossman

Tel (07) 4098 0057
digby@capetrib.com.au
www.capetrib.com.au

Double $140-$160
Children Age 6 and over welcome
Full breakfast
Four cafés are within walking distance
2 nights min
Extra person $30
Max 3ad or 2ad+2 children/cottage
Visa MC accepted
2 Queen 2 Double (2 bdrm) 1 Queen
+ 1 Double folding divan per open-plan cottage
Bathrooms: 2 Ensuite

Two private, high set timber pole-framed cottages, on the edge of our privately owned World Heritage Rainforest, with its own walking trails. Breakfast is a sumptuous repast, based around farm produce. The property is in a remote wilderness area and runs on solar power. We offer a personalized experience, as hosts who know the area and have lived here for 18 years. There is a lot to do - we are one kilometre from the beach and the Great Barrier Reef is 45 minutes offshore.

Daintree - Cow Bay

Cow Bay Homestay *B&B & Homestay*

Marion Esser
160 Wattle Close
Cow Bay
Qld 4873
58 km N of Mossman

Tel (07) 4098 9151
marion@cowbayhomestay.com
www.cowbayhomestay.com

Double $140
Single $140
Children over 6 years
Full breakfast
Dinner please advise
Visa MC accepted
1 Queen 1 Double 1 Twin (2 bdrm)
Bathrooms: 2 Ensuite

Cow Bay Homestay is adjacent to two World Heritage Wilderness areas the Daintree Rainforest and the Great Barrier Reef. Wake up to nature: views into vast tropical gardens and rainforest, swim in our fresh water creek, sit under trees or on the deck spotting birds, stars, butterflies or the goanna. Get active with walks to stunning Cow Bay Beach and big range of guided tours. Great breakfast. Marion can arrange all your tour bookings. Action Packed Relaxation. Two friendly cats may make friends with you.

The Glasshouse Mountains

The Glasshouse Mountains are ancient volcanic plugs about 25-27 million years old and form the backdrop to the beautiful hinterland region forty minutes North of Brisbane. The area is popular with bushwalkers, climbers, cyclists, bird-watchers, artists, photographers and people who just want to get away from it all and breathe some fresh mountain air.

It's also a great base to explore the other attractions of the Sunshine Coast such as the Australia Zoo, hinterland towns such as Maleny and Montville, beaches, the Ettamongah Pub, the Big Pineapple, Eumundi markets and Noosa. The surrounding agricultural industry provides fruit for Brisbane and Sydney, including strawberries, paw paws, mangos, limes, macadamias, avocados and pineapples.

Bill Rogers, Glasshhouse on Glasshouse, Qld.

Gold Coast Hinterland - Nerang

Riviera Bed & Breakfast *B&B & Retreat*
Robert & Caroline Marchesi
53 Evanita Drive
Gilston/Nerang
Qld 4211
6 km S of Nerang

Tel (07) 5533 2499
or 0421 853 189
Fax (07) 5533 2500
rivbandb@bigpond.net.au
www.rivierabandb.com.au

Double $115-$140 Single $95-$115
Children $15-$30
Continental breakfast
Dinner B/A $25-$55, children $10-$35
Extra person $45
Visa MC Eftpos accepted

4 Queen 3 Single (4 bdrm) 3 rooms have queen + single bed
Bathrooms: 1 Ensuite 1 Guest share 1 Private Ensuite has bath & shower

Unique French Experience on the edge of Gold Coast Hinterland. Close proximity to all Theme Parks and National/Wildlife Parks. Peaceful, secluded and exotic location in an Exquisite 100 year old Queenslander on 7 acres of sub-tropical bushland. Franco-Australian hosts offer sumptuous breakfasts of organic eggs, homemade breads and jams with weekend specialities of French crepes and omelettes. Exotic native birds to handfeed from deck while kangaroos graze nearby. Authentic French Gourmet meals by arrangement. Aussie host offers Therapeutic Massage. Pet friendly.

Hervey Bay

Hervey Bay is one of the most sought after holiday destinations a scenic three and a half hours drive north of Brisbane and only 45 minutes by air.

Hervey Bay's pristine environment and expansive sheltered waters enhance its reputation as the Whale Watch Capital of the world for the Humpback Whales from late July to November. With beautiful Beaches, calm stinger-free waters you can enjoy an experience you will never forget.

Visit World Heritage listed Fraser Island, the wonderful Great Sandy Straits. Hervey Bay also offers great access to Lady Elliot Island and the Sout hern Great Barrier Reef.
Pauline & Max Harriden, Alexander Lakeside B&B

Hervey Bay

Alexander Lakeside B&B *B&B & Separate Suite*
Pauline & Max Harriden
29 Lido Parade
Hervey Bay
Qld 4655
1 km N of Hervey Bay

Tel (07) 4128 9448
Fax (07) 4125 5060
alexbnb@bigpond.net.au
www.herveybaybedandbreakfast.com

Queen rooms $130-$140
S/C suites $150-$160
Full breakfast
Visa MC Eftpos accepted
4 Queen (4 bdrm)
2 Queen Rooms & 2 S/C Suites
Bathrooms: 4 Ensuite

  AAA Tourism
★★★★☆

Luxury accommodation located beside a peaceful wildlife lake. Wake up and enjoy a full tropical breakfast while watching our wildlife. Guests can participate in turtle feeding. Indulge yourself in our heated Lakeside Spa. Fully equipped kitchen and laundry. BBQ facilities. We can organise your tours to view the majestic Humpback Whales Aug, Sept, Oct. World Heritage listed Fraser Island the largest sand Island in the world and Lady Elliott Island beginning of the Great Barrier Reef. A warm welcome awaits you. Your Home Style Resort.

Hervey Bay

Bay Bed & Breakfast *B&B*
Michel & Cheryll Lecointre
180 Cypress Street
Hervey Bay
Qld 4655
1 km E of Hervey Bay

Tel (07) 4125 6919
or 0401 041 661
Fax (07) 4125 3658
baybedandbreakfast@bigpond.com
www.hervey.com.au/baybedandbreakfast

Double $120-$150
Single $75
Full breakfast
Visa MC accepted
2 King/Twin 3 Queen 1 Single (5 bdrm)
Bathrooms: 2 Ensuite 1 Guest share

Recommended by the Lonely Planet Qld. Quality accommodation in an idyllic tropical setting. Salt water swimming pool, continental and cooked breakfast in our dining room or shady rear terrace. Quality bedrooms with ensuite/shared bathroom or suite with private lounge, bathroom and laundry for that extra touch of privacy. One street from the beach, close to shops, restaurants and clubs. Tours and transfers arranged free of charge. Courtesy pick up from Hervey Bay Airport or Coach Terminal. On parle français.

Hervey Bay - Howard

Melvos Country House *B&B & Country House*
Yvonne & Paul Melverton
20 Pacific Haven Circuit
Howard
Qld 4659
30 km N of Maryborough

Tel (07) 4129 0201
or 0428 290 201
Fax (07) 4129 0201
melvos1@bigpond.com.au
www.bbbook.com.au/melvos.html

Double $90-$110
Full breakfast
Dinner B/A
1 Queen 1 Double (2 bdrm)
Bathrooms: 1 Ensuite 2 Guest share
1 Private

  AAA Tourism ★★★★

Centrally located between Maryborough - Hervey Bay - Childers on 44 acres in comfortable and affordable accommodation. Home cooked meals - BBQ facilities - BYO alcohol. Tropical gardens - inground pool/spa, TV, DVD, Video. Two saltwater rivers, boat ramp, laundromat, golf course, tennis court nearby. Tours arranged - Fraser & Elliott Islands - whale watching - 4x4 hire, deep-sea fishing, camel rides. Complimentary tea/coffee anytime. Free pickup from Howard Tilt train or bus terminal. Dinner by arrangement. We have small well behaved dogs. Not suitable for children. Smoking outdoors. A warm welcome awaits you.

Hervey Bay - Howard

Montrave House B&B Home & Pet Stay *B&B*

Jackie & George Adams
20 Pacific Haven Drive
Howard
Qld 4659
30 km N of Maryborough

Tel (07) 4129 0183
or 0407 930 106
montrave@bigpond.com
www.bbbook.com.au/MontraveHouse.html

Double $95-$105
Full traditional Aussie or Scottish
breakfast included
Refreshments on arrival included,
tea/coffee, evening Port
2 Queen 1 Double 2 Twin (4 bdrm)
Bathrooms: 2 Guest share Spa bath

Enjoy the elegance of a bygone era, traditional Scottish hospitality in the ambiance of a high set historic Queenslander in a tranquil atmosphere on rural acreage. Modern comforts, spa bath, wide verandahs and comfortable air conditioned tastefully decorated federation rooms. Close to the golf course boat ramps for two saltwater rivers and within walking distance of Howard CBD. Bookings available for all tours of Fraser Island also Lady Elliot Island and whale watching trips as well as vehicle and boat hire. Central for Hervey Bay and the historic towns of Maryborough and Childers.

Kuranda - Cairns

Koah Bed & Breakfast *B&B & Homestay & Farmstay & Self Contained Chalets*

Greg Taylor
Lot 4 Koah Road
MSI 1039 Kuranda
Qld 4881
40 km W of Cairns

Tel (07) 4093 7074
Fax (07) 4093 7074
koah@ozemail.com.au
www.kurandahomestay.com

Double $77 Single $55
Children 50% (under 15)
Continental breakfast
Cabin $95 double, $125 for four
Visa MC accepted
2 Queen 2 Double 4 Twin 2 Single
(6 bdrm) 2 cabins sleep 4 each, 2 dbl in homestead
Bathrooms: 1 Ensuite 1 Private

Comfortable country home on 10 acres 10 mins from Kuranda the township in the Rainforest Kuranda and 30 mins from Cairns and Great Barrier Reef. Offering fully self contained cabins for families with balconies overlooking native bushland and large dam. Also homestead accommodation of 2 double bedrooms with double opening doors onto verandah 1 guest bathroom (ensuite) fully insulated and screened with ceiling fans. Each bedroom can be fitted with single folding bed for children, pets also welcomed.

Noosa - Lake Weyba

Eumarella Shores Lake Retreat *B&B & Self Contained Cottages and Pavlions*

Bill & Christine Tainsh
251 Eumarella Road
Lake Weyba, Qld 4562
7 km SW of Noosa

Tel (07) 5449 1738
Fax 07 5449 1738
stay@eumarellashores.com.au
www.eumarellashores.com.au

Double $132-$265
Children $12-$22 Full provisions
Dinner Seafood or BBQ Hampers
Cold drink and snacks available
Extra adults $28-$46 per night
Visa MC accepted
5 King/Twin5 King 7 Queen 8 Double
1 Single (14 bdrm) 7 queen & 7 king twin or king
Bathrooms: 7 Private 3 x pavlions with king single spa

AAA Tourism
★★★★

A unique lake front retreat, nestled in temperate rainforest on the shores of pristine Lake Weyba. Only minutes from cosmopolitan Noosa: world class beaches, national parks, restaurants and boutiques. Enchanting traditional cottages and contemporary pavilions on the lake's edge; self contained to preserve your privacy with individual lake access and beach area. Explore the creeks and lake in a canoe; go bushwalking; bird & wildlife watching; fish virtually from your doorstep; or simply relax on your verandah, listening to the gently lapping lake. Sheer bliss!

Noosa - Noosa Valley

Noosa Valley Manor Luxury B&B *Luxury B&B*

Kathleen & Murray Maxwell
115 Wust Road
Doonan, Noosa Valley
Qld 4562
6 km SW of Noosa

Tel (07) 5471 0088
or 0400 280 215
Fax (07) 5471 0066
noosavalleymanor@bigpond.com
www.noosavalleymanor.com.au

Double $195-$230
Full breakfast
Candlelight dinners by arrangement
Visa MC Eftpos accepted
1 King/Twin 3 Queen (4 bdrm)
All with air conditioning
Bathrooms: 4 Ensuite

  AAA Tourism
★★★★☆

Noosa Valley Manor is a custom built Bed & Breakfast that truly reflects its 4.5 star AAA rating. Set in 1.5 acres of award winning tropical gardens yet you are only 10 minutes pleasant drive to the heart of Noosa. All bedrooms are air conditioned with ensuites. Gourmet fresh food is a feature of your stay with us. Here is what some guests have said: "Divine food, beautiful house, perfect hosts." "So lovely to be spoilt by wonderful people in a beautiful setting."

Noosa - Peregian

Lake Weyba Cottages *B&B & Self Contained Cottages*

Philip & Samantha Bown
79 Clarendon Road
Peregian Beach
Qld 4573
14 km S of Noosa

Tel (07) 5448 2285
or 0404 863 504
Fax (07) 5448 1714
info@lakeweybacottages.com
www.lakeweybacottages.com

Double $260-$400
Full breakfast Dinner $85
Extra person $75
Visa MC Amex Eftpos accepted
4 King/Twin 5 Queen 2 Single (10 bdrm)
Bathrooms: 8 Ensuite 1 Guest share
Double spa in each cottage

AAA Tourism
★★★★☆

Luxury cottages for couples with double spas, wood fires, air-conditioning and fabulous views. Peace and privacy assured. Enjoy breakfast on your private verandah, perfect for relaxing and watching passing kangaroos and the abundant bird life. LCD televisions with home theatre systems and digital reception in all cottages. Only 5 minutes to Peregian Beach and 15 minutes south of Noosa. Complimentary facilities include canoeing, cycling, fishing and a DVD library. Additional services include in-house dinners, massage treatments and eco tours. Perfect for weddings and conferences.

Noosa Hinterland - Cooroy

Cudgerie Homestead B&B *B&B*

Veronica & Steve Hall
42 Cudgerie Drive
Cooroy, Qld 4563
7 km W of Cooroy and Pomona

Tel (07) 5442 6681
or 0408 982 461
Fax (07) 5442 6681
cudgerie@hotmail.com
www.cudgerie.com

Double $155-$167 Single $90-$95
Infants free with cot in parent bedroom
Full breakfast
Delicious evening meals available B/A
Visa MC accepted
3 Queen 1 Double 2 Twin 1 Single
(6 bdrm) Wonderfully comfortable
Bathrooms: 5 Ensuite 1 Private

Multi-award winning Cudgerie Homestead is one of the Sunshine Coast's most popular bed and breakfasts, offering you a unique blend of relaxation, ambience and cuisine. Unwind by the sensational swimming pool in summer or around the pot belly in winter. A quiet and secluded location with fantastic views across the Noosa Hinterland. Guest Comments: A place to indulge, superb breakfasts on the verandah. Charming hosts with helpful touring advice." "It doesn't get any better than this, splendid location, warm and friendly hosts and top notch food."

Rockhampton - Capricorn Coast

Brae Bothy B&B *B&B*
Judy & Keith Brandt
1184 Yeppoon Road
Iron Pot, Rockhampton
Qld 4701
20 km NE of Rockhampton

Tel (07) 4936 4026 or 0427 364 026
Fax (07) 4936 4038
stay@braebothy.com.au
www.braebothy.com.au

Double $110-$130 Single $95-$110
Children $15 or B/A
Full breakfast
Dinner $25 B/A
Visa MC accepted
1 King/Twin 2 Queen (3 bdrm)
Bathrooms: 2 Ensuite 1 Private

    AAA Tourism ★★★★☆

Brae Bothy is an award winning traditional B&B located on 4.2 hectares of Central Queensland Bush. Relax in a quaint Scottish bothy nestled in a peaceful tranquil setting with abundant bird and animal life. Bedrooms tastefully furnished, air-conditioned, Queen size beds, ensuite and private outdoor garden settings. Each room has a television set. The King room has an external heated spa. Guest BBQ facility and swimming pool. Fifteen minutes to Yeppoon's beautiful beaches and ten minutes to Rockhampton shopping centres. Brae Bothy has the very friendly Kelpie dog called Molly and a beautiful ginger cat called Rusty.

~

Stanthorpe

The Granite Belt, so called because of its spectacular granite outcrops, is situated just north of the New South Wales border, around the small town of Stanthorpe. Because of its altitude, the area has become well-known as the coldest place in Queensland, when locally produced red wines, 'Christmas in July' dinners and cosy log fires attract large numbers of tourists to the area.

The four National Parks in the area, Girraween, Bald Rock, Boonoo Boonoo and Sundown, each with its own individual character, offer plenty of opportunity for walking, climbing, photography and bird-watching.
Margaret Taylor, Jireh B&B

Stanthorpe

Jireh *B&B & Homestay*
Margaret Taylor
89 Donges Road
Severnlea
Qld 4352
8 km S of Stanthorpe

Tel (07) 4683 5298
ktaylor3@vtown.com.au
www.bbbook.com.au/jireh.html

Double $90-$110
Single $65-$75
Children $30
Full breakfast
Dinner $25
Extra adult $50
3 Double 1 Single (3 bdrm)
Bathrooms: 1 Ensuite 1 Guest share

Old-fashioned country hospitality in a quiet rural setting, close to the wineries and national parks of the Granite Belt. Antiques and country decor reflect family history and include many examples of Margaret's embroidery, patchwork, dolls and bears. Hearty country breakfasts are served and dinner (Traditional or Indian) is by arrangement. The combination of country home, personal attention, household pets, farm animals, and country rambles offers both a unique experience and value for money. "Wonderful friendly atmosphere and simply great food." B&B Book Commended, 2004, 2005.

Sunshine Coast

The Sunshine Coast is located an easy one hour drive north on the Bruce Highway of Queensland's capital city of Brisbane. Discover the delights of coastal towns from Caloundra to Noosa and the lush green hinterland areas of the Noosa Hinterland, the Blackall Ranges, Buderim and the Mary Valley.

The Sunshine Coast Hinterland boasts lavish scenery with breathtaking views, ancient rainforest, waterfalls and lakes, enticing markets and restaurants, local produce, art galleries and museums, boutiques and an array of shopping catering for tastes refined or earthy.
David Mathers.

Sunshine Coast - Ninderry - Yandina - Coolum

Ninderry House *B&B*
Mary Lambart
8 Karnu Drive
Ninderry
Qld 4561
5 km E of Yandina

Tel (07) 5446 8556
Fax (07) 5446 8556
enquiries@ninderryhouse.com.au
www.ninderryhouse.com.au

Double $145
Single $90
Full breakfast
Dinner if requested on booking $20-$30
Visa MC accepted
2 King/Twin 1 Queen (3 bdrm)
Bathrooms: 3 Ensuite

Central Sunshine Coast location, views overlooking Mt Ninderry and Maroochy Valley to the Ocean. Close to beaches, native plant nurseries, ginger factory, art galleries, craft and produce markets of Eumundi and Yandina. First class restaurants nearby. Three ensuite guestrooms, comfortable sitting room with fire, deck for summer breezes or winter sun. Imaginative meals using fresh local produce. Special diets catered for. Dinner available if requested on booking. Full breakfast included in tariff. Ph/Fax: 07 5446 8556. Email: enquiries@ninderryhouse.com.au.

Sunshine Coast Hinterland - Glasshouse Mountains

Glass on Glasshouse *B&B Cottages with kitchenettes*
Bill & Misao Rogers
182 Glasshouse-Woodford Road
Glasshouse Mountains, Qld 4518
45 km N of Brisbane

Tel (07) 5496 9603
or (07) 5496 9608
info@glassonglasshouse.com.au
www.glassonglasshouse.com.au

Double $180-$300 Single $165-$285
Additional person $70 per night
Full provisions
Nearest restaurants are 6 km away
Maximum of 3 people per cottage
(3rd on sofa bed)
Visa MC Eftpos accepted
3 King (3 bdrm) King or Twin beds
Bathrooms: 3 Ensuite Freestanding spa

We're building 3 beautiful self-contained cottages in a mango orchard. Completion is January but ring/email first! Magnificent views of the two grandest mountains (Beerwah and Coonowrin). Watch the kangaroos, or listen to the Kookaburras and Black Cockatoos. Great for walkers, birdwatchers, artists and those who want to relax. Floor-to-ceiling glass walls, a gorgeous freestanding spa, romantic gas fire, HiFi. flat-screen TV, kitchenette and a gas BBQ. Breakfast in our café or in your cottage. Nearby are Australia Zoo, beaches, Woodford, Maleny, Eumundi markets and Noosa.

Sunshine Coast Hinterland - Maleny

Braeside Bed & Breakfast *Luxury B&B*

Ken & Elizabeth Smith
305 Maleny Stanley River Road
Maleny
Qld 4552
3.5 km SW of Maleny

Tel (07) 5494 3542
Fax (07) 5494 2403
enquiries@braesidebnb.com.au
www.braesidebnb.com.au

Double $200-$270
Single $150-$205
Full breakfast
Dinner by arrangement
Visa MC Eftpos accepted
2 King/Twin 2 Queen (4 bdrm)
Reverse cycle air-conditioning to all suites
Bathrooms: 4 Ensuite Spas in King suites

Perched on the ridge overlooking the spectacular Glasshouse Mountains, Braeside is a spacious, modern home 75 minutes north of Brisbane and 30 minutes from Sunshine Coast beaches. A retreat for adults to enjoy exceptional hospitality, pre-dinner treats by the fire or on the deck and scrumptious breakfasts featuring local produce. Chill out in one of our stylish, air-conditioned suites or guest lounges, CD & DVD collection and games included. Close to restaurants, wineries, galleries, bush walks and shops.

Sunshine Coast Hinterland - Maleny - Montville

Lillypilly's Country Cottages *5 B&B Cottages with kitchenettes*

Josef & Adele Gruber
584 Maleny-Montville Road
Maleny
Qld 4552
6 km S of Town

Tel (07) 5494 3002
or 0408 943 002
Fax (07) 5494 3499
lillypillys@bigpond.com
www.lillypillys.com.au

Double $187-$297 Single $176-$286
Full breakfast
Dinner $28.60-$33.00 (Main Course)
$1/2$ to 1 hour massage $44-$77
Visa MC Diners Amex Eftpos accepted
5 Queen (5 bdrm)
Bathrooms: 5 Ensuite 5 Private

Lillypilly's Cottages for couples overlook picturesque Lake Baroon or are situated in a rainforest garden setting. All cottages are air conditioned and feature log fires, dual-system double spas, separate ensuite, lounge area with television, video, DVD and CD player, kitchenettes, and private verandahs with double hammocks. Gourmet Breakfasts are included in the rate and Candlelit Dinners are available Tues-Sat and served to your individual cottage. An on-site masseuse and saltwater pool are also features of Lillypilly's.

Sunshine Coast Hinterland - Montville

Secrets on the Lake *Luxury B&B & Luxury Treehouse Cabins*

George and Aldy Johnston
208 Narrows Road
Montville
Qld 4560
5 km SW of Montville

Tel (07) 5478 5888
Fax (07) 5478 5166
aldy@secretsonthelake.com.au
www.secretsonthelake.com.au

Double $295-$395
Continental provisions
Visa MC Amex Eftpos accepted
1 King/Twin 13 Queen
2 Single (14 bdrm)
Bathrooms: 1 Ensuite 11 Private

Secrets on the Lake offers the perfect opportunity for romance, relaxation and intimate accommodation. Elevated wooden walkways lead you through the rainforest to 10 individually themed treehouses offering total privacy, superb attention to detail and a completely unique world-class experience. Each retreat features carved cedar furniture, double shower, kitchen facilities, special home baked treats, toasty log fire, AC, TV, CD/ DVD, sunken double spa and your own balcony with BBQ. What a way to indulge... we provide a stunning view, chocolates, roses & champagne. All you need to bring is that special someone to share it with.

Sunshine Coast Hinterland - Mooloolah Valley

Mooloolah Valley Holidays *Guest House & Self contained House & Cottage*

Atalanta Moreau
93 King Road
Mooloolah Valley
Qld 4553
1 km SW of Mooloolah

Tel (07) 5494 7109
or 0408 224 668
info@mooloolahvalley.com
www.mooloolahvalley.com

Double $150-$250
Accommodation only
Visa MC accepted
3 Double 4 Single (3 bdrm)
2 Romantic Bedrooms 1 bedsitter
Bathrooms: 3 Private
3 Guest House, 1 Cottage

Discover the glorious pleasures of a country horse riding holiday at Mooloolah Valley. For romantic couples, JACARANDA COTTAGE is charming and full of olde-world splendor. For Families and celebrations, FRANGAPANI HOUSE is dazzling! Guests are treated to a fun-filled holiday. Try the tropical Hot-tub Jacuzzi spa, fabulous heated swimming pool and wood-fire pizza oven. Great for parties! There are fun games like giant chess set, bikes to explore picturesque Mooloolah Valley, safe Horses and cute Ponies to trek into Rainforest and Mountain-tops. Come and enjoy!

Yeppoon - Capricorn Coast

While Away B&B *B&B*

Sharyn McClelland
44 Todd Avenue
Yeppoon
Qld 4703
2.4 km N of Yeppoon

Tel (07) 4939 5719
Fax (07) 4939 5577
whileaway@bigpond.com
www.whileawaybandb.com.au

Double $110-$130
Single $95
Full breakfast
Visa MC Eftpos accepted
1 King 3 Queen 1 Twin (4 bdrm)
Bathrooms: 4 Ensuite

AAA Tourism
★★★★☆

While Away B&B is a purpose built B&B. We offer style, comfort and privacy in a modern home less than 100 m to beach. This property is ideal for couples but unsuitable for children under 10. All rooms have ensuites, television plus air-conditioning. We offer a generous tropical/cooked breakfast - tea/coffee-making facilities with cake/biscuits are available at all times. Dining room facilities available for use of guests. We will do our best to ensure you enjoy your stay in this area.

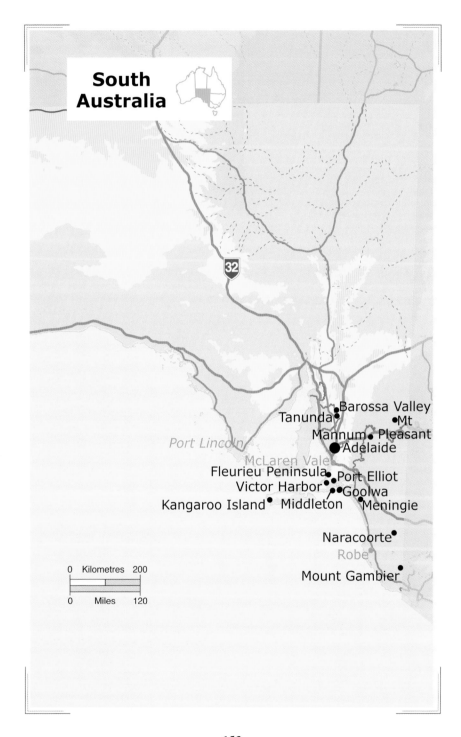

South
Australia

32

Barossa Valley
Tanunda
Mt
Mannum Pleasant
Port Lincoln
Adelaide
McLaren Vale
Fleurieu Peninsula
Port Elliot
Victor Harbor
Goolwa
Kangaroo Island Middleton Meningie

Naracoorte
Robe
Mount Gambier

0 Kilometres 200

0 Miles 120

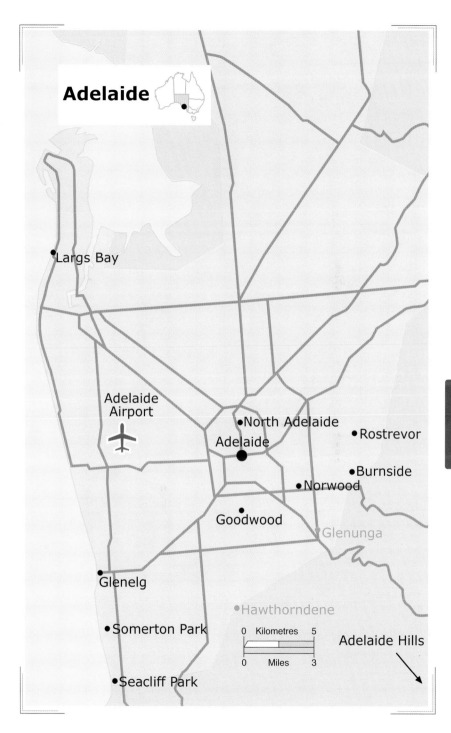

Adelaide - Burnside - St Georges

Kirkendale *B&B & Self Contained Apartment*
Jenny & Steve Studer
16 Inverness Avenue
St. Georges
SA 5064
5 km SE of Adelaide

Tel (08) 8338 2768
or 0413 414 140
Fax (08) 8338 2768
kirkendale@ozemail.com.au
www.kirkendale.com.au

Double $135-$145
Single $115-$125
Children $20-$30
Continental provisions
Visa MC accepted
1 Queen 2 Twin (2 bdrm)
Bathrooms: 1 Private

Idyllic "Country-style" 3 room apartment, nestled in peaceful, leafy garden, sun-dappled patio, French doors, terracotta floors, rose garden. Hint of the Provence. Fresh flowers, fruit basket, generous breakfasts, books, tourist information. Separate entrance, private bathroom, living room, kitchenette, sole occupancy. Quiet location. 5km city, near restaurants, wineries, wildlife parks. Jenny and Steve are extremely well travelled, this is reflected by their gracious but unobtrusive hosting. Smoking outdoors. "We loved our accommodation - our best yet in 6 weeks of travel," SS & DC, USA.

Adelaide - Glenelg

Water Bay Villa Bed & Breakfast *Luxury B&B - Self Contained Suite*
Kathy & Roger Kuchel
28 Broadway
Glenelg South
SA 5045
11 km SW of Adelaide

Tel 0412 221 724
glenelg@waterbayvilla-bnb.com.au
www.waterbayvilla-bnb.com.au

Double $240-$275
Single $200
Children $20-$45
Full provisions
Visa MC Diners Amex accepted
2 Queen 2 Single (2 bdrm)
Bathrooms: 1 Ensuite

Indulge! Experience the luxury of this 1910 Queen Anne Villa in seaside Glenelg. 'The Attic' - your upstairs 4 room suite with private entry and off street parking. Welcoming bottle of wine, fresh flowers, fruit and chocolates. Antiques, open fire, claw foot bath and laundry. Kitchenette with cooking facilities. Living area with tourist info, TV, video, CD/Radio. A few minutes stroll via the award winning garden to the nearby beach, Jetty Road, trams, restaurants, cinema, 7-day shopping, summer markets, fun park and marina. Close to airport and public transport. Come and enjoy! "A little piece of heaven." HF, Canada.

Adelaide - Goodwood

Rose Villa *B&B & Homestay*
Doreen Petherick
29 Albert Street
Goodwood
SA 5034
2 km S of Adelaide

Tel (08) 8271 2947
Fax (08) 8271 2947
doreen@rosevilla.com.au
www.rosevilla.com.au

Double $120-$145
Single $95-$110
Full breakfast
1 King 1 Queen (2 bdrm)
Bathrooms: 1 Ensuite 1 Private

Treat yourself to a romantic candle lit breakfast in my newly decorated Tea Rose salon. Rose Villa offers an elegant private suite (own entrance) overlooking the garden. Inside is an additional guest room with the use of the exquisite Blue-White-Russian Tea Cup bathroom. Stroll to trendy Hyde Park Road with its delightful cafés and coffee shops, boutiques and flower shops. Close by are buses and trams (to the Bay) and city and The Ghan Terminal. "Rose Villa" is roses, romance and caring hospitality. You are most welcome. "A romantic and warm place to be. Great hospitality." Erwin Zwijnenburg, The Hague, Holland.

Adelaide - Largs Bay

Seapod B&B *B&B*
Bernadette McDonnell
146 Esplanade
Largs Bay
SA 5016
18 km NW of Adelaide

Tel (08) 8449 4213
or 0418 851 680
info@seapod.com.au
www.seapod.com.au

Double $180-$195
Single $150-$160
Children $50
Full breakfast
Visa MC Diners Amex Eftpos
JCB accepted
1 Queen (1 bdrm)
Bathrooms: 1 Private

AAA Tourism
★★★★

Seapod is wonderful hosted bed & breakfast accommodation in a superb seaside setting with great views and within walking distance of shops, restaurants, cafés, and public transport. Delicious breakfasts served daily in your suite overlooking the sea. Natural, free range and organic produce with unlimited freshly brewed coffee and tea are standard. See dolphins and magnificent sunsets from your table, go for a run on the track across the road, walk along the jetties, swim with the dolphins, or stroll along the beach for miles.

Adelaide - North Adelaide

Cornwall Park Heritage Accommodation *B&B & Self Contained Apartment*

Judy Fitzhardinge
84 Mills Terrace
North Adelaide
SA 5006
1 km N of Adelaide city centre

Tel (08) 8239 0155
or 0411 171 807
judy@seekshare.com.au
www.seekshare.com.au

Double $135-$250 Single $120-$165
Children B/A
Special breakfast
Visa MC Diners Amex Eftpos accepted
1 King/Twin1 King 5 Queen
1 Twin (7 bdrm)
Bathrooms: 5 Ensuite 1 Private 3 with spa suites

Cornwall Park is an 1873 state heritage listed property, situated around north Adelaide golf course and parklands. Only 1 kilometre from Adelaide city and 500m from some of the best restaurants and cafés in Adelaide. The bluestone residence was sympathetically renovated in 2002-3 to include four lovely spacious bedrooms, two with large spa and two other bedrooms with ensuites in the heritage side. A stunningly modern apartment offers either 1 to 3 bedrooms with 2+ bathrooms including one with spa. Open fireplaces and reverse-cycle air-conditioning throughout. A romantic place suitable for people on holiday, weddings as well as the business person. Internet is available for guests. Secure off street parking

Adelaide - Seacliff Park - Brighton

Homestay Brighton *B&B & Homestay*

Ruth Humphrey & Tim Lorence
PO Box 319
Brighton
SA 5048
2 km S of Brighton

Tel (08) 8298 6671
or 0417 800 755
0405 092 701
Fax (08) 8298 6671
ruthhumphrey001@hotmail.com
www.bbbook.com.au/brighton.html

Double $65-$75
Single $45-$55
Children by arrangement
Full breakfast
1 Double 2 Single (2 bdrm)
Bathrooms: 1 Guest share 1 Private

Spacious home and grounds in a quiet suburb close to Brighton beach. Close to bus and trains to the city or trips to the southern Fleurieu Peninsula. Guest rooms are upstairs and include a television lounge area with heating and cooling. Laundry and off-street parking available. We have a friendly Border Collie dog, who stays outside. "Home from home." LJ, UK. "It was a lovely stay." SH, Germany. "Great value in a relaxing suburb of Adelaide. Outstanding host, helpful, supportive and friendly." J&GB, UK.

Adelaide - Somerton Park

Forstens Bed & Breakfast *B&B & Homestay*
John & Marilyn Forsten
19 King George Avenue
Somerton Park
SA 5044
2.5 km S of Glenelg

Tel (08) 8298 3393
forstens_bandb@hotmail.com
www.bbbook.com.au/forstensbb.html

Double $77
Single $60
Full breakfast
1 King 2 Single (2 bdrm)
Bathrooms: 1 Ensuite 1 Guest share

AAA Tourism
★★★☆

Located in a residential area 600 metres from beautiful Somerton Beach, 2.5km south of the bustling seaside resort of Glenelg with its 'mile' of shopping and dining along Jetty Road. A city bus passes the house en route to Glenelg and Adelaide. Guests are accommodated in a lovely bedroom with a rear garden view, ensuite bath, TV, private entrance, reverse cycle air conditioning, and off-street parking. Warm fresh bread is included in the cooked breakfast. Laundry facilities available.

Adelaide - Rostrevor

Morialta Bed & Breakfast *Luxury Self Contained Apartment*
Claire Viscione
5 Baroota Avenue
Rostrevor
SA 5073
In Rostrevor

Tel (08) 8365 2707
Fax (08) 8365 2707
jviscione@bigpond.com
www.morialtabnb.com.au

Double $95-$110
Special breakfast
10% discount for 1 week stays
1 Queen (1 bdrm)
Bathrooms: 1 Ensuite

AAA Tourism
★★★☆

Situated on the edge of Morialta Conservation Park this self contained unit offers complete privacy. Relax and recharge while experiencing the tranquillity of bush land 20 minutes from the CBD of Adelaide. Sit under the vine covered pergola for a meal or read a book or watch and listen to the birds

Adelaide Hills - Mt Pleasant

Saunders Gorge Sanctuary *Family cottage & 5 Self contained buildings for couples*

Brenton & Nadene Newman
18km east of Mt Pleasant
Mt Pleasant, SA 5237
18 km E of Mt Pleasant

Tel (08) 8569 3032
nature@saundersgorge.com.au
www.saundersgorge.com.au

Double $110-$160 Single $90-$130
Children in family cottage $10 per night
Continental provisions
Restaurant availbile on the property
Family Cottage (sleeps 6) extra adult $20pp
Visa MC accepted
4 King 3 Queen 2 Single (7 bdrm)
Bathrooms: 5 Ensuite 1 Guest share
1 bathroom in family cottage All other
buildings ensuite

AAA Tourism ★★★☆

ECO Tourism accredited Saunders Gorge Sanctuary is a private property of 1364 ha on the rugged Eastern slopes of the Mt Lofty Ranges (Adelaide Hills). Offering visitors the opportunity to experience the rugged Australian landscape, learn about and enjoy the natural environment. The property is now a combination of conservation and sheep grazing. The owners Brenton & Nadene Newman are dedicated to Natural Habitat Preservation. Relax in self contained accommodation, explore the property on many scenic walks. Relax in your room by the wood fire & enjoy an evening meal with your hosts in there licensed restaurant.

Barossa Valley - Lyndoch - Tanunda

Bellescapes *Self Contained B&B Cottages*

Mandy & Mark Creed
PO Box 481
Lyndoch, SA 5351
1 km N of Lyndoch

Tel (08) 8524 4825
or 0412 220 553
Fax (08) 8524 4046
escape@bellescapes.com
www.bellescapes.com

Double $150-$250 Single $140-$220
Children welcome in properties with more
than one bedroom
Full provisions
Dinner platters & BBQ packs B/A
Tours can be arranged
Visa MC accepted
10 properties to choose from, ranging from 1 bedroom to 3 bedrooms
Each property has its own bathroom facilities

Bellescapes properties are exclusively yours, private & self contained. Indulge in one of our stunning B&B's; there's Bluebelle, a quaint 1850's stone cottage; Cherrywood Log Cabin, nestled in Tanunda; Casa Rossa, secluded overlooking a vineyard; Christabelle, a stunning 1849 ironstone chapel; Daisybelle, a delightful stone cottage built in 1855; Hall Manor has 3 contemporary suites, centrally located; Jandas Lake View, on 30 acres with its own lake; Jasmine's Cottage, C1880's quaint shabby chic decor. All properties feature fine furnishings, air-con, kitchen facilities, provisions for breakfast, 6 with spas and 7 with log fires.

Barossa Valley - Tanunda

Goat Square Cottages *B&B & Self Contained Apartment*
Edward Wright, Manager
33 John Street
Tanunda
SA 5352
75 km N of Adelaide

Tel 1800 227 677
info@goatsquarecottages.com.au
goatsquarecottages.com.au

Double $190
We can provide a baby's cot at no extra cost
Full provisions
Close to the 1918 Restaurant
Visa MC Diners accepted
3 King 1 Queen (4 bdrm)
4 enormous beds
Bathrooms: 3 Private
Fully heated, with modern double spa and shower

Set in the historic centre of Tanunda, these 3 adjoining cottages date from 1867, incorporating features from an original structure built in the 1840s, including the old baker's oven. Recent renovations include a modern spa in each cottage, under-floor heating and a superbly appointed kitchen. You are welcomed with warm country hospitality and a selection of local products for your breakfast. Very close to some of SA's most famous wineries - a great chance to visit this historic area and then relax sitting in the flowery garden, where you can pick your own fruit in season.

Goolwa

Vue de M B&B *B&B*
Pam & Bob Ballard
11 Admiral Terace
Goolwa
SA 5214
0.1 km S of Goolwa

Tel (08) 8555 1487
or 0414 760 232
vuedemerde@iprimus.com.au
www.vuedemerde.com.au

Double $170 Single $160
Full breakfast
Visa MC accepted
2 Queen (2 bdrm)
Bathrooms: 2 Ensuite

M?? Mysterious, Mighty, Murray, Mouth, Muesli, Milo, Milk or Munchies?? Ask us about the real name of our 1850's Riverside Cottage. Relax and enjoy the superb river view from the balcony adjoining your room. Two Queen-sized bedrooms, each with Ensuite. Breakfast is served in the Sun Room with magnificent views from the Hindmarsh Island Bridge to the Goolwa Barrage.

Kangaroo Island

Kangaroo Island is renowned for its spectacular scenery and abundant and diverse variety of wildlife and flora. The spectacular South Coast is buffeted by winds from the Southern Ocean that have produced incredible rock formations, whilst the calmer north coast has rolling hills, secluded bays and beautiful beaches.

Blessed with a temperate 'Mediterranean' climate not unlike the French Riviera, the warm dry summers and cool mild winters make it a year round destination. Average daytime summer temperature is 25°C and winter average is 15°C. Kangaroo Island is a 30 minute flight from Adelaide Airport or 4 hours SW of Adelaide by car & ferry.
Jenny Bloemendal

Kangaroo Island
Cape Cassini Wilderness Retreat *Homestay & Ecolodge*
David & Pat Welford
PO Box 609
Kingscote
SA 5223
38 km N of Kingscote

Tel (08) 8559 2215
or 0428 152 401
Fax (08) 8559 2109
retreat@capecassini.com.au
www.capecassini.com.au

Double $210
Single $130
Special breakfast
Visa MC Eftpos accepted
2 Queen 1 Single (3 bdrm)
Bathrooms: 2 Ensuite 1 Private

AAA Tourism ★★★★

Discover our secret little paradise tucked away in the bush with fantastic ocean views, 1000 acres of wilderness and wildlife, excellent food, great walks, crystal clear water, cosy fires, interesting books, healthy breakfasts and peace and quiet. You will find a special retreat with a self sufficient lifestyle, solar and wind energy, an organic orchard and filtered rain water in a wild, untamed setting with the comforts of home. Come and experience the perfect blend of exclusive touring, hosted homestay and gracious hospitality.

Meningie - Narrung

Poltalloch Station *B&B & Self Contained House & Self Contained Heritage Cottages*

Beth and Chris Cowan
Poltalloch Road, Narrung,
Meningie
SA 5264
29 km N of Meningie

Tel (08) 8574 0043
Fax (08) 8574 0065
info@poltalloch.com.au
www.poltalloch.com.au

Double $170-$195
Single $155-$180
Children from $25 per night
Full provisions
Dinner by special arrangement only
Visa MC accepted
1 King 3 Queen 9 Single (8 bdrm)
2x2 bedroom cottages, 1x4 bedrooom cottage
Bathrooms: 4 Ensuite large cottage has 2 bathrooms
All cottages have 2 toilets

Tranquil and historic farm estate on the shore of freshwater Lake Alexandrina. Enjoy canoes, wood fires in winter, jetty and beach, tennis, walks, 22 historic buildings and some of the very best bird watching in the Coorong area. Our guests stay in private cottages with charm, character and a high level of comfort. An ideal holiday base, or treat yourself to a relaxing retreat and soak up the spectacular scenery.

Middleton - Fleurieu Peninsula

Wenton Farm Holiday Cottages *Farmstay & Fully Self Contained Cottages*

Tony & Wendy Crosby
Sect 163 Burgar Road
Middleton
SA 5213
10 km W of Goolwa

Tel (08) 8555 4126
or 0438 642 157
Fax (08) 8555 4126
wentonfarm@hotmail.com
www.bbbook.com.au/
WentonFarmHolidayCottages.html

Double $110-$130
Children 4-15 $11 each per night
Full provisions
3 Queen 2 Twin (5 bdrm)
3 bedroom cottage sleeps 6
2 bedroom cottage sleeps 4
Bathrooms: 2 Private

 AAA Tourism ★★★

Two fully self contained cottages fully fenced on 1 acre beef cattle property. One 2 bedroom and one 3 bedroom. Each cottage has own decking and outdoor furniture. A shared undercover bbq area is nearby. Enjoy views of hillsides and dam. See kangaroos in far paddocks and wonderful native birds. Chickens and ducks are kept on the farm. Peaceful and quiet - five minutes drive to the beach and shops. Guests are able to join farm activities if desired.

Mount Gambier

Apartments on Tolmie *Self Contained Apartment*
Sandra Parsons & Martin Svec
27A Tolmie Street
Mount Gambier
SA 5290
1.5 km N of Mount Gambier

Tel (08) 8725 1429
or 0418 816 876
Fax (08) 8725 1852
mail@apartmentsontolmie.com.au
www.apartmentsontolmie.com.au

Double $160 Single $150
Children $15
Breakfast by arrangement
Extra adult $30
Visa MC Diners Amex Eftpos accepted
1 Queen 1 Double 1 Single (2 bdrm)
3x2 B/R Apts & dbl sofabed each sleeps 7
Bathrooms: 1 Private

 AAA Tourism ★★★★

3 x 2 br apartments, each sleeps 7. Full kitchen with dishwasher and spacious living area. Washing Machine/Dryer. Queen bed, double & single bed & double sofa bed. All linen and towels supplied. Espresso coffee & gourmet tea selection. Telephone/Internet access. Gas heating/ducted cooling. Private gardens, Gas BBQ and lock up garages. Pets welcome. No smoking indoors. Cooked breakfast provisions can be supplied on request, $30 per couple, extra Adults $15 & Children $5. Located 1.5km North of the city centre of Mount Gambier.

Mount Gambier

Mount Gambier Serviced Apartments *Luxury Self Contained Apartment & Self Contained House*
Miss Carol Downing
PO Box 8424
Mount Gambier East
SA 5291
2 km NE of Post Office

Tel 0409 250 577
or (08) 87247026
cdowning@datafast.net.au
www.mountgambierservicedapartments.
com.au

Double $150-$180 Single $150-$160
Children $15each if using a bed
Porta cot available
Provisions first night
Visa MC Amex Eftpos accepted
2 Queen 2 Double (4 bdrm)
Comfortable quality beds & ensuite to main bedrooms
Bathrooms: 1 Ensuite 1 Private

AAA Tourism ★★★★☆

Mount Gambier Serviced Apartments offer a variety of properties in different locations throughout Mount Gambier, catering for individuals, couples, families and groups of up to 12 people. Properties are fully equipped and offer modern conveniences including Ensuites, Dishwashers, Austar, Dial-up Internet access, Outdoor entertaining areas and private secure parking. Comfort is a priority for me and this is reflected throughout the properties.

Naracoorte

Dartmoor Homestead *B&B*
Lorraine & Andrew Oliver
30 McLay Street
Naracoorte
SA 5271
1 km W of Naracoorte

Tel (08) 8762 0487
or 0416 210 645
Fax (08) 8762 0487
dartmoorhomestead@rbm.com.au
www.dartmoorhomestead.com.au

Double $207-$217
Single $187-$207
Children not suitable
Full breakfast
Visa MC Diners Amex accepted
1 King 3 Queen (4 bdrm)
Bathrooms: 1 Ensuite 1 Guest share 1 Private

AAA Tourism
★★★★☆

Heritage listed and award winning Dartmoor Homestead is a magnificent property - just a short drive from the heart of the Coonawarra wine region. The homestead comprises of three suites, they are all opulently furnished and each room has its own individual furnishings keeping in line with the Victorian theme. There is also a circa 1842 cottage that has been restored to reveal its original charm and character. The enchanting self contained cottage includes a bedroom and comfy living room with a cosy fireplace and a bathroom added that adds to the heritage décor.

South Australia

Victor Harbor

Parkfield Lodge B&B *B&B & Homestay*
Jill Fairchild
66 Rapid Drive
Victor Harbor
SA 5211
5 km S of Victor Harbor

Tel (08) 8552 7270
or 0409 527 270
Fax (08) 8552 8386
jill@encounterhideaway.com
www.encounterhideaway.com

Double $110-$140
Single $80
Full breakfast
Visa MC accepted
3 Queen (3 bdrm)
Bathrooms: 2 Ensuite 1 Private

Parkfield Lodge is a traditional B&B overlooking the sixth green of the McCracken Golf Course. The three well appointed bedrooms each have a queen-sized bed, two with ensuite and one with a private bathroom. This well-established B&B's many guests have enjoyed the opportunity to relax and unwind, play a round of golf or just catch up on some reading in the guest lounge room with its panoramic view of the golf course and surrounding hills. A three-course breakfast is prepared daily by the host/chef.

Victor Harbor

Encounter Hideaway Cottages *B&B & 2 Self Contained Cottages*
Jill Fairchild
66 Rapid Drive
Victor Harbor
SA 5211
5 km S of Victor Harbor

Tel (08) 8552 7270
or 0409 527 270
Fax (08) 8552 8386
jill@encounterhideaway.com
www.encounterhideaway.com

Double $150 Single $100
Full provisions
Extra person $50 per night
Visa MC accepted
1 Queen 2 Single (2 bdrm)
Bathrooms: 1 Private Bathroom includes spa

Encounter Hideaway has two self-contained cottages. Ruby and Bud Cottages are situated just one street back from the sea in the historic part of Encounter Bay, only five minutes drive from the centre of Visitor Harbour. Set in a charming garden, each cottage has a queen-size bed in the main bedroom, plus twin beds (Ruby) or double bed (Bud) in the second bedroom, a sparkling bathroom with a large spa, a well equipped kitchen with generous provisions for a cooked breakfast, a comfortable living room with A/C, TV, VCR, CD player, flowers, port and fresh fruit.

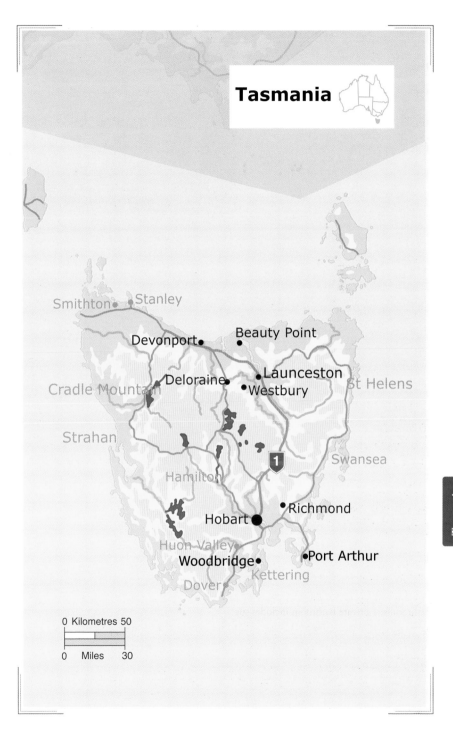

Beauty Point

Pomona Spa Cottages *Luxury B&B & Self Contained Cottages*

Paula & Bruce Irvin
77 Flinders Street
Beauty Point
Tas 7270
40 km N of Launceston

Tel (03) 6383 4073
Fax (03) 6383 4074
relax@pomonaspacottages.com.au
www.pomonaspacottages.com.au

Double $180-$250
Single $180-$240
Full provisions
Visa MC Diners Amex Eftpos accepted
4 King/Twin 2 Single (4 bdrm)
Spacious bedrooms with river views
Bathrooms: 4 Ensuite
Spa and seperate shower

   AAA Tourism ★★★★☆

Relax and enjoy a wine or a delicious breakfast in your private Rotunda, overlooking beautiful views of the Tamar River/valley. Spoil yourself in the new luxurious, spacious, sunny S/C Spa Cottages. Water views from your king bed or in front of your cosy wood fire. Stroll in the rambling gardens, orchard, vines and along river to Restaurants, Seahorses, Platypus House. Explore the Tamar Valley Scenic Wine Route, National Parks, Penguins. Ferry & Airport - within 1 hour. Ideally located between Freycinet and Strahan. BBQ.

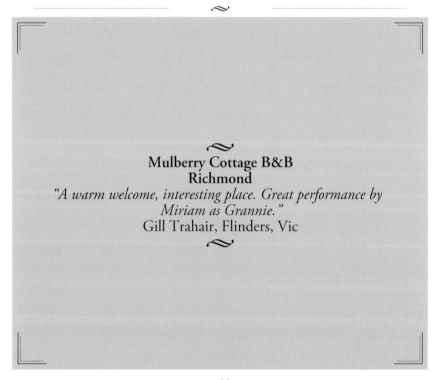

Mulberry Cottage B&B
Richmond
"A warm welcome, interesting place. Great performance by Miriam as Grannie."
Gill Trahair, Flinders, Vic

Deloraine

Bowerbank Mill B&B *Heritage B&B, Self Contained Cottages and Separate Suites*
Anne and JD
4455 Meander Valley Road
Deloraine, Tas 7304
2 km E of Deloraine

Tel (03) 6362 2628
bowerbank@iinet.net.au
www.bowerbankmill.com.au

Double $135-$225 **Single** $125-$200
Children $25-$55 depending on age
Special breakfast
Extra adult $45-$55
Visa MC accepted
7 Queen 1 Double 5 Single (9 bdrm)
Bathrooms: 3 Ensuite 2 Guest share

STOP the clock - on entering Bowerbank Mill B&B and Fine Art Gallery you leave the hecticness behind and experience the 'olde worlde' rustic charm of an 1853 flour mill. The Mill's impressive features - huge pit-sawn beams, meter thick stone walls, log fire in the towering six storey chimney--have been lovingly combined in a poetic blend of antiques, personal 'objets d'art', and modern comforts. Here guests slow down, breath fresh country air and enjoy old fashioned hospitality. "Loved it so much . . . don't want to go home," a guest commented. From upstairs to downstairs, each Cottage, Suite, or Room has a unique, charming feel, oozing their own individuality--there is a place here to suit singles, couples, newlyweds, business clients, and groups up to 20 people. Easy to find in the idyllic Meander Valley, Bowerbank Mill B&B, is surrounded by farmland with the backdrop of Mountains - exquisitely beautiful in all seasons. Conveniently located (central north) near pristine lakes, rivers, wilderness, fishing, wildlife, colonial building, galleries and wineries, but only minutes to the township of Deloraine. Thirty five minutes to Launceston and Devonport (Airports and Ferry).

Devonport - Port Sorell

Tranquilles *Luxury B&B*
John Kumm & Barbara Walsh-Kumm
9 Gumbowie Drive
Port Sorell
Tas 7307
14 km E of Devonport

Tel (03) 6428 7555
Fax (03) 6428 7775
enquiries@tranquilles.com
www.tranquilles.com

Double $120-$205 Single $110-$195
Full breakfast
Dinner available by prior arrangement
Luncheon hampers by prior arrangement
Visa MC Diners Amex Eftpos accepted
1 King 2 Queen (3 bdrm)
2 queen bedrooms, 1 king suite
Bathrooms: 3 Ensuite 1 shower, 2 double spas

A unique blend of elegance and relaxation, three beautifully appointed bedrooms (two with double spas), log fire and conservatory with enclosed courtyard, set in two acres of sweeping gardens. 15 minutes from Devonport, an hour to Launceston. Port Sorell is renowned for beaches, walking tracks and the Narawntapu National Park. A perfect location to unpack once, and explore the many highlights of the region - eg Cradle Mountain, Stanley, Tamar Wine Route. Meals serving fresh Tasmanian produce available by prior arrangement - fully licensed.

Hobart - Battery Point - Sandy Bay

Grande Vue & Star Apartments *Private Hotel, Apartments & Townhouses*
Annette & Kate McIntosh
8 Mona Street Battery Point
22 Star Street, Sandy Bay, Tas 7005
0.8 km S of Hobart Central

Tel (03) 6223 8216 or 0419 104 417
0400 591 457
Fax (03) 6224 1724
jarem8@bigpond.com
www.grande-vue-hotel.com

Double $165-$280 Single $125-$145
Children and extra guests $30
Continental provisions
Winter specials available
Weekly rates in apartments on request
Visa MC Diners Amex Eftpos accepted
2 King/Twin 7 Queen 2 Double (7 bdrm)
Bathrooms: 7 Ensuite 5 spa suites

G rande Vue Private Hotel is located in Hobart's historic Battery Point. (8 Mona Street). This gracious Edwardian mansion c1906 has spectacular views of the Derwent River, Mount Wellington, just 5 minutes walk to the city, restaurants, Salamanca Place and Hobart's waterfront. We also offer studio, water view rooms and spa suites. Star Apartments (22 Star Street Sandy Bay) are modern contemporary design 1 and 2 bedroom stylish apartments and townhouses with kitchens, washer/dryer and central heating. Some have water views, balconies/courtyards, spas and secure undercover car parking. Walking distance to Battery Point, restaurants, Salamanca Place and the city centre.

Hobart - Lindisfarne

Orana House *B&B*
Colin & Leonie Chung
20 Lowelly Road
Lindisfarne
Tas 7015
6 km E of Hobart

Tel (03) 6243 0404
or 0416 250 357
Fax (03) 6243 9017
welcome@oranahouse.com
www.oranahouse.com

Double $120-$170
Single $90-$135
Children $50
Full breakfast
Visa MC Eftpos accepted
7 Queen 3 Double 4 Single (10 bdrm)
Bathrooms: 10 Ensuite

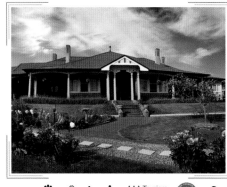

   AAA Tourism ★★★★☆

A large Federation home circa 1909 offering warm hospitality. Orana House is 12 minutes from the airport and six minutes to Hobart. Situated near picturesque Lindisfarne Bay, it is a convenient base to explore southern Tasmania. Some of our many features include superb breakfasts, great views from the verandah and guest lounge, afternoon tea daily, genuine antiques and open fire. A choice of standard, deluxe or spa rooms, all with ensuites. Pets on property.

Hobart - Rose Bay

Roseneath Bed & Breakfast *B&B & Self Contained Apartment*
Susan & Alain Pastre
20 Kaoota Road
Rose Bay
Tas 7015
3.5 km NE of Hobart

Tel (03) 6243 6530
or 0418 121 077
Fax (03) 6243 0518
pastre@bigpond.com
www.roseneath.com

Double $115-$165 Single $100-$155
Full breakfast
Dinner $35 - $50 BA
Low season/long stay available
Visa MC Diners Amex Eftpos
JCB accepted
2 King/Twin 1 Queen 2 Double (5 bdrm)
Bathrooms: 5 Ensuite 2 rooms have baths, 1 spa, 5 showers

    AAA Tourism ★★★★

For true Tasmanian hospitality and warmth with a French accent. Only 5 minutes from CBD/Salamanca and 10 from airport. Spectacular views of Mt Wellington, the Tasman Bridge and Derwent River. An ideal base for exploring southern Tasmania or for business. Choose from a SC studio (kitchenette) or in-house accommodation with ensuites (1 spa). Guest lounge with log fire; conservatory; inground heated (summer) pool; spacious, secluded gardens; BBQ; off street parking. Dinner BA with your French chef host. Pet on property.

Launceston

Trevallyn House B&B *Luxury B&B*
Janie & Brett Reynolds
83a Riverside Drive
Launceston
Tas 7250
4 km N of Launceston City Centre

Tel (03) 6327 3771
Fax (03) 6327 3700
info@trevallynhouse.com.au
www.trevallynhouse.com.au

Double $140-$190
Children $35
Full breakfast
Visa MC Amex Eftpos accepted
2 Queen 1 Single (2 bdrm)
Bathrooms: 2 Ensuite

 AAA Tourism ★★★★☆

With 7 hectares of gardens and bushland and sweeping views of the Tamar River this secluded and peaceful new luxury accommodation is only five minutes from Launceston's City Centre. Located on the Tamar Valley Wine Route Trevallyn House offers comfort and convenience. You are assured of a special experience with two beautifully appointed guest rooms. The Guest Lounge with open fire is a perfect place to experience the changing seasons of the Tamar Valley and your gourmet cooked breakfast served in the Dining Room.

~

Launceston

Edenholme Grange *Luxury B&B & Self contained apartments & 2 bed cottage*
Paul & Rosemary Harding
14 St Andrews Street
Launceston
Tas 7250
1.5 km SW of Post Office

Tel (03) 6334 6666
or 0419 894 269
Fax (03) 6334 3106
sales@edenholme.com
http://wwww.edenholme.com

Double $150-$240 **Single** $130-$220
Children up to age 12 $25
Full breakfast
Dinner nearby restaurants
Visa MC Diners Amex Eftpos JCB accepted
2 King/Twin 2 King 4 Queen 3 Double 2 Twin (10 bdrm)
Themed Heritage
Bathrooms: 10 Ensuite

  AAA Tourism ★★★★

Edenholme Grange, Settlers Cottage and The Coachhouse Apartments. Experience past times in this private Victorian mansion. set amongst secluded and substantial grounds, on the edge of the City and near the magnificent Cataract Gorge. There are uniquely themed rooms, furnished with antiques & some with spa baths. Close to the City yet secluded in the spacious grounds of the House are a self-contained rustic cottage, with modern amenities, including double spa bath and extra ensuite and 2 luxury apartments.

Port Arthur

The Tasman Peninsula has it all. The coastal rock formations, forests, bays and beaches, and towering sea cliffs will have you pointing your camera in no time. The historic remains at Port Arthur, Point Puer, the Isle of the Dead, the Salt River Coal Mines and Eaglehawk Neck will have you pondering the sometimes sad saga of human history.

Just five minutes from Port Arthur is one of the Peninsula's best kept secrets, Safety Cove, with its crystal clear waters and sparkling white sand which have to be seen to be believed. Visit Remarkable Cave, less than one minute away, take a leisurely stroll to Crescent Bay with its massive sand dunes or enjoy a round of golf at the Tasman Golf Course just two minutes away.
Rex & Sue Mapley

Port Arthur - Taranna

Norfolk Bay Convict Station *B&B & Homestay & Guest House*
Lynton Brown & Lorella Matassini
5862 Arthur Highway
Taranna
Tas 7180
10 km N of Port Arthur

Tel (03) 6250 3487
Fax (03) 6250 3701
norfolkbay@convictstation.com
www.convictstation.com

Double $110-$170 **Single** $80-$120
Children 2-15 yo $40-$55
Continental breakfast
Dinner Nearby restaurants
Visa MC Eftpos accepted
2 Queen 2 Double 1 Twin 3 Single
(5 bdrm) All beds with electric blankets
Bathrooms: 3 Ensuite 2 Private Private
dedicated bathrooms but not connected to bedroom

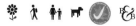

Stay in living history and indulge yourself. Nature, adventure, history, culture, it's all here! Convict built in 1838 on this picturesque waterfront location, we are just minutes from Port Arthur, Eaglehawk Neck and all that the Tasman Peninsula has to offer. We offer warm, comfortable rooms, a guest sitting room with a log fire and a wonderful breakfast. This friendly B&B has history, charm and all the modern comforts. Enjoy a complimentary glass of Port, watch a DVD or explore our extensive library.

∼

Port Sorell

A sweep of golden beaches; sheltered inlets; a seaside holiday haven and magnificent outlooks - that's Port Sorell. Protected by hills and with Bass Strait to the north, the district enjoys a particularly mild climate with low rainfall and a high average of sunshine.

Port Sorell is an ideal gateway to enable you to undertake any number of day tours in the North of Tasmania, including Narawntapu National Park, Cradle Mountain, Cataract Gorge and Tamar Valley Wine Route.
John Kumm, Tranquilles

Richmond

Mulberry Cottage B&B *B&B & Homestay*

Miriam Cooper
23a Franklin Street
Richmond, Tas 7025
In Richmond

Tel (03) 6260 2664 or 0407 473 015
miriam23@bigpond.net.au
www.mulberrycottage.com.au

Double $110-$160 Single $85-$110
Children B/A Full breakfast
Dinner or platters B/A with Grannie
Seasonal Specials   Show included in
Grannie Rhodes Cottage
Visa MC accepted
1 King 2 Queen 2 Twin 1 Single (4 bdrm)
Old English, French Boudoir, Attic
Bathrooms: 2 Ensuite 1 Family share
1 Guest share can be shared or private

Charming, hosted B&B, in 'old worlde' cottage, built from the reclaimed wall of Hobart's Old Penitentiary. Excellent Tourism Award Winning show included (Highly Commended, Cultural Heritage section). Valley views. Rustic gardens. Glass of wine on arrival. Cosy guest sitting room (pet free). Host lounge shared with greeting retrievers, cuddly cat. For the history & theatre lover; unique entertainment, by your hostess, a performance of 'Turn the Key of Time' about a cottage, a key and a convict in Grannie Rhodes' Cottage, on site 1830.

Richmond

Mrs Curries Bed and Breakfast *B&B*

Cheryl and Steven
4 Franklin Street
Richmond
Tas 7025
In Richmond

Tel (03) 6260 2766
Fax (03) 6260 2110
mrscurries@optusnet.com.au
www.mrscurrieshouse.com.au

Double $140
Single $100
No children under 10 years old
Full breakfast
Visa MC Diners Amex Eftpos
JCB accepted
1 Queen 3 Double 1 Single (4 bdrm)
Elegantly appointed
Bathrooms: 3 Ensuite 1 Private

   AAA Tourism ★★★★

Mrs Curries House, a lovely Georgian home built in the 1820's. Two storey with bedrooms upstairs and down. All have their own bathroom and their own charm. Tastefully decorated with antiques throughout. Open fires in the lounge and dining area. Complimentary port and sherry. Manicured gardens and lawns for all to enjoy. A great place to stay a while and wind down and enjoy the hospitality of Cheryl and Steve. We pride our selves on looking after you.

Westbury

Westbury Gingerbread Cottages *5 Self Contained Cottages*

Karen and John Madge
52 William Street
Westbury
Tas 7303
33 km W of Launceston

Tel (03) 6393 1140
Fax (03) 6393 1752
info@westburycottages.com.au
www.westburycottages.com.au

Double $150-$170
Single $150-$170
Children over 5 welcome
Full provisions
Pet free cottages
Visa MC Eftpos accepted
(11 bdrm)
Bathrooms: 5 Private

The Westbury Gingerbread Cottages - "Not just a room - a complete colonial cottage for your exclusive use!" Five delightfully individual colonial cottages dating from the 1850s with from one to four bedrooms. Our cottages have fully equipped kitchens and we supply everything you need for a big breakfast. The quaint little village of Westbury being centrally located is the perfect base from which to explore Launceston, Devonport, Tamar wineries, Cradle Mountain, the Caves and the Northwest. Courtyard BBQ and cosy gas log fires.

Woodbridge

Orchard Lea Woodbridge *B&B*

Carol & Steve
11 Weedings Way
Woodbridge
Tas 7162
39 km S of Hobart

Tel (03) 6267 4108
or 0400 522 193
Fax (03) 6267 4797
stay@orchardlea.com.au
www.orchardlea.com.au

Double $130-$150
Single $110-$120
Continental breakfast
Visa MC Eftpos accepted
2 Queen 1 Twin (3 bdrm)
Queen with ensuite, Twin with ensuite
Bathrooms: 3 Ensuite

The Orchard Lea Guest House is located in the picturesque village of Woodbridge overlooking Bruny Island and the Dentrecasteaux Channel. Unwind, relax and Experience the tranquil country setting - only a short drive from Hobart. Why not stay with us longer and explore the region? Use Orchard Lea as your base to visit Bruny Island, The Tahune Airwalk, Hastings Caves and the many quality vineyards and restaurants in the district. Country Tasmanian hospitality at its best.

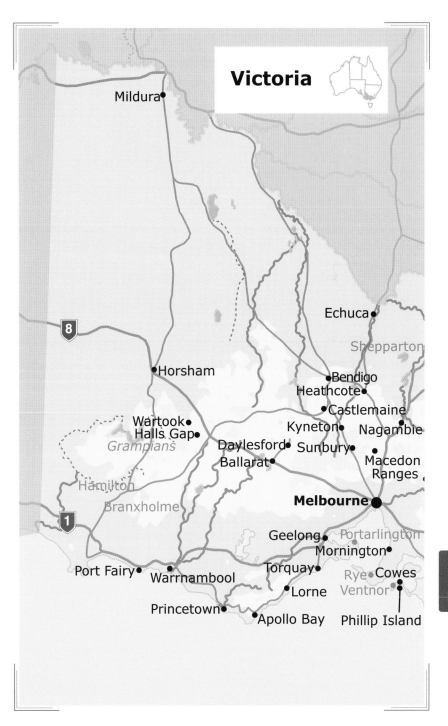

Victoria

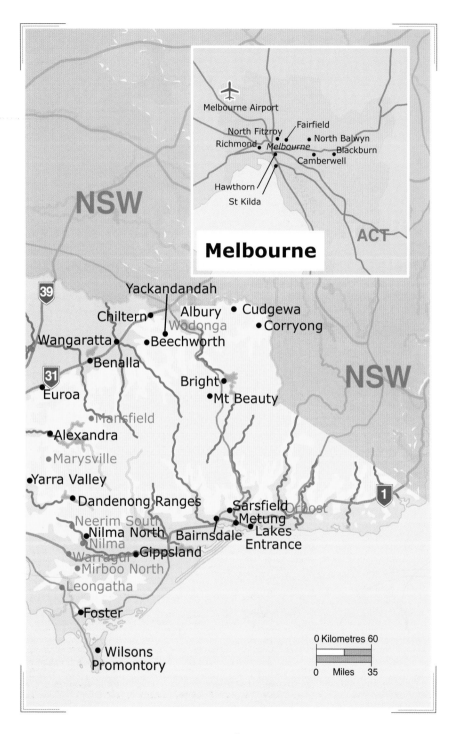

Melbourne Airport

North Fitzroy   Fairfield
Richmond   *Melbourne*   North Balwyn
                              Blackburn
                         Camberwell

Hawthorn
St Kilda

Melbourne

NSW

ACT

39

Yackandandah

Chiltern   Albury   Cudgewa
         Wodonga   Corryong
Wangaratta   Beechworth

Benalla

31

Euroa

Bright
Mt Beauty

Mansfield

Alexandra

Marysville

Yarra Valley

Dandenong Ranges   Sarsfield
                     Metung
Neerim South   Orbost
Nilma North   Bairnsdale   Lakes
Nilma   Entrance
Warragul   Gippsland
Mirboo North

Leongatha

NSW

1

Foster

Wilsons
Promontory

0 Kilometres 60

0   Miles   35

Victoria

Victoria
Inn.House Bed and Breakfast Australia Inc

I nn.House. Victoria's Best Boutique Accommodation.
50 of the best B&Bs in Victoria.
Quality assured by the Inn.House Assessment Team

Gift Vouchers Available: Telephone (03) 5598 8169
or order on line: www.innhouse.com.au/giftvouchers.html
Full details on the Award Winning website: www.innhouse.com.au

---

Alexandra

Idlewild Park Farm Accommodation *Farmstay & Self Contained House*
Elizabeth & Don Deelen
RMB 1150
Alexandra
Vic 3714
5 km N of Alexandra

Tel (03) 5772 1178
or 0400 030 677
idlewild@virtual.net.au
www.idlewild.com.au

Double $130-$160
Single $80-$100
Children $20
Children enjoy egg collecting
Full provisions
1 King/Twin 1 Queen (2 bdrm)
Bathrooms: 1 Ensuite twin spa bath

   AAA Tourism ★★★★

E njoy this 3,000 acre grazing property 128 km NE of Melbourne. The beautiful district offers horse riding, fishing, water and snow sports, bush walking, golf & adventure activities. Stay in a fully equipped two bedroom cottage with a double spa, wood heater, full kitchen air/con. The location is superb with magnificent panoramic views. There is tennis, gas BBQ and a beautiful garden. Property has sheep, cattle, horses and poultry (also native animals and birds). Owners have two friendly Jack Russel dogs.

Apollo Bay

Arcady Homestead *Homestay & Farmstay*
Marcia & Ross Dawson
925 Barham River Road
Apollo Bay - Great Ocean Road
Vic 3233
10 km W of Apollo Bay

Tel (03) 5237 6493
or 0408 376 493
Fax (03) 5237 6493
arcady2@bigpond.com
www.bbbook.com.au/arcadyhomestead.html

Double $110-$120
Single $75-$85
Children 50%
Full breakfast
Dinner B/A
2 Queen 1 Double 3 Single (4 bdrm)
Bathrooms: 1 Guest share

Set on sixty scenic acres, part farmland and part natural bush. Share breakfast with our Kookaburras, explore the Otway Forest trails, tree-fern and glow worm gullies and waterfalls, see some of the tallest trees in the world or visit Port Campbell National Park, which embraces Australia's most spectacular coastline. The Otway Ranges are a bushwalkers paradise. Bird-watchers? We have identified around thirty species in the garden alone! Many visit our kitchen window! Our home has wood fires & spring water. Our beds are cosy, our meals country-style, and our atmosphere relaxed and friendly.

Apollo Bay

Paradise Gardens *B&B & Self Contained Cottages*
Jo and Jock Williamson
715 Barham River Road
Apollo Bay
Vic 3233
7.5 km W of Apollo Bay

Tel (03) 5237 6939
or 0417 330 615
Fax (03) 5237 6105
paradisegardens@bigpond.com.au
www.paradisegardens.net.au

Double $120-$220
Full breakfast
Continental provisions provided in Cottages
Visa MC Eftpos accepted
1 King/Twin2 King 1 Queen (4 bdrm)
Bathrooms: 4 Ensuite

AAA Tourism
★★★★☆

Situated on 3 acres of landscaped gardens in a lush rainforest valley, our facility is only 10 minutes from Apollo Bay on a (sealed) scenic road. Our charming self-contained cottages (one and two bedroom) are built over a lake and feature wood fires, spas, bar-b-cues on the decking and air conditioning. Continental breakfast provided in tariff. Laundry facilities available. Our in-house B&B unit is comfortable with double spa and external entrance. Complementary Devonshire tea with all accommodation. Enjoy walks, birdlife and glow-worms.

Victoria

Apollo Bay

Point of View *Luxury B&B & Self Contained Apartment*
Alan & Glenda Whelan
165 Tuxion Road
Apollo Bay
Vic 3233
1 km N of Apollo Bay

Tel 0427 376 377
Fax (03) 5237 6377
info@pointofview.com.au
www.pointofview.com.au

Double $250-$340
Continental provisions
2 night minimum stay ($600)
Visa MC Diners Eftpos accepted
5 King (5 bdrm) modern, open plan
Bathrooms: 5 Ensuite Double shower and
spa

Breathtaking views from every location in our architect designed luxury villas. Perfect retreat for couples for those special occasions.

Features wood fire, king beds, double shower, full kitchen, dishwasher, satellite TV, large therapeutic spa, DVD, electric heating, air conditioning, robes, toiletries, surround sound, spacious sundecks, BBQ, washing machine, dryer, fresh flowers, beach towels, hairdryer, continental breakfast supplies.

Ideal base to explore the 12 Apostles, Great Ocean Road or as a romantic, secluded getaway for you and your partner. Wine and chocolates on arrival. Spoil yourself.

Apollo Bay - Great Ocean Road

Glenoe Cottages *Luxury Self Contained Apartment*
Dianne Beggs
235 Tuxion Road
Apollo Bay
Vic 3233
2 km N of Apollo Bay

Tel (03) 5237 6555
or 0438 376 410
Fax (03) 5237 6555
dianne@glenoe-cottages.com
www.glenoe-cottages.com

Double $240-$300
Continental provisions
Exclusively for adults
2 night minimum stay
Visa MC Eftpos accepted
3 King (3 bdrm) 3 cottages
Bathrooms: 3 Private

Simply the best and none better for intimate classic relaxed romance. Only the ancient poets could find the words to give justice in describing these captivating cottages. The coastal views are absolutely entrancing.

Features wood fire, ducted central heating, TV/DVD stereo and surround sound. King size bed, large spa with rain shower, bath robes, toiletries, hairdryer and beach towels. Full kitchen with dishwasher, microwave oven, espresso coffee maker, washing machine and drier. Continental breakfast basket provided with complementary wine, chocolates and ice-cream. BBQ, surround veranda and undercover car park.

The limestone built cottages may be millions of years old but on entry you are introduced to a modern contemporary experience of space, comfort and quality.
Ideal home base to explore the Great Ocean Road, Otway National park and 12 Apostles, or simply an intimate, romantic secluded escape for you and your partner.

Apollo Bay - Great Ocean Road

Claerwen Retreat *Self Contained Apartment & Self Contained House & Guest House*

Cornelia Elbrecht
480 Tuxion Road
Apollo Bay
Vic 3233
5 km N of Apollo Bay

Tel (03) 5237 7064
Fax (03) 5237 7054
cornelia_elbrecht@claerwen.com.au
www.claerwen.com.au

Double $99-$350 Single $99-$220
Pre-school children only in cottages
Full breakfast
Cheese and wine upon request
Cottage (sleeps up to six) $295-$350
Visa MC Diners Amex Eftpos JCB accepted
4 King 5 Queen 3 Twin (12 bdrm)
Bathrooms: 10 Ensuite
The cottages have a double spa with ocean view

Exclusively situated on top of the highest hill overlooking the coast with panoramic ocean views from all rooms we offer spacious suites, self contained three-bedroom cottages or one-bedroom studios. Set in the peaceful solitude of 130 acres of park, bush and rainforest, it features saltwater swimming pool, hot spa and tennis court. It is close to the famous Great Ocean Road to the Twelve Apostles and the Otway National Park. We offer in-house massages, facials and art classes. In winter every third night is free.

∽

Bairnsdale

Tara House *B&B*

Phillip
37 Day Street
Bairnsdale
Vic 3875
1.2 km W of town centre

Tel (03) 5153 2253
Fax (03) 5153 2426
enquiries@tarahouse.com.au
www.tarahouse.com.au

Double $160-$170 Single $130-$140
Children fold out bed in parents room $60
Full breakfast
Dinner be arrangement
Visa MC accepted
2 King/Twin 1 Queen (3 bdrm)
traditionally decorated
Bathrooms: 3 Ensuite one ensuite with claw foot bath

Share a beautiful garden with a retired gardener. Be welcomed by the hostess, Tara, a seven year old Sydney Silky. A relaxing and refreshing time is assured. Sit on the verandah and watch the setting sun or have a glass of wine. Many areas to sit and forget your troubles. Come and smell the roses. Two hours to the snow, 20minutes to lake, 30minutes to sea. The perfect place to stay.

Beechworth

Kinross Guest House *Luxury B&B*
Terry and Gail Walsh
34 Loch Street
Beechworth
Vic 3747
39 km S of Albury/Wodonga

Tel (03) 5728 2351
Fax (03) 5728 3333
kinross@dragnet.com.au
www.innhouse.com.au/kinross.html

Double $160-$180
Single $130-$145
Full breakfast
Off-street parking for 4 vehicles
Visa MC Eftpos accepted
1 King/Twin 4 Queen (5 bdrm)
Bathrooms: 5 Ensuite

   AAA Tourism ★★★★☆

Experience the style, warmth and charm of Kinross, in the centre of Beechworth, close to excellent restaurants, specialty shops and historic precinct. Kinross (c1858) has five large fully-serviced guestrooms furnished with period pieces. Enjoy the luxury of your own ensuite, open fireplace, heating/cooling, TV/DVD, comfortable seating, tea/coffee making facility. Whether sitting with a book and glass of wine beside an open fire, or on the verandah enjoying the beauty of the cottage garden, you cannot help but feel the peace and quiet.

Beechworth

Country Charm Swiss Cottages *Self Contained House*
Judy and Greg Lazarus
22 Malakoff Road
Beechworth, Vic 3747
1.4 km W of Beechworth

Tel (03) 5728 2435
or 0417 376 899
Fax (03) 5728 2436
info@swisscottages.com.au
www.swisscottages.com.au

Cottage $175-215 per day
Children under 4
Full breakfast
Visa MC Amex Eftpos accepted
5 Queen 6 Single (8 bdrm)
Five 1 or 2 Bedroom S/C Cottages
Bathrooms: 5 Ensuite 2 Family share
2 Guest share Double spas

  AAA Tourism ★★★★☆

Delightful, well appointed self-contained cottages set high overlooking the Beechworth Gorge. Our 1 or 2 Bedroom cottages offer tranquillity, privacy and a perfect setting for any occasion. Each cottage has open fires in winter, reverse cycle air conditioning, spa baths, along with TV, CD/DVD players. A guest laundry and outdoor BBQ area are available. Enjoy generous breakfast provisions to be prepared at your leisure. Along with the complimentary treats provided, the ambience of the property and wonderful hosts will ensure a wonderful stay.

Victoria

Beechworth

Freeman on Ford *Luxury B&B*
Heidi Freeman & Jim Didolis
97 Ford Street
Beechworth
Vic 3747
In Beechworth

Tel (03) 5728 2371
or (03) 5728 2055
0409 958 340
Fax (03) 5728 2504
freemanford@westnet.com.au
www.freemanonford.com

Double $195-$250
Single $165-$195
Full breakfast
Visa MC Diners Amex accepted
4 Queen (4 bdrm)
Bathrooms: 4 Ensuite 1 with spa bath

 AAA Tourism ★★★★★

The hosts provide gourmet breakfast and afternoon tea and their mission statement is to make guests feel thoroughly spoilt. They have a love of history and have a wealth of information to offer about the historical and unique township of Beechworth. Gourmet Traveller magazine recommends the venue as "excellent" (April May 2007). Onsite parking and AUSTAR channels, wide selection of DVDs, WiFi Internet, split systems, TVs in all bedrooms and all modern conveniences making it 5-star comfort.

Bendigo

Arbroath Lodge *B&B & Self Contained Apartment*
Heather & Rod MacLeod
30 Clearing Court
Mandurang, Bendigo
Vic 3551
8 km S of Bendigo PO

Tel (03) 5439 3054
or 0407 349 733
Fax (03) 5439 3054
heatherandrod@bigpond.com
www.skyeglenbendigo.net.au

Double $120 Single $80-$90
Children $15
Full provisions
1 Queen (1 bdrm)
1 trundle bed for child
Bathrooms: 1 Ensuite

Arbroath Lodge's "Highlander" Studio Apartment for two people has the best of both worlds. Close to Bendigo Central (8 km) but set on a tranquil three acres overlooking the majestic redgums on Sheepwash Creek. The Highlander, with its Scottish flavour is very spacious with s/c kitchenette, a/c, heating, private entrance and balcony views of the beautiful Mandurang Valley "Loch Duck", abundant with waterfowl and birdlife. An outdoor gazebo and spa tub is for the exclusive use of guests. A barbecue is also available and full breakfast provisions are supplied. "Ceid m'ille failte" or one hundred thousand welcomes awaits you.

Bright

Bright is the town of four seasons and has something special to offer at anytime of year.

It is located on the North East Gourmet Trail and the town and district abound in wineries and top class restaurants. There are 3 chefs hatted restaurants in the area. The wineries of Rutherglen, Beechworth and Milawa are all just a day trip away.

Bright itself, has miles of magnificent walking tracks along the banks of the gurgling Ovens River. The Autumn Festival, when the multitude of European trees change their colours, is known Australia wide.

Catherine Falcke, Tyntynder Lodge

Bright

The Buckland - Studio Retreat *Luxury B&B & Self Contained Chalet*

Sabine Helsper & Eddie Dufrenne
116 McCormacks Lane
Buckland Valley
Vic 3740
12 km SW of Bright

Tel (03) 5756 2383
or 0419 133 318
Fax (03) 5755 2283
stay@thebuckland.com.au
www.thebuckland.com.au

Double $250-$340
Children only small babies travelling with
own port-a-cot or similar
Full breakfast
Visa MC Eftpos accepted
4 King (4 bdrm)
Bathrooms: 4 Ensuite

 AAA Tourism
★★★★☆

The Buckland - Studio Retreat features luxury accommodation tucked away in the picturesque Buckland Valley close to Bright, Mt. Buffalo and the wineries of the Victorian High Country. Each of the 4 individual studios has an open plan lounge/kitchen area, king size bedroom and funky bathroom with double rainwater showers and private bush outlook. The décor is contemporary and stylish and creature comforts are well catered for: goosedown doonas, espresso coffee machine, seductive mood lighting, plush robes and L'Occitane aromatherapy products.

Bright

Tyntynder Lodge Holiday Cottages *Luxury Self Contained House*

Catherine
4 Tyntynder Lane
Bright
Vic 3741
0.5 km W of Bright

Tel 0408 476 046
falcke@ecn.net.au
www.tyntynderbright.com.au

Double $185-$250
Children $10 per night
Accommodation only
Visa MC accepted
1 Queen 1 Double 1 Single
Four @ 2 bedroom cottages
Bathrooms: 1 Private

Tyntynder Lodge Cottages won the 2006 Award for Best Holiday Accommodation in Victoria. Surrounded by 1 acre of magnificent, private mature gardens they are located in a tranquil tree lined country lane running beside the beautiful Ovens River. The cottages are fully equipped - gourmet kitchens & modern bathrooms, airconditioning & log fires, quality beds & comfortable lounges. All linen is provided. Each cottage has its own fully fenced, private garden. Two cottages have been set aside for those who like to travel with their pets.

Chiltern

The Mulberry Tree B&B & Tea Rooms *B&B*

Regina Welsh
28 Conness Street
Chiltern
Vic 3683
20 km S of Albury - Wodonga

Tel (03) 5726 1277
www.chilternbusinessjournal.com.au

Double $150-$170
Single $120-$140
Special breakfast
Dinner by arrangement
Tearooms next door
2 Queen (2 bdrm)
Bathrooms: 1 Ensuite 1 Private

Indulge yourself in the heart of Country Victoria. At The Mulberry Tree you will find a haven to relax and enjoy delightful accommodation with gourmet breakfast. Choose from "The Bank Residence" with it's own lounge with open fire, private bathroom or "The Henry Handel Richardson Suite" with ensuite dining area. This delightful building was built in 1879 as "The Bank of Australasia" and is on the Historic Building Register. Be assured of a warm welcome with special attention to every detail. Situated in the centre of town. Come and see our beautiful cats, 'Paris' and 'Tina'.

Cudgewa - Corryong

Elmstead Cottages *B&B & Farmstay & Self Contained House*

Marja & Tony Jarvis
61 Ashstead Park Lane
Cudgewa
Vic 3705
12 km W of Corryong

Tel (02) 6077 4324
or 0427 774 324
Fax (02) 6077 4324
elmstead@corryongcec.net.au
www.bbbook.com.au/elmstead.html

Double $80
Single $60
Children under 12 $10
Breakfast by arrangement
Extra person $15
Eftpos accepted
2 Queen 4 Single (3 bdrm)
1 in Elmstead Cottage, 2 in Arthur's Cottage
Bathrooms: 2 Private

Elmstead Cottage: A one room cottage set amongst magnificent elm trees on a working farm, cute cosy and affordable. Arthur's Cottage: An eco-friendly, historic two bedroom cottage (circa 1887). Secluded location on the banks of the Cudgewa Creek where platypus and trout abound. Fully equipped kitchen, BYO linen.

Dandenong Ranges

An hours' drive from Melbourne, you'll find a timeless sanctuary of the Dandenong Ranges. Towering gum trees, fern forests, parks and gardens are just a slice of the spectacular scenery on offer. Take a stroll through the nature trails in the forest or in Spring you can visit gardens of tulips, daffodils and rhododendrons.

William Ricketts Sanctuary and Alfred Nicholas Gardens have native trees, bird life, waterfalls and spectacular lakes. Puffing Billy Train departs Belgrave and takes you through thick forests, fern gullies and over trestle bridges. Spectacular panoramic views are waiting, just around the next bend. You will enjoy your stay in this beautiful natural countryside.
Wendy Bramley

Victoria

Dandenong Ranges

Candlelight Cottages Retreat *B&B & Self Contained Cottages*

Peta & Laurie Rolls
7-9 Monash Avenue
Olinda Village, Vic 3788
0.3 km N of Olinda

Tel (03) 9751 2464 or 1300 553 011
Fax (03) 9751 0552
stay@candlelightcottages.com.au
www.candlelightcottages.com.au

Double $210-$330 Single $200-$310
Children 0-3 yrs n/c; 4-10 yrs $15p/n
Full provisions Mini bar dinner service
Woolrich: not suitable for children/pets
Extra couple $50 per night
Visa MC Diners Amex Eftpos accepted
4 Queen 1 Double (5 bdrm)
Two 2 bedroom cottages, One 1 bedroom
Bathrooms: 3 Ensuite 1 Guest share
Two 2 bed/bath cottage; 1 2 bed/1bath cottage; 1 ensuite

Two exquisite cottages right in Olinda Village in the Dandenong Ranges - offering privacy, serenity and discreet service. The owners provide you with cottages which have spa baths, delightful romantic antique beds, lounge rooms, open log fires, full kitchens, outdoor sitting areas - within minutes of restaurants, shops, cafés and galleries. Woolrich - set in 5 acres of historic gardens Woolrich is wonderful light filled, spacious, newly renovated with 2 bedrooms, bathrooms, jacuzzi spa for four, a kitchen to dream of, lounge with open fire, deck with BBQ overlooking gardens and hills. ~

Arabella Country House
Princetown
"From the welcome on our arrival, afternoon tea, spotless comfy room with glorious views over green fields to the sea, sumptuous dinner and fulfilling breakfasts, we felt very special."
Pat and Jan Dawes, Conder, NSW

~

Dandenong Ranges - Mount Dandenong

Observatory Cottages *4 Self Contained Cottages*
Leeanne & Daniel Gazzola
8 Observatory Road
Mt Dandenong
Vic 3767
2 km N of Mt Dandenong

Tel (03) 9751 2436
Fax (03) 9751 2904
enquiries@observatorycottages.com.au
www.observatorycottages.com.au

Double $220-$320
Children $25 each
Full provisions
Extra person $50
Visa MC Eftpos accepted
4 Queen (4 bdrm)
Open plan living
Bathrooms: 4 Ensuite

Sip wine by the twinkling night light views of the city skyline on a lazy summers evening. Slide into a deep hot bubbling spa with a good book or your true love. Curl up in an ultimately romantic four posted bed and watch the mountain mist roll in through the winter nights. Feel the silent touch of snow flakes on your cheeks in a white winter panorama. Sleep late and enjoy a hearty breakfast to the serenade of the birds, the fragrance of the forest, and the tranquillity of a stunning garden paradise.

Daylesford

Ambleside On The Lake *Luxury B&B*
Linda and Frank Carroll
15 Leggatt Street
Daylesford
Vic 3460
0.8 km SE of Post Office

Tel (03) 5348 2691
or 0417 213 913
ambleside@netconnect.com.au
www.amblesideonthelake.com

Double $165-$250
Single $140-$190
Children under 5 not catered for
Full breakfast
Visa MC accepted
3 Queen 2 Single (3 bdrm)
2 deluxe, 1 standard
Bathrooms: 3 Ensuite

Overlooking Lake Daylesford and offering stunning views, Ambleside On The Lake is a boutique Edwardian B&B offering 4 star luxury accommodation. Boasting absolute lake frontage, Ambleside On The Lake is centrally located and is walking distance to several restaurants, galleries and attractions. Featuring 3 guestrooms only, we are located on the quiet side of Lake Daylesford. Daylesford is an easy 80min drive from the Melbourne CBD. Come away and enjoy old world comforts, relaxing breakfasts and some of the best views Daylesford has to offer.

Daylesford - Hepburn Springs

Pendower House *B&B*
Renee Ludekens
10 Bridport Street
Daylesford
Vic 3460
0.1 km NW of Daylesford PO

Tel (03) 5348 1535
or 0438 103 460
Fax (03) 5348 1545
bookings@pendowerhouse.com.au
www.pendowerhouse.com.au

Double $150-$380
Single $105-$290
Children B/A
Full breakfast
Visa MC accepted
3 Queen 1 Twin (4 bdrm)
Bathrooms: 4 Ensuite

Pendower House, a beautifully restored Victorian House, situated in the heart of Australia's Spa Capital - Daylesford. RACV Rated 4.5 Pendower House offers first class amenities: fine linen, antique furnishings, big brass beds, loungeroom /library with open fire. Our luxurious Spa Suite, with corner spa, TV/DVD & private courtyard is perfect for privacy, peace & pampering. Fantastic country breakfast, Muffins, hollandaise sauce drizzled on Eggs - more like brunch than breakfast! Easy walk to restaurants/galleries. Close to Spa resort. Massages & Spa packages or Gift Vouchers available.

Euroa

Euroa, nestled into the Strathbogie Ranges, easily accessible on the Hume Highway, is only one and a half hours from Melbourne and Albury. Once the domain of bushrangers, goldminers and loggers, the Ranges became a major wool-growing region, pioneered by the legendary Eliza Forlonge.

Today the region is recognized for its renowned horse studs, outstanding wineries and a feast of local restaurants, and an abundance of wildlife (koalas, kangaroos, wombats and echidnas) in their natural habitat.

Euroa's history is preserved with historic buildings, heritage trails, rustic homesteads and outbuildings and in the natural beauty of the land--ancient, mystical and uniquely Australian. Euroa is a four-season town--close to the winter snow, with magnificent autumns, brilliant spring and warm summers.
Jenny Tehan, Forlonge B&B

≈

Euroa

Forlonge Bed & Breakfast Euroa *B&B & Separate Suite*
Jenny & Michael Tehan
76 Anderson Street
Euroa
Vic 3666
0.5 km SE of Post Office

Tel (03) 5795 2460
Fax (03) 5795 1020
forlongebb@eck.net.au
www.innhouse.com.au/forlonge.html

Double $150-$200
Single $100-$150
Full breakfast
Dinner by arrangement
Visa MC Amex Eftpos accepted
1 King/Twin 1 King 1 Queen (3 bdrm)
Bathrooms: 1 Ensuite 1 Guest share
1 Ensuite with spa

 AAA Tourism
★★★★☆

Forlonge is set in half acre garden with large trees, tennis court, gazebo BBQ, just minutes away from shops, restaurants, hotels and the renowned Sevens Creek Park. Choice of 2 air-conditioned suites. Garden room with ensuite spa, and private terrace. Courtyard suite with 2 bedrooms, sitting room and private facilities. Euroa is a charming country town nestled into the Strathbogie Ranges. It is an ideal environment for relaxation. An easy drive to local wineries, Nagambie Lakes Rowing Course, Winton Raceway, Goulburn Valley and snowfields.

Victoria

Geelong

Baywoodbyne B&B *B&B*
Nola Haines
41 The Esplanade
Geelong
Vic 3215
1.5 km N of Geelong

Tel (03) 5278 2658
www.greatoceanroad.org

Double $115-$140
Single $110
Children over 6 welcome
Full breakfast
Visa MC Diners accepted
2 Double 1 Twin (3 bdrm)
Bathrooms: 1 Ensuite 1 Private

Centrally located accommodation in a lovely 1921 California Bungalow style home. Superb view overlooking Corio Bay; a short stroll to city centre and colourful waterfront precinct. Warmth, comfort, convenience are yours, together with books and music. Offering: Ground floor, double bedroom with ensuite (extra bed available), sitting and breakfast room, open fire, picture window. First floor, two double bedrooms, sitting area and beautiful view. Tea/coffee making facilities. Off-street parking. Easy access to Melbourne, (train or car one hour) and the famous Great Ocean Road. Direct bus service to Geelong from Melbourne (Tullamarine and Avalon) airports.

Gippsland - Nilma North

Springbank B&B *B&B & Cottage*
Kaye & Chris Greene
240 Williamsons Road
Nilma North
Vic 3821
8 km E of Warragul

Tel (03) 5627 8060
or 0437 350 243
Fax (03) 5627 8149
bookings@springbankbnb.com.au
www.springbankbnb.com.au

Double $150-$180 Single $120-$135
Full breakfast
Dinner & massage by arrangement
Res liquor license
Cottage Double $140-$150
Cottage Single from $115
Visa MC Eftpos accepted
3 Queen (3 bdrm) 2 in House, 1 in Cottage
Bathrooms: 3 Ensuite Includes claw foot bath

AAA Tourism
★★★★☆ INN·HOUSE

Springbank, a delightful 1890's Victorian Farmhouse offers luxury and boutique accommodation for a maximum of 3 couples set on 20 acres close to Warragul. Quiet, private & restful with extensive cottage gardens provides the perfect setting. Gourmet breakfasts, BBQ and outdoor cooking facilities, warm and friendly atmosphere. Open fires in the winter and reverse cycle airconditioning. Superb dining by arrangement.

Grampians

A spectacular area, and one of the largest National Parks in Victoria, where you can see majestic waterfalls, rugged ranges and placid lakes. The region includes about 160km of walking tracks.

There is a great diversity of vegetation with well in excess of 1000 plant species - This is one of Australia's richest flora areas. The warmer northern and western sides of the Grampians are the best areas to view the wonderful wildflowers in the spring.

There are over 200 species of birds, large mobs of kangaroos as well as many other animals.
The area is also rich in Aboriginal culture with most of Victoria's rock art sites.
Royce & Jeanne Raleigh, Wartook Gardens B&B

Grampians - Halls Gap

Welch's on Wildflower *B&B*
Graeme & Pauline Welch
39 Wildflower Drive
Pomonal, Vic 3381
12 km SE of Halls Gap

Tel (03) 5356 6311
or 0428 402 131
Fax (03) 5356 6122
welchs@netconnect.com.au
www.innhouse.com.au/welchs.html

Double $160-$195
Single $110-$150
Children POA
Full breakfast
Dinner from $45 pp by arrangement
pets outside only
Visa MC accepted
3 Queen 2 Single (4 bdrm) 2 queen, 1 family suite
Bathrooms: 2 Ensuite 1 Private

AAA Tourism
★★★★☆

INN·HOUSE

Victoria

Of unique octagonal design, Welch's on Wildflower offers peace, tranquillity and warm hospitality in 4 acres of native gardens filled with birdsong and wildlife. Only 10 mins from Halls Gap we are the ideal base for Grampians activities such as bushwalking, sightseeing, wildflowers, climbing and visiting wineries. Enjoy gourmet country breakfasts including home made jams and preserves, and home baked afternoon teas. Evening meals are by arrangement with your hosts - we are happy to cater for special occasions and specific dietary requirements.

Grampians - Halls Gap

Mountain Grand Boutique Hotel *Guest House*

Kay & Don Calvert
Main Road Town Centre
Halls Gap
Vic 3381
In Halls Gap

Tel (03) 5356 4232
or 1800 192 110
don@hallsgap.net
www.mountaingrand.com

Double $128-$155
Full breakfast
Dinner, B&B from $196 dbl
Indulgence Getaway (all meals) $218 dbl
Visa MC Eftpos accepted
3 King 3 Queen 7 Double (13 bdrm)
Most rooms can become twin/triple
Bathrooms: 12 Ensuite Spa Rooms available

  AAA Tourism ★★★★

The Mountain Grand is a boutique hotel/guest-house/conference centre set amongst the picturesque Grampians mountains. Rooms have ensuites some with spas, suiting the era of the guesthouse. Guests may serenely relax in three lounge areas with a book or DVD. An al fresco courtyard, upstairs balcony and a mezzanine sundeck offer alternative places to be served afternoon teas or enjoy fine wines & beers from the club bar. "The Balconies" Restaurant provides a Delightful Dining experience. Cool Jazz musicians feature Saturday nights.

Grampians - Wartook

Wartook Gardens *B&B & Homestay*

Royce & Jeanne Raleigh
2866 Northern Grampians Road
Wartook
Vic 3401
29 km NW of Halls Gap

Tel (03) 5383 6200
Fax (03) 5383 6240
bookings@wartookgardens.com.au
www.grampiansnationalpark.com

Double $130-$160
Single $110-$120
Full breakfast
Dinner From $35
Visa MC accepted
1 King/Twin 2 Queen (3 bdrm)
Bathrooms: 1 Ensuite 2 Private

 AAA Tourism ★★★★

Just minutes from the Grampians National Park and set on 70 acres in the beautiful Wartook Valley famed for its mobs of kangaroos, Wartook Gardens offers elegant country living in a tranquil 5 acre garden of native and exotic plants and 118 bird species. Enjoy our delicious breakfast before visiting waterfalls, walks, wineries, lookouts, wildflower areas. Ceiling fans, air conditioning, saltwater pool, underfloor heating, wood heater, make your stay a very comfortable one - an all seasons destination. Enjoy friendly hospitality. Please phone.

Grampians - Wartook Valley

The Grelco Run *Self Contained Luxury Cottages and Homestead B&B*
Graeme & Liz McDonald
520 Schmidt Road
Brimpaen
Vic 3401
15 km W of Wartook

Tel (03) 5383 9221
Fax (03) 5383 9221
grelco@netconnect.com.au
www.grampiansgrelcorun.com

Double $143 Single $71.50
Children $27.50
Full provisions   Dinner $66
Homestead: Single $110, Double $220
and includes full breakfast
Visa MC accepted
 4 King/Twin1 King 4 Queen 2 Twin 1 Single (5 bdrm)
Bathrooms: 4 Ensuite 2 Guest share

The Grelco Run offers 2 s/c cottages set apart in natural bush, sleeping 6 in each, and a luxuriously appointed homestead with 3 guest bedrooms each with an ensuite. By prior arrangement we serve elegant hosted dinners in a convivial atmosphere. Our son Cameron operates the renowned Grampians Horse Riding Centre with escorted tours from the property. As we are adjacent to the National Park there are superb opportunities for bushwalking, 4WD driving, fishing, viewing abundant wildlife and wild flowers and visiting all major scenic attractions and nearby wineries.

Heathcote

Once a gold mining region, Heathcote's new gold is Shiraz. Quickly becoming the Shiraz capital of Australia, winemakers and locals alike are keen to talk about the Cambrian soil and the big, beautiful red wines that come from grapes grown here.

Heathcote is surrounded by both National and State forests. Open-cut mining was popular in the 1850's, and its marks are still evident. Tread carefully thought the forests, and fossick if you like, as we're told there's still gold among the trees!

If it's gentle walking you enjoy, Heathcote boasts the longest main street in the southern hemisphere, and it's flat! Wander the shops, the galleries, have a coffee or enjoy a glass of wine.
Leslye Thies, Emeu Inn B&B, Restaurant and Wine Centre

Heathcote

Hut on the Hill *Luxury B&B & Farmstay & Self Contained House*
David & Astrid
720 Dairy Flat Road
Heathcote
Vic 3523
120 km N of Melbourne

Tel (03) 5433 2329
asalter@bordernet.com.au
www.hutonthehill.com

Double $200-$250
Full provisions
Add $100 pn if 2nd bedroom required
Visa MC Diners Amex Eftpos accepted
1 King/Twin 1 Queen (2 bdrm)
Bathrooms: 1 Ensuite Spa bath
Separate shower & separate toilet

 AAA Tourism ★★★★☆

If its luxury, exclusive privacy and total indulgence you're looking for, welcome to Hut on the Hill. From the solar heated swimspa to the king size bedroom, every room offers you spectacular views. The only 4+ star 2-bedroom accommodation in the area with separate lounge and dining areas, where you can relax and watch the sunset with a glass in hand whilst enjoying the blissful serenity of Heathcote's Hut on the Hill. For bookings visit our website at www.hutonthehill.com

Heathcote - Goldfields

Emeu Inn Bed & Breakfast, Restaurant and Wine Centre *Luxury B&B & Self Contained Cottage w/ mini kitchen*
Fred & Leslye Thies
187 High Street
Heathcote
Vic 3523
45 km SE of Bendigo

Tel (03) 5433 2668
Fax (03) 5433 4022
info@emeuinn.com.au
www.emeuinn.com.au

Double $180-$255 Single $150-$220
Children $40
Continental breakfast
Dinner From $29 main courses
Cottage $420/couple: two nights
Extra person $40 per night
Visa MC Diners Amex Eftpos JCB accepted
7 Queen (7 bdrm) Cottage sleeps four in queen-size bed and double sofa bed
Bathrooms: 6 Ensuite Deluxe cottage with double spa and separate shower

Indulge yourself in luxury at the Award-winning Emeu Inn. Relax in the spacious suites with queen beds, private ensuites with spas or open fires and all the extras gourmet travellers expect. Dine in our Good Food Guide-recommended restaurant where international cuisine and local wines are standard fare. Our Wine Shop is stocked with local wines to take away! Enjoy some golf, Lake Eppalock, the forests, the shops or the wine! Part of the Goldfields, Heathcote's an easy weekend getaway!

Horsham

Orange Grove B&B *B&B & Self Contained Cottage*

Graeme and Nola Hill
123 Keatings Road
Horsham
Vic 3401
8 km NW of Horsham

Tel (03) 5382 0583
or 0427 536 346
Fax (03) 5382 7238
bookings@orangegrovebandb.com.au
www.orangegrovebandb.com.au

Double $150-$200
Single $100-$120
Full provisions
Pet-Friendly
Visa MC Amex Eftpos accepted
2 Queen 1 Twin (3 bdrm)
Bathrooms: 1 Private

Conveniently located approximately halfway between Melbourne and Adelaide, Orange Grove offers luxury accommodation in a restored historic mudbrick homestead (early 1900s) located on 25 acres just minutes drive from Horsham. Enjoy a relaxed friendly welcome to a spacious quiet country setting with renovated gardens for your pleasure. The whole cottage is available exclusively, and features an open living area with cooking facilities and lounge with open fire (air-conditioning in summer). There is also a private enclosed outdoor courtyard with BBQ facilities. Pets are welcome.

Lorne - Aireys Inlet

Lorneview B&B *B&B & Separate Suite*

Nola & Kevin Symes
677 Great Ocean Road
Eastern View
Vic 3231
14 km E of Lorne

Tel (03) 5289 6430
Fax (03) 5289 6735
lorneview@bigpond.com
www.lorneview.com.au

Double $130-$170
Single $120-$160
Continental breakfast
Visa MC accepted
2 Queen (2 bdrm)
Bathrooms: 2 Ensuite

 AAA Tourism ★★★★☆

Lorneview has two spacious guest rooms, separate from main house, one overlooking the ocean and the other overlooking the bush. Each room has QS bed, ensuite, TV, CD/DVD player, heating, air conditioning, refrigerator, iron, ironing board, tea and coffee facilities. Delicious breakfast of fresh fruit, homemade muesli, muffins and croissants is served in your room or on balcony overlooking beach. Dinner unavailable, but many excellent restaurants nearby. Barbecue and Games Room provided. Enjoy walks along the beach and go to sleep listening to the waves.

Lorne - Otway Ranges - Birregurra

Elliminook *Luxury B&B & Heritage*
Jill & Peter Falkiner
585 Warncoort Road
Birregurra
Vic 3242
38 km N of Lorne

Tel (03) 5236 2080
Fax (03) 5236 2423
enquiries@elliminook.com.au
www.elliminook.com.au

Double $150-$230
Single $130-$190
Full breakfast
Visa MC Diners Amex accepted
3 Queen 1 Double 3 Single (4 bdrm)
Bathrooms: 3 Ensuite 1 Private
Spa Bath in private Bathroom

  AAA Tourism ★★★★☆   INN·HOUSE

Award winning Elliminook c1865 is a beautifully restored and decorated National Trust classified homestead providing a great relaxing getaway. Guests will enjoy the historic garden, croquet, boules, tennis court, open fires, liquor service, sumptuous cooked breakfast, fresh flowers in your room, and welcoming hospitality.

From Elliminook you can explore the Great Ocean Road, Twelve Apostles, Shipwreck Coast, Otway Fly Tree Top Walk, including Birregurra's historic walk, waterfalls and rain forest of the scenic Otway Ranges. For a unique accommodation experience be our welcome guest. "Guests enjoy the serenity of a flourishing garden and the grandeur or a magnificent historic home as seen in Australian House & Garden."

Macedon Ranges - Mount Macedon

Craigielea Mountain Retreat *Luxury Self Contained Apartment & Self Contained Suites*

Simone & Richard Graham
109 Mountain Road
Cherokee
Vic 3434
15 km E of Woodend

Tel (03) 5427 0799
or 0411 444 449
Fax (03) 5427 0669
info@craigielea.com.au
www.craigielea.com.au

Double $275-$365
Children not suitable
Full provisions
Gourmet dinner from $65pp
Elegant small functions by arrangement
Visa MC Diners Amex Eftpos accepted
3 King (3 bdrm)
Bathrooms: 3 Ensuite Luxury double spa

  AAA Tourism ★★★★★ INN·HOUSE

F ive Star Craigielea Mountain Retreat, only 45 minutes from Melbourne, is a romantic getaway for couples, perched high on the mountain with magnificent views of the city and the bay from each of its self contained spa suites. All have a king-size bed, double spa, wood fire, air conditioner and verandah. Gourmet dinners are available and served in the privacy of your suite. You need bring nothing but each other.

Macedon Ranges - Sunbury

Rupertswood Mansion *B&B*

Margaret McLelland
3 Macedon Street
Sunbury
Vic 3429
10 km N of Melbourne Airport

Tel (03) 9740 5020
Fax (03) 9740 3686
info@rupertswood.com
www.rupertswood.com

Double $160-$495
Full breakfast
Dinner by arrangement
Visa MC Amex Eftpos accepted
11 Queen (11 bdrm)
Bathrooms: 11 Ensuite

 AAA Tourism ★★★★☆

R upertswood is undoubtedly one of the most beautiful Victorian mansions in Australia. If you are a lover of heritage architecture then Rupertswood Mansion is something you must experience. The mansion offers exclusive accommodation in beautifully appointed rooms, all featuring exquisite antique furnishings, ensuites and heating/air conditioning. All accommodation tariffs include a Full Country Breakfast. Situated in Sunbury, the gateway to the Macedon Ranges, guests staying at Rupertswood will have the opportunity to explore the delights of the region by day and relax in the mansion at night.

Melbourne - Blackburn

Treetops Bed & Breakfast *B&B*
Sue & Jim Chambers
16 Linum Street
Blackburn, Vic 3130
18 km E of Melbourne Central

Tel (03) 9877 2737 or 0418 380 633
Fax (03) 9894 3279
treetops@alphalink.com.au
www.treetopsmelbourne.com

Double $121-$155 **Single** $95
Children $22
Continental breakfast, full available for
additional charge
King Honeymoon Suite:
Double $185-$220 Single $165
Visa MC Diners Amex accepted
1 King 3 Queen 2 Double (3 bdrm)
Bathrooms: 3 Ensuite

   AAA Tourism ★★★★☆ INN·HOUSE

Treetops B&B is a picturesque homestead with a rustic half acre garden set in a unique National Trust classified area. There are three spacious suites with private entrance, ensuite and their own comfortable lounge area for relaxation or entertainment includes honeymoon suite with spa. A pool and heated spa also available. Each suite has a refrigerator, microwave, TV, Video, CD Player, Queen sized bed, fresh fruit basket and fresh flowers. A light breakfast is provided daily. Suites have airconditioning and heating. It's a short walk to shops, restaurants, train and bus.

Melbourne - Camberwell

Springfields *B&B*
Robyn & Phillip Jordan
4 Springfield Avenue
Camberwell
Vic 3124
9 km E of Melbourne

Tel (03) 9809 1681
or 0434 353 750
Fax (03) 9809 1681
the.jordans@pacific.net.au
www.bbbook.com.au/springfields.html

Double $120 **Single** $80
Children welcome - contact us for prices
Full breakfast
1 King/Twin 1 Twin (2 bdrm)
Bathrooms: 1 Guest share 1 Private
Guest bathroom is located between the
two guest bedrooms.

AAA Tourism ★★★☆ B&B

Springfields is our attractive and spacious family home in a quiet avenue in one of Melbourne's finest suburbs. Guests comment on the quietness, and the fresh fruit salad at breakfast! Guests can enjoy the peace and privacy of their own lounge - or join us for friendly chat. Public transport is nearby. Children are most welcome. Make our home your home when you next visit Melbourne.

Melbourne - Fairfield

Fairfield Guest House *Guest House*
Clare & Lindsay Nankivell
18 Station Street
Fairfield
Vic 3078
5 km N of Melbourne

Tel (03) 9482 2959
or 0438 891 817
Fax (03) 9482 1956
fairfieldguesthouse@hotmail.com
www.babs.com.au/fairfield

Double $85-$180
Single $70-$160
Continental provisions
Visa MC Eftpos accepted
5 Queen 1 Twin 1 Single (7 bdrm)
Bathrooms: 3 Ensuite 2 Guest share

AAA Tourism ★★★★

Fairfield Guest House offers seven rooms ranging between rooms with shared bathroom facilities to rooms with private bathrooms and lovely self contained suite with double spa bath and all the comforts of home. We are only ten minutes from Melbourne CBD a short stroll to all public transport and the beautiful Fairfield Park Boathouse offering the best Devonshire Teas in Melbourne overlooking the Yarra River. We cater for all budgets and we are pet friendly for those that love travelling with their animals.

Melbourne - North Fitzroy

Slattery's North Fitzroy B&B *B&B & Self Contained Apartment*
Jacqui & Ron Slattery
41 Rae Street
North Fitzroy
Vic 3068
2 km N of Melbourne

Tel (03) 9489 1308
www.bbbook.com.au/slatterysnthfitzroybb.
html

Double $120
Single $95
Continental breakfast
Visa MC accepted
1 Twin (1 bdrm)
Bathrooms: 1 Private

AAA Tourism ★★★★

Slattery's offers superior self-contained accommodation in Melbourne's first suburb, 2 km from Melbourne's CBD. Air-conditioned, centrally heated accommodation comprises bedroom with twin beds, separate sitting room, bathroom, kitchenette and meals area. Tea & coffee facility, toaster, microwave, fridge, TV, video, hair-dryer, iron and ironing board, electric blankets, garage parking and roof garden with city views. Close to public transport, theatres, Edinburgh Gardens, Royal Exhibition Buildings and Brunswick Street cafés. Breakfast is your choice of juice, cereals, breads, and home-made jams and marmalades. Credit cards.

Melbourne - Richmond

Rotherwood *B&B & or Self Contained Apartment*

Flossie Sturzaker
13 Rotherwood Street
Richmond, Melbourne
Vic 3121
1.5 km E of Melbourne Central

Tel (03) 9428 6758
Fax (03) 9428 6758
rotherwoodbb@bigpond.com.au
www.bbbook.com.au/rotherwood.html

Double $145-$180
Single $120-$175
Children additional
Special breakfast
Visa MC accepted
1 Queen (2 bdrm)
Own dining room and drawing room
Bathrooms: 1 Private bath per apartment

On the Hill in Richmond, "Rotherwood" is at the heart of Melbourne's attractions. Walking distance of the MCG, Royal Botanic Gardens, National Tennis Centre, Royal Tennis Centre, shops and restaurants. Only a 5 minute tram ride to City. Easy access to National Gallery, Concert Hall, Crown Casino, and Southbank. Private entrance to Victorian era apartment. Large sitting room with French doors leading to terrace overlooking garden. Bedroom (Q.S. Bed), private bathroom, and separate dining room with cooking facilities. Special French Breakfast provided. Extra fold-out bed. Airport transport available. TV, Video, DVD. Suitable for short or long term stay.

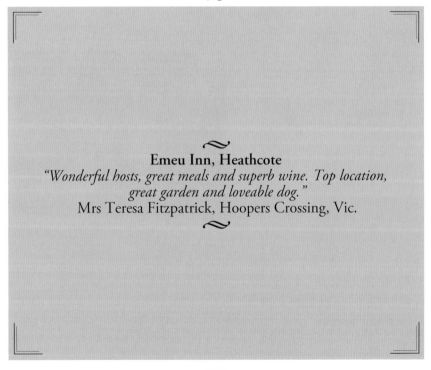

Emeu Inn, Heathcote
"Wonderful hosts, great meals and superb wine. Top location, great garden and loveable dog."
Mrs Teresa Fitzpatrick, Hoopers Crossing, Vic.

Melbourne - Richmond

Villa Donati *B&B*
Gayle Lamb & Trevor Finlayson
377 Church Street
Richmond
Vic 3121
2.5 km E of Melbourne CBD

Tel (03) 9428 8104
or 0412 068 855
Fax (03) 9421 0956
email@villadonati.com
www.villadonati.com

Double $175-$225 **Single** $150-$175
Full breakfast
Visa MC Diners Amex Eftpos accepted
1 Queen 2 Double (4 bdrm)
Bathrooms: 4 Ensuite

 AAA Tourism ★★★★☆

Cool classic exterior, rich stylish interior- Villa Donati is a chic, inner city bed and breakfast. Previously home to distinguished architects, archbishops and the 'Moulin Rouge' massage parlour, Villa Donati has been restored to capture the essence of the European pensione. Today, this historic and charming property is a stunning mix of contemporary and antique design. Each of the en-suite bedrooms has its own unique style and furnishings - fine bed linen, imported toiletries, antiques and original art works. The guest sitting room offers city views and the café style breakfast room is the perfect place for indulgent breakfasts. Villa Donati is situated in cosmopolitan Richmond, only minutes from the CBD and Melbourne's main shopping, entertainment and sporting precincts.

From the Visitors' Book: Divine - everything!

Melbourne - St Kilda

Bishopsgate House *B&B & Self Contained Apartment*
Margaret Tudball & Ross Bishop
57 Mary Street
St Kilda West
Vic 3182
5 km S of Melbourne

Tel (03) 9525 4512
or 0402 057 351
Fax (03) 9525 3024
marg@bishopsgate.com.au
www.bishopsgate.com.au

Double $165-$195 Single $145-$175
Special breakfast
Dinner B/A Licensed property
Visa MC Amex accepted
1 King/Twin1 King 4 Queen 3 Single (5 bdrm)
Bathrooms: 2 Ensuite 3 Private

 AAA Tourism ★★★★☆

A s featured on the national travel show 'Getaway' Bishopsgate is a stunningly renovated two storey 1890's terrace home furnished with antiques and original art work. The three individually themed guest rooms and 2 bedroom apartment are luxuriously appointed with quality fittings. Facilities include en-suites, TV, tea and coffee making facilities, and individually controlled heating and cooling. Enjoy using Bishopsgate's own designer toiletries. Bishopsgate is located in a grand, broad, tree-lined street. One block from St Kilda's Fitzroy Street and just two blocks to the beach, rollerblading and bike riding. Bishopsgate is the perfect accommodation for both tourism and business.

~

Melbourne - St Kilda

Alrae Bed & Breakfast *B&B*
Vivienne Wheeler
7 Hughenden Road
St Kilda East
Vic 3183
5 km SE of Melbourne

Tel (03) 9527 2033
or 0409 174 132
Fax (03) 9527 2044
alrae2@bigpond.com
www.visitvictoria.com/alrae

Double $165-$205 Single $99-$121
Children $33-$66
Special breakfast   Dinner $44 B/A
Spare sofa bed $66-$121
Visa MC Amex JCB accepted
1 Queen 1 Twin (2 bdrm) Twin room 3 & 1/2 stars
Bathrooms: 1 Ensuite 1 Private

  AAA Tourism ★★★★

A lrae, a well kept secret, is 5 km. from Melbourne CBD, handy public transport including daytime suburban airport shuttle bus, beach, shops, sports venues, restaurants and theatres. It features a Queen bedroom with ensuite, air-conditioning, fridge, private entrance. The Twin bedroom with a view has adjoining private bathroom with spa shower over bathtub, aircond. Air-conditioned guests' dining room cum lounge, specialty breakfasts and dietary variations. All rooms have TV/VCR, TV/DVD, clock radios, books etc. BBQ, OSP. Corporate, Seniors, Medical profession, Members Motor Organisations, Conditions apply.

Mildura

Mildura's Linsley House *B&B & Homestay*
Colin & Desley Rankin
PO Box 959
Mildura
Vic 3502
15 km E of Mildura at Trentham Cliffs

Tel (03) 5024 8487
or 0417 593 483
Fax (03) 5024 8914
www.visitvictoria.com/mildouraslinsley

Double $110
Single $66
Full breakfast
Visa MC accepted
2 Queen 2 Single (3 bdrm)
Bathrooms: 2 Ensuite

Linsley House B&B has a magnificent river view. Colin and Desley Rankin take pleasure in welcoming you to their charming and tranquil home which is situated in a quiet rural setting and has panoramic views of the garden and Murray River from the bedrooms. The large lounge/dining area includes: full kitchen facilities, TV, fridge, woodfire, air-conditioning and comfortable antiques. Mildura is renown for its oranges, dried fruits, wineries and Mediterranean weather.

Mornington - Mount Eliza

Sartain's at Mornington *Luxury Self Contained Cottage and Bungalow*
Sally Sartain
75 Oakbank Road
Mount Eliza, Vic 3930
5 km SW of Mount Eliza & 5 km E of
Mornington

Tel (03) 5975 1014
Fax (03) 5975 1014
sally@sartains.com.au
www.sartains.com.au

Double $130-$190
Continental provisions
Lunch & dinner B/A
Cooked full breakfast $20 per couple
Double $130 Bungalow
Double $190 Cottage
Visa MC Eftpos accepted
2 Queen (2 bdrm) 1 Queen Cottage 1 Queen Bungalow
Bathrooms: 2 Private 1 Private The Cottage, 1 Private The Bungalow

AAA Tourism
★★★★

You are invited to share the Sartains' Experience. Stylishly renovated self-contained air-conditioned cottage and bungalow. First class facilities set in private gardens including tennis court with pavilion and excellent barbecue. Close to beaches and shops (5 minutes), golf and wineries. As much or as little as you would like to do. All set in a relaxing country atmosphere. Sartain's is licensed and in addition to breakfast can also provide lunch and evening meals. Prices from $130 per couple for bungalow or $190 per couple for cottage, per night.

Mount Beauty

Towns including Bright, Myrtleford, Beechworth and Mount Beauty are synonymous with the northeast and have their own charm and appeal to the visitor. Crystal clear mountain streams with elusive trout, fabulous mountain scenery many wineries with cellar doors, restaurants showcasing locally grown products such as chestnuts, berries and olive oils.

The northeast has a rich history of farming, timber, tobacco and hops, high country mountain cattlemen, goldmining and hydro electricity. More recently the area is becoming known for its cool climate wines with many vineyards and cellar doors being established.
Isla MacLeod

Phillip Island

Abaleigh on Lovers Walk *Self Contained Apartment*
Jenny & Robert Hudson
6 Roy Court
Phillip Island,
Vic 3922
0.4 km E of Cowes PO

Tel (03) 5952 5649
Fax (03) 5952 2549
info@abaleigh.com
www.abaleigh.com

Double $170-$250
Single $160-$250
Full provisions
Apartment from $190 double
Visa MC accepted
 2 King/Twin1 King 2 Queen (5 bdrm)
Bathrooms: 5 Ensuite 5 Private spa

 AAA Tourism
★★★★☆

A baleigh's FSC absolute beach frontage apartment and studios offer the finest accommodation. Featuring: spas, water views, Jetmaster log fires, double showers, breakfast-stocked kitchens, laundries, courtyards with barbecues for outdoor living, TV, DVD, stereo and more. Five minutes foreshore stroll to restaurants and central Cowes. Peaceful, private, ideal for couples or small groups of adults. Winner Best New Business, Best Hosted Accommodation Regional Tourism Awards. AAA ****¹/₂, "In one word perfect." J&M, Malvern.

Phillip Island

Glen Isla House *Small Luxury Hotel Country House*
Madeleine & Ian Baker
230-232 Church Street
Cowes, Vic 3922
0.15 km W of Cowes

Tel (03) 5952 1882
Fax (03) 5952 5028
infobbb@glenisla.com
www.glenisla.com

Double $265-$395
Not suitable for children
Special chef-prepared breakfast
Table D'Hote Dinner B/A
Single Tariff POA
Visa MC Diners Amex Eftpos accepted
1 King 6 Queen 2 Twin (9 bdrm)
1 Heritage Suite 6 Glen Isla Rooms, 1 SC Cottage
Bathrooms: 7 Ensuite 1 Guest share Spa Bath in Anderson Suite

 AAA Tourism ★★★★★ INN·HOUSE

Set in the secluded heritage gardens of the historic Glen Isla homestead (circa 1870). Award winning small luxury hotel country-house offering elegant surroundings. Absolute privacy, 100 meters to the beach. "Arguably the island's best accommodation" - Melbourne Age. The Anderson Heritage Suite cottage with four-poster king bed, log fire, spa, period furnishings and TV/DVD system. Six purpose-architected Glen Isla "classic" rooms with walk-in robe/luggage room, private en-suite, superb garden vistas & separate entrances. Resident chefs, gourmet breakfast and private cellar. Intimate weddings & corporate conferences.

Phillip Island - Cowes

Genesta House *B&B & Guest House*
Gay Langrish
18 Steele Street
Cowes
Vic 3922
0.3 km E of Post Office

Tel (03) 5952 3616
or 0413 013 766
genesta@nex.net.au
http://genesta.com.au

Double $150-$160
Full breakfast
Visa MC Eftpos accepted
4 Queen (4 bdrm)
Own entrance and balcony
Bathrooms: 4 Ensuite

 AAA Tourism ★★★★

Historic guesthouse in the heart of Cowes, four houses from the beach and close to the main street with cafés and restaurants. Own entrance and balcony, outdoor spa, fully cooked English breakfast. Peaceful fountain and water feature in beautiful garden. Relax and unwind on the verandah.

Victoria

Port Fairy

Cherry Plum Cottages B&B *B&B & Self Contained Cottages*
Ruth and Doug Maxwell
Albert Road
Port Fairy
Vic 3284
2 km N of Port Fairy Central

Tel (03) 5568 2595
Fax (03) 5568 2591
cherryplumcottages@bigpond.com
www.port-fairy.com/cherryplum

Double $130-$280
Single $105-$160
Special breakfast
Port Fairy has a good range of dining choices
Visa MC accepted
2 Queen 1 Double (3 bdrm)
1 bedroom cottage and 2 bedroom cottage
Bathrooms: 1 Ensuite 1 Private bath x1

AAA Tourism
★★★★

On a quiet country lane in Port Fairy our cottages Cherry Plum and Arrondoon (c1862) are situated on four acres in a leafy garden amongst historic buildings. We deliver breakfast baskets of local produce to your cottage. Our accommodation features period furnishings, private entrance, guest sitting rooms, verandahs and off street parking. We are 3 mins by car [20 minutes walk] to the main street and well located to enjoy the town, restaurants, beaches, or trips to the 12 Apostles, regional wineries.

≈

Princetown - The Great Ocean Road

The Great Ocean Road is one of our international visitors must see areas. It begins at Torquay and boarders the edge of the ocean, with many stops at vantage points to enjoy the views. From Apollo Bay the road leaves the coast and enters the Otway Ranges, one of Australia's best examples of Cool Temperate Rainforest.

A visit to Cape Otway Light House to learn about the shipwrecks that give the coast its name, and a walk in the treetops at the Otway Fly is a must. On leaving the Otways the road joins the coast again for a different spectacle. The "12 Apostles", one of many seascape attractions to be discovered on this part of the Great Ocean Road.
Lyn Boxshall, Arabella Country House

Princetown - Twelve Apostles

Arabella Country House *B&B & Homestay*

Lynne & Neil Boxshall
7219 Great Ocean Road
Princetown
Vic 3269
6 km E of Princetown

Tel (03) 5598 8169
Fax (03) 5598 8186
arabella.ch@bigpond.com
www.innhouse.com.au/arabella.htm

Double $145-$160
Single $80
Children $25
Full breakfast
Dinner $15-$30
Visa MC Eftpos accepted
3 Queen 1 Double 2 Single (4 bdrm)
Bathrooms: 4 Ensuite

   AAA Tourism ★★★★☆ INN·HOUSE

Arabella Country House is situated within sight of 12 Apostles, Port Campbell N.P. and Otway N.P. All are must see attractions for visitors to Victoria. Our promise is that our superior B&B experience will add to our guests' adventure along the Great Ocean Road. With comfortable relaxing surroundings, quality fittings and the freshest food, plus local knowledge make special memories. Together with our dogs, we really enjoy our guests' visit and hope to see you soon.

Sarsfield - Bairnsdale

Stringybark Cottages B&B *B&B & Self Contained B&B cottage*

Lois & Neil Triggs
77 Howards Road
Sarsfield
Vic 3875
19 km N of Bairnsdale

Tel (03) 5157 5245
Fax (03) 5157 5639
neil@stringybarkcottages.com
http://stringybarkcottages.com

Double $154-$170
Single $100
Children under 2 stay for free
Full provisions
Dinner is avaliable by prior arrangement
Extra person $35 per night
Visa MC accepted
3 Queen 5 Single (5 bdrm)
2 Cottages have 2 bedrooms, 1 cottage has 1 bedroom
Bathrooms: 3 Private 1 cottage has double shower and bath

  AAA Tourism ★★★★

Experience that little piece of paradise, tranquil and delightfully different. Enjoy those cool evenings snuggled up in front of the wood fire, warmer nights spent relaxing on your verandah with a ceiling of millions of stars. Multi Award winning Stringybark Cottages are situated 19kms from Bairnsdale just off The Great Alpine Road. There are four cottages, accommodating from two to five people. Each cottage is fully self contained.

Sorrento - Mornington Peninsula

Tamasha House *B&B*

Naomi & Peter Nicholson
699 Melbourne Road
Sorrento
Vic 3943
1 km E of Sorrento

Tel (03) 5984 2413
Fax (03) 5984 0452
tamasha@ozemail.com.au
www.peninsulapages.com/tamasha

Double $180-$200
Single $120
Full breakfast
Dinner by arrangement
Visa MC Diners Amex JCB accepted
1 King/Twin 1 Double (2 bdrm)
Modern seaside décor with sittingroom
Bathrooms: 2 Ensuite

   AAA Tourism ★★★★

Tamasha House, set in a beautiful garden, is situated between Ocean and Bay beaches and is a short distance from historic Sorrento. An ideal place to stay while exploring the Mornington Peninsula. Take the ferry to Queenscliff or go swimming with the dolphins, visit the wineries or discover the galleries and restaurants, all within a short distance. Your caring hosts offer a warm welcome, fine food and local knowledge.

Torquay - Surf Coast

Ocean Manor B&B *Luxury B&B & Separate Suite*

Helen & Bob Bailey
3 Glengarry Drive
Torquay
Vic 3228
17 km S of Geelong

Tel (03) 5261 3441
or 0407 597 100
Fax (03) 5261 9140
oceanmanor@bigpond.com
www.bbbook.com.au/oceanmanorbb.html

Double $110-$160
Single $90-$100
Children $20
Continental breakfast
2 bedroom suite $130-$190
Visa MC accepted
1 Queen 1 Twin (2 bdrm)
Bathrooms: 1 Ensuite 1 Family share

 AAA Tourism ★★★★☆

The 2 bedroom suite is situated upstairs to ensure privacy and take maximum advantage of the ocean view. The master bedroom features a queen sized bed, en suite bathroom. Adjoining is a combined lounge and dining area which leads onto a decked balcony with sweeping ocean views. The air conditioned lounge has Foxtel, TV and DVDs. The mini kitchen with fridge and microwave leads to a second bedroom with separate toilet facilities and 2 single beds. A continental breakfast is included.

Wangaratta

The Pelican *B&B & Farmstay*
Margaret & Bernie Blackshaw
606 Oxley Flats Road
Wangaratta
Vic 3678
6 km E of Wangaratta

Tel (03) 5727 3240
or 0413 082 758
pelicanblackshaw@hotmail.com
www.bbbook.com.au/thepelican.html

Double $120-$150
Single $75
Children $40
Full breakfast
Dinner $30 per person by arrangement
Extra person in double room $40
Visa MC accepted
1 Queen 1 Twin 2 Single (3 bdrm)
Bathrooms: 1 Guest share 1 Private

The Pelican is a charming historic homestead set in parklike surroundings. Cattle and horses are raised on the 400 acres and early risers can go "trackside" to watch the harness horses at work. Guest rooms are in an upstairs wing of the home and have lovely country views where peacocks and pelicans are often spotted. The main bedroom has its own private balcony overlooking a lagoon fringed with giant red gums. Hearty breakfasts feature home grown produce and evening meals are available on request.

Warrnambool

Merton Manor Exclusive B&B *B&B & Separate Suite*
Pamela & Ivan Beechey
62 Ardlie Street
Warrnambool
Vic 3280
1 km N of Warrnambool PO

Tel (03) 5562 0720
or 0417 314 364
Fax (03) 5561 1220
merton@ansonic.com.au
http://members.datafast.net.au/merton

Double $160-$180
Single $130-$150
Full breakfast
Visa MC Diners Amex Eftpos
JCB accepted
1 King/Twin 5 Queen 2 Single (6 bdrm)
Bathrooms: 6 Ensuite 6 double spas

Merton Manor is a traditional B&B with mews style accommodation set within an historic Victorian villa. It features antiques, open fires, billiard and music rooms and grand dining room and is located mid way between Adelaide and Melbourne. All suites feature private entrances, climate control heating and air conditioning, private lounge rooms and ensuites with double spas. Merton Manor is situated close to the cultural attractions and restaurants of Warrnambool. The 12 Apostles, whale viewing, Tower Hill State Game Reserve and the Maritime Museum are all close by. AAAT 4 1/2 stars. Beach and Botanical Gardens nearby.

Warrnambool

Manor Gums *B&B & Separate Suite*
Michael & Kittipat Esposito
170 Shadys Lane, Mailors Flat
Warrnambool
Vic 3275
8 km NW of Warrnambool

Tel (03) 5565 4410
Fax (03) 5565 4409
manorgum@standard.net.au
www.travel.to/manorgums

Double $135-$165 Single $120-$135
Children $20
Continental breakfast
Dinner $35+
Visa MC Eftpos accepted
3 Queen 1 Double (4 bdrm)
Bathrooms: 4 Ensuite
Ensuite with bath and spas available

M anor Gums is a quality and unique retreat surrounded by tall majestic gums and abundant birdlife. The distinctive architectural style and unique features offer couples luxury in private self contained suites, all designed to be different and capture the tranquillity of the bushland setting and views. Suites have fully equipped kitchenette, microwave, TV, VCR, CD player, climate control air conditioning. Some have a woodfire, balconies or large bath. A generous breakfast hamper is provided. Spa, sauna, gym and BBQ are available.

Warrnambool

Quamby Homestead *B&B & Self Contained House*
Julie & Karl Mischkulnig
3223 Caramut Road
Woolsthorpe
Vic 3276
32 km N of Warrnambool

Tel (03) 5569 2395
Fax (03) 5569 2244
quambyhomestead@bigpond.com
www.quambyhomestead.com.au

Double $140-$181.50
Single $121-$165
Children 3-12 $22, Free baby cot provided
Full breakfast
Dinner available by prior arrangement
Additional adult in Carriage House $33
Visa MC Diners Amex Eftpos JCB accepted
1 King 5 Queen 1 Twin 2 Single (8 bdrm)
Bathrooms: 7 Ensuite

L ocated just 20 mins from Great Ocean Road and Warrnambool, Quamby provides an ideal two night destination for exploring this fascinating region, which includes volcanic Tower Hill, historic Port Fairy and whale watching at Logan's Beach, Warrnambool, before travelling on to The Grampians, Ballarat Goldfields, Melbourne or Adelaide. Relax and enjoy local native wildlife (kangaroos, wallabies, koalas, cockatoos, possums), watch cattle and horses graze in the paddocks, or take a stroll around the 2km property walk. Whatever your preference, come experience 'Quamby', Aboriginal for resting place.

Wilsons Promontory

saltwater @ sandypoint *Beach house/self contained house*
Bonny & Graeme Francis
16 Anderson Avenue
Sandypoint
Vic 3959
0.5 km S of Sandypoint

Tel (03) 5783 1939
Fax (03) 5783 1937
gbef@bigpond.com.au
www.bbbook.com.au/saltwater@
sandypoint.html

Accommodation only $400-$500
Children no extra charge
Peak and off peak rates
Weekly family rates apply
Visa MC accepted
2 Queen 1 Double 1 Single (3 bdrm)
Q/B bed downstairs and upstairs, D/B, S & Sofa/B upstairs
Bathrooms: 1 Guest share

Sandy Point beach in South Gippsland has to be the most beautiful, secluded beach in Southern Australia. Stretching in an arc from Waratah Bay to Shallow Inlet, Sandy Point overlooks Cape Liptrap to the West and the magnificent Wilson's Promontory to the South. SALTWATER is a new addition to accommodation at Sandy Point. Only 4 minutes walk to the beach; contemporary but very comfortable & sleeps 6 in 3 bedrooms. Great for a weekend for two or a family summer holiday.

~

Wilsons Promontory - Waratah North

Bayview House *B&B & Separate Suite*
Ellen Fabel & Paul Greco
202 Soldiers Road
Waratah North
Vic 3959
16 km S of Foster

Tel (03) 5687 1246
bayview@iprimus.com.au
www.bayviewhouse.com.au

Double $140-$180 Single $130-$170
Children under 12 months old free
Full breakfast
Extra Person $30-$40
Specials for extended stays
Visa MC Diners Amex Eftpos
JCB accepted
2 Queen 1 Double 1 Single (4 bdrm)
One 2 bedroom suite, two 1 bedroom suites
Bathrooms: 3 Ensuite

 AAA Tourism
★★★★

Bayview House sits in three acres of gardens overlooking the magnificent Wilsons Promontory National Park, (one of the worlds oldest with its beaches, mountains and wilderness areas - only a fifteen minute drive away). We offer three private suites within our large house, 2 with kitchenettes, all with superb views and their own lounge area. Breakfast is served in the main kitchen. Warm hospitality, pancakes, tranquility, space, and good design have become our trademarks. We also speak Dutch, German, Swiss German and a little Cornish!

Yackandandah - Beechworth - Albury

Time After Time *B&B & Self Contained Cottage*
Robyn McCulloch & Jen Haberecht
43 Back Creek Road
Yackandandah
Vic 3749
1.2 km SE of Yackandandah

Tel (02) 6027 1786
or 0419 616 112
robynmc@dragnet.com.au
www.tat.dragnet.com.au

Double $125
Single $115
Additional person/child $20
Full breakfast
Specials are available for longer stays
1 Queen 1 Double (1 bdrm)
Queen bedroom, plus double sofa
Bathrooms: 1 Private

She-Oaks cottage is designed for comfort and relaxation, with ever changing views to the hills beyond! Great sitting room with kitchen and dining room. There is a luxurious queen bedroom, and up to 2 extra can be accommodated in the living area. TV, DVD, heating, airconditioning, private BBQ and outdoor sitting areas. The verandah on three sides provides a wonderful place to enjoy the view. A great country breakfast, either a well-stocked hamper, or you can choose from the daily breakfast menu. Dog friendly!

~

Yarra Valley

Kalorama is set in the beautiful Dandenong Ranges near Olinda where you can visit all the local attractions the Dandenong Ranges has to offer, including art and craft markets, specialty gift and antique shops.

Wander through our picturesque walking trails and enjoy the wonderful surroundings such as, William Ricketts Sanctuary, Healesville Sanctuary, and Puffing Billy, plus various Yarra Valley Wineries. Indulge yourself with fine food and wine amongst the wide variety of local restaurants and cafes.
Loraine Potter, Holly Gate House

Yarra Valley - Dandenong Ranges

Holly Gate House Bed and Breakfast *Luxury B&B*

Loraine Potter
1308 Mt Dandenong Tourist Road
Kalorama
Vic 3766
5 km NE of Olinda

Tel (03) 9728 3218
or 0415 192 690
Fax (03) 9728 3218
reception@hollygatehouse.com.au
www.hollygatehouse.com.au

Double $145-$225 Single $120-$160
Full breakfast
Complimentary restaurant transfer
Visa MC Eftpos accepted
3 Queen (3 bdrm)
Bathrooms: 3 Ensuite
1 ensuite with spa bath

AAA Tourism
★★★★

Luxury adult retreat in the romantic Dandenong Ranges, the gateway to the Yarra Valley. Three beautifully appointed QB's with private ensuite (one with spa). All rooms have TV, Video, CD/Radio, robes, luxury toiletries. Tariff includes afternoon tea on arrival, fully cooked breakfast served in the guests' dining room. Sitting room with log fire. Outside pool in a pleasant garden setting. BBQ facilities. Complimentary transport to and from any local restaurant/function venue. Adult Retreat only/no pets. 45k from Melbourne. Melways Ref: Page52 J9.

Yarra Valley - Dandenong Ranges

Stringybark *B&B & Self Contained House*

Bonny & Graeme Francis
35 Lords Road
Upper Plenty
Vic 3756
10 km N of Whittlesea

Tel (03) 5783 1939
Fax (03) 5783 1937
stringybarkbab@bigpond.com.au
babs.com.au/stringybark

Double $285-$370
Single $265-$360
Children 6-15 $15
Full provisions
Extra adult $25 per night
2 night minimum stay
Visa MC accepted
2 Queen 1 Single (2 bdrm)
Bathrooms: 1 Guest share Double Spa

AAA Tourism
★★★★

Stringybark sits in a sunlit little gully surrounded by classic Australian bush yet only an hours drive from Melbourne... guests here have complete privacy. In Summer the hammocks slung in the trees are a great place for a read or a snooze. When it's cool, start the day with a delicious farmer's breakfast in front of the fire or watch the morning sun filter through the trees from the spa ... you'll never want to go home!!!

Yarra Valley - Yarra Glen

The Gatehouse at Villa Raedward *Luxury Self Contained Unit*

John & Sandra Annison
26 Melba Highway
Yering
Vic 3770
7 km S of Yarra Glen

Tel (03) 9739 0822
or 0425 730 624
info@villaraedward.com.au
www.villaraedward.com.au

Double $200-$240
Single $200-$240
Full provisions
Visa MC accepted
1 Queen (2 bdrm)
Large, comfortable bedroom
Bathrooms: 2 Private
2 person spa, large shower in marble bathroom

AAA Tourism
★★★★☆

Two architect-designed fully self contained units with undercover parking and private entrance and patio looking out over the Yarra Valley. Marble bathroom with large shower and two person spa overlooking a private courtyard garden. Fully equipped kitchen, reverse cycle air conditioning, DVD/TV. Complimentary bottle of Yarra Valley Bubbly, slippers, bathrobes, port, fresh coffee, sumptuous 3 course breakfast provisions, DVD library.

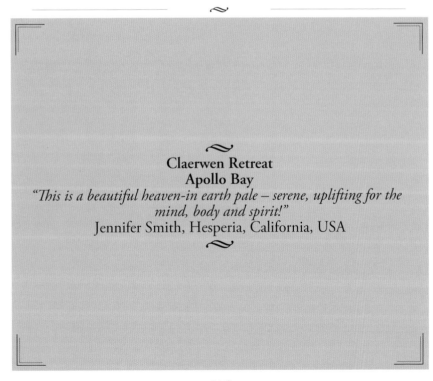

~
Claerwen Retreat
Apollo Bay
"This is a beautiful heaven-in earth pale – serene, uplifting for the mind, body and spirit!"
Jennifer Smith, Hesperia, California, USA
~

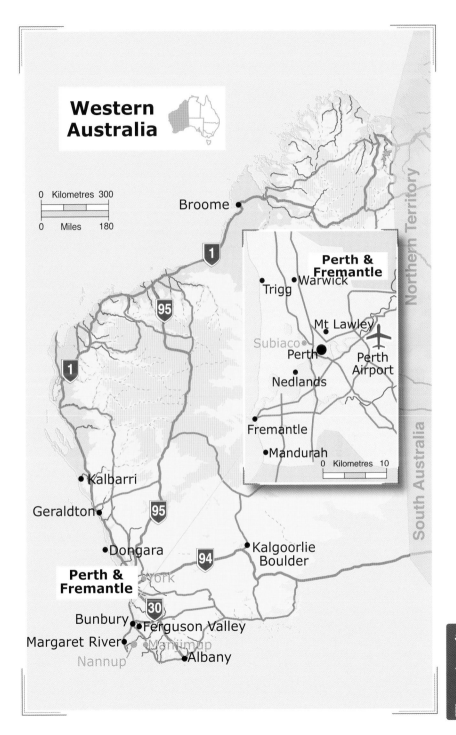

Albany

Situated on Princess Royal Harbour and King George Sound, Albany is Western Australia's oldest town. Albany's spectacular rugged coastline is unique in its own way, located around Frenchman's Bay is the Natural Bridge and the Gap and Blow Holes.

You can see all the history of a bygone era, explore the Cheynes IV one of the last whaling ships at the old Whaling Station, which is now a recognised whaling museum.

Historical old Albany Town has many Heritage listed buildings, like the old Goal and Courthouse. Just out of town is Mt Clarence, which features the Old Forts and the Light Horse Memorial to the soldiers and horses, departing for Gallipolli. There are many local wineries, beautiful beaches and the scenic whale walk around King George sound which joins the Bibbulmun Track.
Betty Ramsell

~

Albany

Albany View St Lodge B&B/Art Studio *B&B*
Lew and Margaret Dowdell
35 View Street
Albany
WA 6330
1 km W of Town Hall

Tel (08) 9842 8820
or 0427 428 820
Fax (08) 9842 8820
stay@albanyviewstbb.com.au
www.albanyviewstbb.com.au

Double $110-$120
Single $90-$95
Full breakfast
Discount for longer stays
Visa MC Eftpos accepted
3 Queen 1 Single (3 bdrm)
Suite 1 has a queen & single bed
Bathrooms: 3 Ensuite

  AAA Tourism ★★★★

L ew & Margaret welcome you to our lovely B&B. Reception is part of Margaret's Art Studio & Gallery. We offer quality accommodation just a short walk to shops, restaurants etc. We have 3 suites (2 with kitchenette-no cooker), fridge, microwave, tea/coffee making, TV, DVD, quality linen, crockery etc. Relax & enjoy breakfast upstairs with beautiful views of the harbour. Lovely gardens at rear with covered patio and BBQ. Guests are welcome to use our laundry. Off street parking and separate guest entrance.

Albany

Charnigup Farm Bed & Breakfast *B&B & self-catering*

Charmaine and Nigel Hickman
86 Mawson Road
Napier, Albany
WA 6330
20 km NE of Albany

Tel (08) 9844 3441
Fax (08) 9844 3441
charnigup@wn.com.au
www.members.westnet.com.au/charnigup

Double $120
Single $80
Not suited to children under 12
Continental breakfast
Dinner $30.00 per person
1 Queen 2 Twin (2 bdrm)
Bathrooms: 1 Private

What are the important aspects in your accommodation needs? If reasonable tariffs, a quiet, comfortable night's rest, privacy, friendly hosts, healthy home-style meals, lovely outlook and attractive, bird-filled gardens are on your list of priorities - look no further. From here your opportunity to experience unique Australiana, such as kangaroos, wild flowers and indigenous local bird life is assured. Our small cattle farm is central to this beautiful region's main attractions - the Stirling and Porongurup National Parks, pristine, isolated beaches and historical Albany.

Broome

BroomeTown B&B *Luxury B&B*

Toni & Richard Bourne
15 Stewart Street
Broome
WA 6725
In Broome

Tel (08) 9192 2006
or 0429 010 161
Fax (08) 9193 7626
info@broometown.com.au
www.broometown.com.au

Double $235-$285
Single $220-$260
Full breakfast
Visa MC Eftpos accepted
1 King/Twin 2 Queen (3 bdrm)
Bathrooms: 3 Ensuite Separate toilet

  AAA Tourism ★★★★☆

BroomeTown B&B has been built with your complete enjoyment in mind. Unwind and appreciate this unique Kimberley town from the comfort of this beautiful retreat situated close to 'Chinatown' and a short walk to many local attractions. We welcome you to enjoy warm hospitality, friendly service and touring advice in the appealing atmosphere of BroomeTown.

Bunbury

Colomberie B&B *B&B*
Sandra & Edward Pigott
11 Duffield Place
Sleaford Park, Bunbury
WA 6230
7 km S of Bunbury

Tel (08) 9795 7734
or 0417 913 398
Fax (08) 9795 7735
edp@iinet.net.au
www.bbbook.com.au/colomberie.html

Double $85-$110 **Single** $75-$85
Children on application by age
Continental provisions
Dinner by arrangement
Season rates apply Nov-Apr
1 Queen 1 Double 1 Single (2 bdrm)
Bathrooms: 2 Ensuite
Bath available by arrangement

 AAA Tourism ★★★☆

Colomberie B&B is an ideal location for travellers to and from Perth and the south-west. Two ensuite bedrooms, plus a single bed & cot, provide a variety of accommodation, plus a shared kitchenette, dining and lounge area for guests. Within easy travelling distance are the beaches, golf courses, vineyards, lavender farm, olive groves, orchards and berry farms of the Capes Region and the Bunbury amenities. The house, on one acre, is in a quiet cul-de-sac and gardens for the enjoyment of guests.

Dongara - Geraldton

Gracelyn B&B *B&B*
Elaine Summers
6 Delmarge Street
Dongara
WA 6525
65 km S of Geraldton

Tel (08) 9927 1938
or 0409 414 698
info@gracelynbedandbreakfast.com.au
www.gracelynbedandbreakfast.com.au

Double $60-$80
Single $50-$70
Children 50%
Full breakfast
1 Queen 2 Twin (3 bdrm)
Bathrooms: 1 Guest share

Home away from Home at Gracelyn Bed & Breakfast. Enjoy the swimming pool and outdoor living with gas BBQ, wood fire & electric blankets. Your own full size fridge, tea & coffee facilities television and pool table. Laundry facilities. Walk to shops and beach or river trails to ocean. Good choice of restaurants to enjoy Dongara's famous Rock Lobsters. Try our 18 scenic hole golf links with grass greens to rival any.

Fremantle

Terrace Central B&B *B&B & Hotel*

Barry White
79-85 South Terrace
Fremantle
WA 6160
10 km N of Fremantle

Tel (08) 9335 6600
or 0428 969 859
Fax (08) 9335 6600
info@terracecentral.com.au
www.terracecentral.com.au

Double $140-$160
Single $140-$160
Children $20
Continental breakfast
Saturday night only, extra $22
Visa MC Diners Amex Eftpos JCB accepted
10 Queen 6 Double 2 Twin 2 Single (18 bdrm)
Large air-conditioned ensuite
Bathrooms: 16 Ensuite

Heritage house in the city centre of Fremantle with 10 huge air-conditioned en-suite bedrooms and 4 apartments. Close to rail and bus service. 3 minutes walk to Markets, shops. Close to all tourist attractions and ferry to Rottnest Island. All rooms air-conditioned, en-suite bathroom. Free wireless broadband, TV & DVD Player, tea and coffee, fridge. Free parking.

Kalbarri

Gecko Lodge *Luxury B&B*
Sharyn & Graham Geikie
9 Glass Street
Kalbarri
WA 6536
0.3 km SW of Kalbarri

Tel (08) 9937 1900
or (08) 9937 1922
0439 968 305
Fax (08) 9937 1899
stay@geckolodgekalbarri.com.au
www.geckolodgekalbarri.com.au

Double $195-$235 Single $150-$195
Full breakfast
Seasonal tariffs
Discounts for extended stays
Visa MC Eftpos accepted
1 King 3 Queen (4 bdrm)
Airconditioned with ensuite
Bathrooms: 4 Ensuite 2 Spa Suites

   AAA Tourism ★★★★☆

Gecko Lodge is a luxury, romantically appointed purpose built Bed & Breakfast Lodge designed for couples. Located only a stone's throw from the beach, river mouth, shops and cafés, Gecko Lodge provides an ideal base from which to explore Kalbarri's attractions (yet benefits from total seclusion and privacy). Enjoy well appointed ensuite rooms (2 with spas, 2 with double showers), afternoon tea and evening Port and chocolates. Enjoy our high standards of service and comfort in this beautiful part of the world.

Mandurah - North Yunderup

Nautica Lodge *Luxury B&B*
Glenda & Roger Lingard
203 Culeenup Road
North Yunderup
6208
9 km E of Mandurah

Tel (08) 9537 8000
or 0419 944 627
nautica@istnet.net.au
www.nauticalodge.com

Double $120-$130 Single $95-$105
Continental breakfast
Visa MC accepted
1 King/Twin1 King 1 Queen 3 Single
(2 bdrm) ensuite, air-con, WIR, TV, safe
& hairdryer
Bathrooms: 2 Ensuite

    AAA Tourism ★★★★

Situated in a unique and idyllic riverfront location on the beautiful Murray River 10 mins east of Mandurah. You can sit back on your terrace and appreciate an arm chair view of the river through gum trees. It is an ideal place to relax while on holiday or unwind and/or entertain if on business. An exclusive guest lounge, dining, kitchenette and terrace overlook the river. The lounge has internet, plasma HD TV, DVD, wine cellar, refrigerator, microwave, toaster and 24/7 tea & coffee.

Margaret River

The Noble Grape *Luxury B&B & Guest House*
Rodney & Donna Carter
Lot 18, Bussell Highway
Cowaramup
WA 6284
12 km N of Margaret River

Tel (08) 9755 5538
or 0418 931 721
Fax (08) 9755 5538
stay@noblegrape.com.au
www.noblegrape.com.au

Double $130-$160 Single $110-$130
Children $15
Continental breakfast
Extra adult $25
Visa MC Diners Amex Eftpos accepted
7 Queen 4 Single (6 bdrm)
Bathrooms: 6 Ensuite

The Noble Grape is an intimate Guesthouse in the heart of the Margaret River Wine Region. Colonial style charm with quaint antiques nestled in an English cottage garden. Vineyards, beaches, galleries, chocolate and cheese factories minutes away. Enjoy a leisurely breakfast in our dining room overlooking the garden while watching the native birdlife. Spacious country style rooms with ensuite & hairdryer, r.c. air-conditioning, TV, DVD, refrigerator, tea/coffee, comfortable arm chairs and private courtyard. Guest barbecue. Wireless Internet Access. Room with universal access. Smoking outside only.

Margaret River

Rosewood Guesthouse *Luxury B&B & Separate Suite*
Jane & Keith Purdie
54 Wallcliffe Road
Margaret River
WA 6285
1 km W of Post Office

Tel (08) 9757 2845
or 0427 772 911
Fax (08) 9757 3509
info@rosewoodguesthouse.com.au
www.rosewoodguesthouse.com.au

Double $155-$185
Single $149-$185
Special breakfast
Suite $189-$250 double
Extra guests from $39, max 4
Visa MC Eftpos accepted
2 King/Twin4 King 1 Queen (6 bdrm)
5 B&B plus 1 spa suite
Bathrooms: 6 Ensuite Suite has 2 person spa bath

The Rosewood Guesthouse, Silver winners 2006 WA Tourism for Hosted Accommodation, beautifully appointed en-suite guestrooms & Grand Spa Suite. Log fire in guest lounge. Rosewood breakfasts feature the best regional produce. 7 minute walk to restaurants 4 minute drive to wineries. With beaches, caves and wineries we enjoy helping plan itineraries.

Perth

Perth, the capital of the West, embraced by tree clad hills and golden beaches, Experience the sight of molten gold at the Mint or a trip to explore the Cultural Centre or relax in Kings Park's botanical haven with a birds eye view of the city by day or night.

Take a ferry down the Swan River to Fremantle, our historic port. Continue to Rottnest Island and enjoy a swim in a magnificent peaceful bay, watch for whales, dolphins or cycle around the island and meet the quokkas. On your return visit the magnificent new Maritime Museum or the Old Fremantle Jail before choosing a restaurant harbour side or in the cappuccino strip.

Visit the Swan Valley vineyards for wines, cheeses and other fresh products or wander into the hills to experience the wildflowers.
Jack Tucker, Caesia House.

Perth

Pension of Perth *B&B*
Hoon & Steve Hall
3 Throssell Street
Perth
WA 6000
1 km N of Perth

Tel (08) 9228 9049
or 0421 739 443
Fax (08) 9228 9290
stay@pensionperth.com.au
www.pensionperth.com.au

Double $150 Single $120
Children $30
Full breakfast
Discounts for long stays
Visa MC Eftpos accepted
1 King 4 Queen 1 Single (5 bdrm)
1 Flat - Queen plus Single
Bathrooms: 4 Ensuite 1 Private

AAA Tourism
★★★★

The Pension of Perth is the perfect choice for couples looking for a special place to stay or business travellers wanting somewhere that is value for money, sophisticated, homely and private. It has the amenities of a fine hotel. The luxurious refurbishment reflects the elegance and comfort of its origins in 1897. It overlooks Hyde Park. Within walking distance from the centre of Perth. Our A-la-carte breakfast menu will make your stay memorable.

Perth - Mt Lawley

Durack House Bed and Breakfast *Luxury B&B*
Sandra and Bill Durack
7 Almondbury Road
Mt Lawley Perth
WA 6050
3 km N of Perth

Tel (08) 9370 4305
durackhouse@westnet.com.au
www.durackhouse.com.au

Double $150-$180
Single $130-$150
Special breakfast
Visa MC accepted
1 King/Twin 2 Queen (3 bdrm)
Bathrooms: 3 Ensuite

  AAA Tourism ★★★★

Durack House is an Edwardian home in quiet, leafy suburb, only 300m from bus/train and 3km from City. R/C air-conditioning, TVs, DVDs, electric blankets, hairdryers, comfortable beds and a cosy sitting room exclusive to guests. Relax in lush gardens after a busy day. Enjoy a complimentary drink each evening in the open courtyard. Sightseeing, shopping, beautiful Swan River and Kings Park within easy reach. The vibrant café strip on Beaufort Street is within walking distance, with an excellent selection of fine dining and affordable restaurants.

Perth - Nedlands

Caesia House Nedlands *B&B & Homestay*
Jane & David Tucker
32 Thomas Street
Nedlands, Perth
WA 6009
5 km W of Perth Central City

Tel (08) 9389 8174
or 1800 008 206
Fax (08) 9389 8173
tuckers@iinet.net.au
www.caesiahouse.com

Double $110-$140
Single $100-$125
Special breakfast
Visa MC accepted
1 King/Twin1 King 1 Queen (2 bdrm)
Bathrooms: 2 Ensuite

A quiet serene oasis in the city, only 7 minutes from Perth city centre and Kings Park, within walking distance to numerous cafés, or wonderful riverside BBQ/picnic spots. Close to UWA, bus to historic Fremantle, and beaches or Perth City centre. Convenient base for day trips to scenic Rottnest Island, the Swan Valley to savour those wines or wildflowers in Perth Hills. Off street parking, ground floor ensuite room in our guest wing. Enjoy a WA breakfast, in our dining room overlooking the sparkling pool!

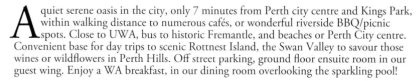

Perth - Trigg

Trigg Retreat Bed and Breakfast *B&B*

Sue Stein
59 Kitchener Street
Trigg
WA 6029
15 km N of Perth

Tel (08) 9447 6726
or 0417 911 048
Fax (08) 9447 6525
sue@triggretreat.com
www.triggretreat.com

Double $130-$150
Single $95-$110
Full breakfast
Visa MC Eftpos accepted
1 King/Twin 3 Queen (4 bdrm)
Bathrooms: 4 Ensuite

AAA Tourism
★★★★☆

An affordable indulgence! 4.5 star tastefully furnished two-storey home. Four bedrooms with ensuite, A/C, luxurious queen or twin beds, TV, DVD, fridge, tea/coffee, broadband wireless access, bedside treats. A gourmet, continental breakfast, served in guest dining room or garden courtyard. Optional hot selection available from enticing menu. A computer and unlimited access to the internet provided free. 'Stroll to the beach', exquisite WA coastline, walking, riding paths and cafés. Airport - 30 min direct route. Guest and owners facilities are separate. Prepare to be pampered!

Colimberie B&B
Bunbury
*"We arrived frazzled and left restored. Perfect for a family.
Comfortably furnished with fresh flowers and books. A delight
for the body and soul."*
Deborah Uzzell, Mtunzine, South Africa.

Peppermint Lane Lodge
Ferguson Valley
*"5 star accommodation on a peaceful and tranquil setting.
Beautifully appointed rooms, comfy beds and excellent friendly
service The evening meal is heartedly recommended."*
Jane Campbell, Alfrick, UK

Index by Location

Y

Index by Name of Acommodation

A

B

C

Accomodation Welcoming Pets

ACT

Canberra - Hall: Surveyor's Hill Winery and B&B

New South Wales

Armidale: Poppys Cottage
Bathurst: Elm Tree Cottage
Bathurst: A Winter-Rose Cottage B&B
Bega Valley - Bemboka: Giba Gunyah Country Cottages
Bermagui: Bellbird Cottage
Berry - Kangaroo Valley: Wombat Hill B&B
Candelo - Bega Valley: Bumblebrook Farm
Cobargo: Old Cobargo Convent
Glen Innes - Ben Lomond: Silent Grove Farmstay B&B
Grafton - Seelands: Seeview Farm
Hunter Valley - Aberdeen - Scone: Craigmhor Mountain Retreat
Hunter Valley - Lochinvar: Lochinvar House
Kangaroo Valley: The Loveshack
Lismore: Suzanne's Hideaway
Manilla Tamworth District: Oakhampton Homestead & Country Holidays
Narooma - Tilba: Pub Hill Farm
Newcastle - Hamilton: Hamilton Heritage
Orange: Greentrees
Port Macquarie - Camden Haven: Penlan Cottage
Port Macquarie - Camden Haven: Cherry Tree Cottage
Port Macquarie - Camden Haven: Benbellen Country Retreat
Sydney: Bed & Breakfast Sydney Central
Taree: Tallowood Ridge
Thredbo - Jindabyne - Snowy Mountains: Bimblegumbie
Ulladulla: Ulladulla Guest House
Yass: Kerrowgair
Young - Cootamundra: Old Nubba Schoolhouse

Northern Territory

Alice Springs: Kathy's Place Bed & Breakfast
Alice Springs: The Hideaway

Queensland

Brisbane - St Lucia - Toowong: Kensington
Cairns - Holloways Beach: Billabong B&B
Cairns - Stratford: Lilybank
Gold Coast Hinterland - Nerang: Riviera Bed & Breakfast

Hervey Bay - Howard: Montrave House B&B
Home & Pet Stay
Kuranda - Cairns: Koah Bed & Breakfast
Stanthorpe: Jireh

South Australia

Adelaide - North Adelaide: Cornwall Park
Heritage Accommodation
Adelaide - Seacliff Park - Brighton: Homestay
Brighton
Adelaide - Somerton Park: Forstens Bed &
Breakfast
Barossa Valley - Lyndoch - Tanunda: Bellescapes
Mount Gambier: Apartments on Tolmie

Tasmania

Port Arthur - Taranna: Norfolk Bay Convict
Station

Victoria

Alexandra: Idlewild Park Farm Accommodation
Bairnsdale: Tara House
Bright: Tyntynder Lodge Holiday Cottages
Cudgewa - Corryong: Elmstead Cottages
Dandenong Ranges: Candlelight Cottages Retreat
Dandenong Ranges - Mount Dandenong:
Observatory Cottages
Grampians - Halls Gap: Welch's on Wildflower
Heathcote - Goldfields: Emeu Inn Bed &
Breakfast, Restaurant and Wine Centre
Horsham: Orange Grove B&B
Melbourne - Fairfield: Fairfield Guest House
Wangaratta: The Pelican
Yackandandah - Beechworth - Albury: Time After
Time
Yarra Valley - Dandenong Ranges: Stringybark

Western Australia

Albany: Charnigup Farm Bed & Breakfast
Mandurah - North Yunderup: Nautica Lodge

Accommodation Welcoming Children

ACT

Canberra - Hall: Surveyor's Hill Winery and B&B

New South Wales

Adaminaby - Snowy Mountains: Reynella

Homestead
Albury: Elizabeth's Manor
Alstonville - Ballina: Hume's Hovell
Armidale: Poppys Cottage
Armidale: Armidale Boutique Accommodation
Batemans Bay: Chalet Swisse Spa
Bathurst: Elm Tree Cottage
Bawley Point: Interludes at Bawley
Bega Valley - Bemboka: Giba Gunyah Country
Cottages
Bellingen: Bellingen Heritage Cottages
Bermagui: Bellbird Cottage
Berry - Kangaroo Valley: Wombat Hill B&B
Blue Mountains - Lawson: Araluen
Blue Mountains - Lithgow: Majic Views B&B
Blue Mountains - Wentworth Falls: Blue
Mountains Lakeside
Blue Mountains - Wentworth Falls: Den Fenella
Lodge
Blue Mountains - Woodford: Braeside
Candelo - Bega Valley: Bumblebrook Farm
Crookwell: Markdale Homestead
Glen Innes: Queenswood - The Quiet One
Glen Innes - Ben Lomond: Silent Grove Farmstay
B&B
Gloucester - Barrington Tops: Arrowee House
B&B
Grafton - Seelands: Seeview Farm
Gunning: Frankfield Guest House
Hunter Valley - Aberdeen - Scone: Craigmhor
Mountain Retreat
Hunter Valley - Lochinvar: Lochinvar House
Hunter Valley - Lovedale - Pokolbin: Hill Top
Country Guest House
Hunter Valley - Pokolbin: Catersfield House
Hunter Valley - Pokolbin: Elfin Hill
Hunter Valley - Wine Country - Wollombi:
Capers Guest House and Cottage
Jervis Bay - Vincentia: Nelson Beach Lodge
Jindabyne - Snowy Mountains: Troldhaugen
Lodge
Kangaroo Valley: The Loveshack
Kiama: Kiama Bed & Breakfast
Kiama: Kiama Sea Mist Cottage
Kiama: Seashells Kiama
Lismore: Suzanne's Hideaway
Manilla Tamworth District: Oakhampton
Homestead & Country Holidays
Merimbula: Robyn's Nest Guest House
Milton - Ulladulla: Meadowlake Lodge
Myall Lakes - Bulahdelah: Bombah Point Eco
Cottages
Narooma - Tilba: Pub Hill Farm
Narromine: Camerons Farmstay
Newcastle: Newcomen B&B

Newcastle - Hamilton: Hamilton Heritage
Newcastle - Merewether: Merewether Beach B&B
Orange: Greentrees
Parkes: The Old Parkes Convent
Parkes: Kadina B&B
Port Macquarie - Camden Haven: Penlan Cottage
Port Macquarie - Camden Haven: Cherry Tree
Cottage
Port Macquarie - Camden Haven: Benbellen
Country Retreat
Southern Highlands - Moss Vale: Heronswood
House
Sydney: Bed & Breakfast Sydney Central
Sydney - Balmain: The Grange B&B
Sydney - Engadine: Engadine Bed & Breakfast
Sydney - Glebe: Cathie Lesslie Bed & Breakfast
Sydney - Hunters Hill: Magnolia House Bed &
Breakfast
Sydney - Newtown: Chloe's Bed & Breakfast
Sydney - Northern Beaches Peninsula: The
Pittwater Bed & Breakfast
Sydney - Parramatta: Harborne Bed & Breakfast
Sydney - Potts Point: Simpsons of Potts Point
Boutique Hotel
Sydney - Rose Bay: Syl's Sydney Homestay
Sydney - Scotland Island: Scotland Island Lodge
Sydney-Chatswood: The Charrington of
Chatswood
Taree: Tallowood Ridge
Thredbo: Alpenhorn
Thredbo - Jindabyne - Snowy Mountains:
Bimblegumbie
Tilba Tilba - Narooma: Green Gables
Ulladulla: Ulladulla Guest House
Wellington: Carinya B&B
Yass: Kerrowgair
Yass - Rye Park: The Old School
Young - Cootamundra: Old Nubba Schoolhouse

Northern Territory

Alice Springs: Kathy's Place Bed & Breakfast
Alice Springs: The Hideaway
Darwin - Malak: Beale's Bedfish & Breakfast

Queensland

Airlie Beach - Whitsunday: Whitsunday Moorings
B&B
Brisbane - Birkdale: Birkdale Bed & Breakfast
Brisbane - Paddington - Rosalie: Fern Cottage
B&B
Brisbane - St Lucia - Toowong: Kensington
Brisbane - West End: Eskdale Bed & Breakfast
Brisbane Central: La Torretta Bed & Breakfast
Cairns - Edge Hill: Galvin's Edge Hill Bed and
Breakfast
Cairns - Lake Tinaroo: Tinaroo Haven Holiday
Lodge
Daintree - Cow Bay: Cow Bay Homestay
Gold Coast Hinterland - Nerang: Riviera Bed &
Breakfast
Hervey Bay - Howard: Montrave House B&B
Home & Pet Stay
Kuranda - Cairns: Koah Bed & Breakfast
Noosa - Lake Weyba: Eumarella Shores Lake
Retreat
Noosa Hinterland - Cooroy: Cudgerie Homestead
B&B
Rockhampton - Capricorn Coast: Brae Bothy
B&B
Stanthorpe: Jireh
Sunshine Coast Hinterland - Glasshouse
Mountains: Glass on Glasshouse

South Australia

Adelaide - Burnside - St Georges: Kirkendale
Adelaide - Glenelg: Water Bay Villa Bed &
Breakfast
Adelaide - Largs Bay: Seapod B&B
Adelaide - North Adelaide: Cornwall Park
Heritage Accommodation
Adelaide - Seacliff Park - Brighton: Homestay
Brighton
Adelaide - Somerton Park: Forstens Bed &
Breakfast
Adelaide Hills - Mt Pleasant: Saunders Gorge
Sanctuary
Barossa Valley - Lyndoch - Tanunda: Bellescapes
Barossa Valley - Tanunda: Goat Square Cottages
Kangaroo Island: Cape Cassini Wilderness Retreat
Meningie - Narrung: Poltalloch Station
Middleton - Fleurieu Peninsula: Wenton Farm
Holiday Cottages
Mount Gambier: Apartments on Tolmie

Tasmania

Deloraine: Bowerbank Mill B&B
Hobart - Battery Point - Sandy Bay: Grande Vue
& Star Apartments
Hobart - Lindisfarne: Orana House
Launceston: Trevallyn House B&B
Port Arthur - Taranna: Norfolk Bay Convict
Station
Richmond: Mulberry Cottage B&B
Richmond: Mrs Curries Bed and Breakfast

Victoria

Alexandra: Idlewild Park Farm Accommodation

Apollo Bay: Arcady Homestead
Apollo Bay - Great Ocean Road: Claerwen Retreat
Bairnsdale: Tara House
Bendigo: Arbroath Lodge
Bright: Tyntynder Lodge Holiday Cottages
Cudgewa - Corryong: Elmstead Cottages
Dandenong Ranges: Candlelight Cottages Retreat
Dandenong Ranges - Mount Dandenong:
    Observatory Cottages
Euroa: Forlonge Bed & Breakfast Euroa
Grampians - Halls Gap: Welch's on Wildflower
Grampians - Wartook Valley: The Grelco Run
Heathcote: Hut on the Hill
Heathcote - Goldfields: Emeu Inn Bed &
    Breakfast, Restaurant and Wine Centre
Horsham: Orange Grove B&B
Macedon Ranges - Sunbury: Rupertswood
    Mansion
Melbourne - Camberwell: Springfields
Melbourne - Fairfield: Fairfield Guest House
Melbourne - St Kilda: Bishopsgate House
Melbourne - St Kilda: Alrae Bed & Breakfast
Princetown - Twelve Apostles: Arabella Country
    House
Sarsfield - Bairnsdale: Stringybark Cottages B&B
Torquay - Surf Coast: Ocean Manor B&B
Wangaratta: The Pelican
Warrnambool: Manor Gums
Warrnambool: Quamby Homestead
Wilsons Promontory: saltwater @ sandypoint
Wilsons Promontory - Waratah North: Bayview
    House
Yackandandah - Beechworth - Albury: Time After
    Time
Yarra Valley - Dandenong Ranges: Stringybark

Western Australia

Bunbury: Colomberie B&B
Dongara - Geraldton: Gracelyn B&B
Fremantle: Terrace Central B&B
Mandurah - North Yunderup: Nautica Lodge
Margaret River: The Noble Grape
Perth: Pension of Perth

Accommodation with Easy Access

ACT

Canberra - Hall: Surveyor's Hill Winery and B&B

New South Wales

Alstonville - Ballina: Hume's Hovell
Armidale: Armidale Boutique Accommodation
Bega Valley - Bemboka: Giba Gunyah Country
    Cottages
Bellingen - Urunga: Aquarelle Bed & Breakfast
Berry - Kangaroo Valley: Barefoot Springs
Berry - South Coast NSW: Broughton Mill Farm
    Guesthouse Berry
Blue Mountains - Lithgow: Majic Views B&B
Blue Mountains - Springwood: Southall
Byron Bay: Victoria's at Ewingsdale & Victoria's
    at Watego's
Candelo - Bega Valley: Bumblebrook Farm
Coffs Harbour: Boambee Palms Bed & Breakfast
Coffs Harbour - Sawtell: Creekside Inn (formerly
    Alamanda Lodge)
Crookwell: Markdale Homestead
Dorrigo: Lisnagarvey Cottage
Glen Innes - Ben Lomond: Silent Grove Farmstay
    B&B
Gloucester - Barrington Tops: Arrowee House
    B&B
Hawkesbury - Colo: Ossian Hall
Hunter Valley - Aberdeen - Scone: Craigmhor
    Mountain Retreat
Hunter Valley - Lochinvar: Lochinvar House
Hunter Valley - Lovedale - Pokolbin: Hill Top
    Country Guest House
Hunter Valley - Pokolbin: Catersfield House
Hunter Valley - Pokolbin: Elfin Hill
Hunter Valley - Wollombi - Laguna: Judsons at
    Laguna
Jervis Bay - Huskisson: Dolphin Sands Jervis Bay
Lismore: Suzanne's Hideaway
Manilla Tamworth District: Oakhampton
    Homestead & Country Holidays
Merimbula: Robyn's Nest Guest House
Myall Lakes - Bulahdelah: Bombah Point Eco
    Cottages
Newcastle - Hamilton: Hamilton Heritage
Orange: Greentrees
Pacific Palms - Coomba: Whitby on Wallis B&B
Southern Highlands - Moss Vale: Heronswood
    House
Ulladulla: Ulladulla Guest House
Wollongong - Mount Pleasant - South Coast:
    Above Wollongong at Pleasant Heights
    B&B
Yass: Kerrowgair

Northern Territory

Darwin - Malak: Beale's Bedfish & Breakfast

Queensland

Cairns - Lake Tinaroo: Tinaroo Haven Holiday Lodge
Cairns - Stratford: Lilybank
Hervey Bay - Howard: Melvos Country House
Kuranda - Cairns: Koah Bed & Breakfast
Noosa - Peregian: Lake Weyba Cottages
Rockhampton - Capricorn Coast: Brae Bothy B&B
Sunshine Coast Hinterland - Maleny: Braeside Bed & Breakfast
Yeppoon - Capricorn Coast: While Away B&B

South Australia

Adelaide - North Adelaide: Cornwall Park Heritage Accommodation
Middleton - Fleurieu Peninsula: Wenton Farm Holiday Cottages

Tasmania

Beauty Point: Pomona Spa Cottages
Hobart - Lindisfarne: Orana House
Richmond: Mrs Curries Bed and Breakfast

Victoria

Apollo Bay: Arcady Homestead
Apollo Bay - Great Ocean Road: Claerwen Retreat
Beechworth: Country Charm Swiss Cottages
Euroa: Forlonge Bed & Breakfast Euroa
Grampians - Halls Gap: Mountain Grand Boutique Hotel
Macedon Ranges - Sunbury: Rupertswood Mansion
Melbourne - Fairfield: Fairfield Guest House
Princetown - Twelve Apostles: Arabella Country House
Sarsfield - Bairnsdale: Stringybark Cottages B&B
Warrnambool: Quamby Homestead

Western Australia

Albany: Charnigup Farm Bed & Breakfast
Margaret River: The Noble Grape

Accomodation with Outstanding Gardens

New South Wales

Alstonville - Ballina: Hume's Hovell
Ballina: Brundah B&B
Batemans Bay: Chalet Swisse Spa
Bathurst: Elm Tree Cottage
Bathurst: A Winter-Rose Cottage B&B
Bawley Point: Interludes at Bawley
Bega Valley - Bemboka: Giba Gunyah Country Cottages
Bellingen: Bellingen Heritage Cottages
Berrima: Berrima Guest House
Berry - Kangaroo Valley: Barefoot Springs
Berry - Kangaroo Valley: Wombat Hill B&B
Berry - South Coast NSW: Broughton Mill Farm Guesthouse Berry
Blue Mountains - Lawson: Araluen
Blue Mountains - Leura: Woodford of Leura
Blue Mountains - Leura: Broomelea
Blue Mountains - Leura: Bethany Manor Bed & Breakfast
Blue Mountains - Springwood: Southall
Blue Mountains - Wentworth Falls: Whispering Pines' Chalet Fontanelle
Byron Bay: Victoria's at Ewingsdale & Victoria's at Watego's
Byron Bay Hinterland: Green Mango Hideaway
Central Coast - Terrigal: AnDaCer Boutique B&B
Coffs Harbour: Boambee Palms Bed & Breakfast
Coffs Harbour - Sawtell: Creekside Inn (formerly Alamanda Lodge)
Corrimal - Wollongong: Corrimal Beach Bed & Breakfast
Crookwell: Markdale Homestead
Gunning: Frankfield Guest House
Hawkesbury - Colo: Ossian Hall
Hunter Valley - Lochinvar: Lochinvar House
Hunter Valley - Morpeth: Morpeth Convent Guest House
Hunter Valley - Pokolbin: Catersfield House
Hunter Valley - Pokolbin: Elfin Hill
Hunter Valley - Wine Country - Wollombi: Capers Guest House and Cottage
Hunter Valley - Wollombi - Laguna: Judsons at Laguna
Jervis Bay - Huskisson: Dolphin Sands Jervis Bay
Jervis Bay - Vincentia: Nelson Beach Lodge
Kiama: Kiama Bed & Breakfast
Kiama: Bed and Views Kiama
Lismore: Suzanne's Hideaway
Manilla Tamworth District: Oakhampton Homestead & Country Holidays
Merimbula: Robyn's Nest Guest House
Milton - Ulladulla: Meadowlake Lodge
Narromine: Camerons Farmstay
Newcastle: Newcomen B&B
Newcastle - Hamilton: Hamilton Heritage
Orange: Greentrees

Port Macquarie: Woodlands Bed & Breakfast
Port Macquarie - Camden Haven: Penlan Cottage
Port Macquarie - Camden Haven: Cherry Tree Cottage
Port Macquarie - Camden Haven: Benbellen Country Retreat
Southern Highlands - Bowral: Chorleywood B&B
Sydney - Engadine: Engadine Bed & Breakfast
Sydney - Glebe: Tricketts
Sydney - Manly - Balgowlah Heights: LillyPilly Cottage
Sydney - Newtown: Chloe's Bed & Breakfast
Tamworth: Jacaranda Cottage Bed & Breakfast
Taree: Tallowood Ridge
Thredbo - Jindabyne - Snowy Mountains: Bimblegumbie
Tilba Tilba - Narooma: Green Gables
Ulladulla: Ulladulla Guest House
Wellington: Carinya B&B
Wollongong - Mount Pleasant - South Coast: Above Wollongong at Pleasant Heights B&B
Yass: Kerrowgair

Northern Territory

Alice Springs: Nthaba Cottage B&B
Alice Springs: Kathy's Place Bed & Breakfast
Darwin - Fogg Dam - Humpty Doo: Eden at Fogg Dam

Queensland

Airlie Beach - Whitsunday: Whitsunday Moorings B&B
Brisbane - Birkdale: Birkdale Bed & Breakfast
Brisbane - Paddington - Rosalie: Fern Cottage B&B
Brisbane - St Lucia - Toowong: Kensington
Bundaberg: Inglebrae
Cairns - Edge Hill: Galvin's Edge Hill Bed and Breakfast
Cairns - Holloways Beach: Billabong B&B
Cairns - Stratford: Lilybank
Cairns Hinterland - Kuranda: Cadaghi Cottage
Daintree - Cow Bay: Cow Bay Homestay
Gold Coast Hinterland - Nerang: Riviera Bed & Breakfast
Hervey Bay: Alexander Lakeside B&B
Hervey Bay - Howard: Melvos Country House
Hervey Bay - Howard: Montrave House B&B Home & Pet Stay
Noosa - Noosa Valley: Noosa Valley Manor Luxury B&B
Noosa - Peregian: Lake Weyba Cottages
Rockhampton - Capricorn Coast: Brae Bothy

B&B
Sunshine Coast Hinterland - Glasshouse Mountains: Glass on Glasshouse
Sunshine Coast Hinterland - Montville: Secrets on the Lake
Sunshine Coast Hinterland - Mooloolah Valley: Mooloolah Valley Holidays

South Australia

Adelaide - Burnside - St Georges: Kirkendale
Adelaide - Glenelg: Water Bay Villa Bed & Breakfast
Adelaide - North Adelaide: Cornwall Park Heritage Accommodation
Alelaide - Rostrevor: Morialta Bed & Breakfast
Barossa Valley - Tanunda: Goat Square Cottages
Goolwa: Vue de M B&B
Naracoorte: Dartmoor Homestead

Tasmania

Beauty Point: Pomona Spa Cottages
Deloraine: Bowerbank Mill B&B
Devonport - Port Sorell: Tranquilles
Hobart - Lindisfarne: Orana House
Hobart - Rose Bay: Roseneath Bed & Breakfast
Launceston: Edenholme Grange
Port Arthur - Taranna: Norfolk Bay Convict Station
Richmond: Mrs Curries Bed and Breakfast

Victoria

Alexandra: Idlewild Park Farm Accommodation
Apollo Bay: Point of View
Apollo Bay - Great Ocean Road: Glenoe Cottages
Bairnsdale: Tara House
Beechworth: Kinross Guest House
Beechworth: Country Charm Swiss Cottages
Bendigo: Arbroath Lodge
Cudgewa - Corryong: Elmstead Cottages
Dandenong Ranges: Candlelight Cottages Retreat
Dandenong Ranges - Mount Dandenong: Observatory Cottages
Gippsland - Nilma North: Springbank B&B
Grampians - Halls Gap: Welch's on Wildflower
Grampians - Wartook: Wartook Gardens
Heathcote - Goldfields: Emeu Inn Bed & Breakfast, Restaurant and Wine Centre
Horsham: Orange Grove B&B
Lorne - Otway Ranges - Birregurra: Elliminook
Macedon Ranges - Mount Macedon: Craigielea Mountain Retreat
Melbourne - Blackburn: Treetops Bed & Breakfast
Mildura: Mildura's Linsley House

Mornington - Mount Eliza: Sartain's at
    Mornington
Phillip Island: Glen Isla House
Phillip Island - Cowes: Genesta House
Sarsfield - Bairnsdale: Stringybark Cottages B&B
Sorrento - Mornington Peninsula: Tamasha House
Warrnambool: Merton Manor Exclusive B&B
Warrnambool: Quamby Homestead
Wilsons Promontory - Waratah North: Bayview
    House
Yackandandah - Beechworth: Time After Time
Yarra Valley - Dandenong Ranges: Holly Gate
    House Bed and Breakfast

Western Australia

Albany: Charnigup Farm Bed & Breakfast
Mandurah - North Yunderup: Nautica Lodge
Margaret River: The Noble Grape
Margaret River: Rosewood Guesthouse
Perth - Mt Lawley: Durack House B&B
Perth - Nedlands: Caesia House Nedlands

Accommodation with Winery Activities

ACT

Canberra - Hall: Surveyor's Hill Winery and B&B

New South Wales

Armidale: Poppys Cottage
Bawley Point: Interludes at Bawley
Hunter Valley - Wine Country - Wollombi:
    Capers Guest House and Cottage
Kiama: Seashells Kiama

South Australia

Barossa Valley - Tanunda: Goat Square Cottages

Tasmania

Devonport - Port Sorell: Tranquilles
Richmond: Mulberry Cottage B&B

Victoria

Grampians - Halls Gap: Mountain Grand
    Boutique Hotel
Heathcote - Goldfields: Emeu Inn Bed &
    Breakfast, Restaurant and Wine Centre

Western Australia

Mandurah - North Yunderup: Nautica Lodge

APPENDIX

1989-2008 – THE BED & BREAKFAST BOOK – 20 YEARS OLD

The Australian Bed & Breakfast Book began when Jim Thomas, publisher of The New Zealand Bed & Breakfast Book, which had its first edition in 1987, and Elaine Taylor a B&B host in Dee Why, Sydney, began working together to compile a collection of B&B hosts across Australia. This was in the days before desk-top publishing software and emails, so in the first few editions text and photos were literally cut and pasted onto sheets of paper before being printed.

The first edition of The Australian Bed & Breakfast Book hit the shelves in 1989. This year is our Twentieth Anniversary Edition, and as a celebration we include two additional features about B&Bs. To begin, a story by one of our original hosts from the first edition. Miriam Cooper and her husband set up and ran Holm Lodge from 1986 to 2000. Located on the waterfront at Bellerive in Hobart, it is still operating to this day. Miriam now runs Mulberry Cottage in Richmond, Tasmania, where she also presents a unique theatre performance for guests depicting the life and times of the many early inhabitants of Mulberry Cottage.

Miriam's story is fascinating in that she is one of the few B&B hosts who run their B&B to provide her major income. Furthermore she was one of the early pioneers of the B&B industry in Australia. There are many hosts who would love to emulate Miriam's achievements; her thorough research, enterprise and good fortune have enabled her to create a successful B&B.

We are often asked by potential hosts, "What do I need to do to open my B&B?" So in celebration of our 20 years we have reprinted out Hints for Getting Started first published many years ago. It was prepared as a basic guide for new hosts and though somewhat dated in its topics on technology, it still encompasses the same essential elements for a successful B&B: a love of people, well presented accommodation and a willingness to offer generous hospitality.

Mulberry Cottage B&B and The Project At Grannie Rhodes' Cottage

Have you ever stayed in a B&B that offers you a show or slept over the site of where 200 sticks of dynamite lay hidden?

In February 2000, I was in Richmond for lunch when I bumped into an acquaintance. "Miriam! I thought I might see you here; you live here don't you?" I can still remember the spot on the pavement where I stood and thought, "No, I don't . . . but I could." I had always wanted to live in Richmond. Thirty years before, we had almost bought two of the village's gracious old homes. Now my marriage had just split, the opportunity just might be here again.

Richmond is one of Australia's best preserved Georgian villages with the oldest bridge, Roman Catholic Church and gaol together with many lovely buildings.

I went straight to the local real estate agent and asked, "What have you got in Georgian Cottages?" He replied, "I have the very thing for you! Reid's or Grannie Rhodes' Cottage, circa 1830 and derelict!" I believe, in the real estate business, this is what is called an emotional buy! I took one look at it and bought it.

The cottage proved to be too much of a challenge to restore and renovate for habitation. So I planned to use it for a museum and build a new copy cottage adjacent to it. Subsequent to fascinating research about Grannie, I abandoned the museum idea to develop the project from a different angle: the theatre. Turn the Key of Time is an award winning innovative and interpretive performance depicting the history of the occupants of the heritage listed building from 1804 to the present day.

In the early 1800's a small number of women came to Van Diemen's Land to join their husbands who were already serving sentences. This story is of Mary Wilby and her three daughters, who were such a family. One of these girls, Maria, became the legendary villager, Grannie Rhodes of Richmond. The performance gives insight into the life of the times, both back in England with the sentencing of the father, the voyage out and the difficult life in the new land. The stories, researched, written and performed by myself, are told to enwrap the visitor in the changing atmospheres of two hundred years of history, including the finding of the key and discovery of enough buried dynamite to blow up all of Richmond!

Subsequently, I designed and built Mulberry Cottage in 2002 as an olde worlde private residence at the rear of the old cottage. It is constructed with reclaimed materials, including the wall from Hobart's Old Penitentiary and windows from Hobart's old Marine Board building. The building and gardens are designed to create a rustic and English country atmosphere and the visitor is truly tricked into believing that Mulberry Cottage is really1800's.

I had always loved the B&B. In the summer of 2003 several local accommodation places, being desperate for extra rooms, asked me to take some visitors to help out. I was so delighted to be offering accommodation again that I obtained permission to use the two attic rooms for accommodation. This proved such a success for one summer that I added two en-suite rooms and a guests' sitting room in a matching extension. Mulberry Cottage now operates as a traditional hosted B&B offering a range of accommodation to visitors both local and overseas.

The attraction at Grannie Rhodes' has become an integral part of the business at Mulberry Cottage B&B.

Bed
&
Breakfast

Hints for getting started

The Australian Bed & Breakfast Book

Hints For Getting Started –
Reprint Of Our Original Guide For New Hosts

First published by Moonshine Press, now included and revised to celebrate 20 years of publishing The Australian Bed & Breakfast Book.

What is Bed & Breakfast?

Bed & Breakfast has become a very popular form of personalised hospitality. Hospitality is defined in the Oxford Dictionary as "the friendly and generous welcome of friends or strangers", and it is the emphasis on friendliness and generosity which typifies Bed & Breakfast hospitality - generosity of a host's time, energy and resources.

B&B began in U.K. and Europe, and was usually a room in someone's home, where guests were treated courteously and generously. B&B has now travelled the world and has become universally popular. In our B&Bs guests are welcomed into a home as friends. We call this form of hospitality homestay or farmstay (when on farm holidays). B&B offered in the private home offers the essence of Bed & Breakfast and continues the tradition begun in Europe. More and more purpose-built facilities are now becoming available, some offering separate suites for privacy or completely self-contained accommodation, and although the levels of hospitality are reduced, they are included as they offer a style of accommodation similar in many ways to B&Bs.

Some B&Bs have changed with demand and become larger establishments, catering to a larger number of guests. Guest houses, as a choice of B&B, have become famous around the world, and are now popular in Australia. Recently we have seen B&B develop even further. Some people have restored grand old homes and now offer luxurious accommodation, where the emphasis is on indulgence and comfort with delicious, sometimes extravagant, breakfasts being served.

So the term "Bed and Breakfast" has come to mean a variety of styles of accommodation over time, but the one ingredient which remains constant is the personalised hospitality which is offered. B&B does not appeal to all travellers all of the time. There are times when we choose the anonymity of a hotel. But the B&B industry is rapidly growing, as people realise the delight of being welcomed into a home as a friend.

What Makes a Good B&B Host?

The main motivation for providing Bed and Breakfast must be that of offering hospitality to visitors. Anyone thinking that home hosting is a chance of an easy income will have to reconsider. To entertain guests takes time and energy, and the rewards are more likely to be personal than financial. In time you will receive a satisfactory number of guests; however the main benefit will be in new friends made and times shared.

The success of your B&B enterprise will depend on the effort you put into making your guests feel welcome. You must be tolerant and understanding and interested in offering generous hospitality. You will be talking with and entertaining people from a wide range of backgrounds, so you must be enthusiastic about chatting with and helping your guests.

In addition to your personal input, you will also need an ability to present your home and the food you prepare, attractively. While genuine friendliness is the most important ingredient, attractive presentation is also very important. It does not take any special training to be a good B&B host. Hosts are all ages from a wide variety of backgrounds. It is part of the delight for guests staying at B&Bs. Each one is a surprise.

Many hosts are in their 50s and 60s because this is the age when children have left home and there is spare room in the house. Many hosts are retired, which gives them time for the B&B demands. B&B requires quite a bit of time for extra cleaning, cooking, laundry, book-keeping, responding to mail and time for chatting to guests.

What Sort Of House is Suitable?

The wonderful thing about being a B&B host is that you need not spend a large amount before beginning your business. Your own home is probably an ideal home for B&B just as it is. The main requirement is a room which will be used exclusively as a guest room, and it must have a comfortable bed. In The Australian Bed & Breakfast Book we have a schedule of standards – Quality Assurance which we expect each host to maintain. The schedule is listed on a following page.

It is helpful if your home is in a centre which is already a source of guests, such as a thriving regional town, or a tourist centre. However this is not essential as these places will already have many accommodation alternatives. A very popular situation for B&Bs (especially the splendid country homes) is within 1-2 hours drive of the main cities. These homes attract visitors from the city who want a quiet time away from the hustle and bustle.

However, if your home is not in a popular area, it does not matter. Homes off the beaten track can be just as popular. The important thing is to begin. And it need not cost a lot to do it. Your home will be more popular if you can offer guests their own bathroom, but it is not necessary. Some of the most successful B&Bs are those with shared bathrooms. Your home must be clean and tidy, but it need not be grand. Some hosts have bought big colonial mansions to establish as B&Bs; but unless you are very comfortable financially, I suggest you cut your teeth from where you are and progress from there.

If a guest complains do not take it personally. Apologise and try to put it right if it is in your power to do so. Be knowledgeable about your area: be able to recommend walks and places to visit. If you haven't already been there, go soon before you are asked about them. Keep a supply of maps and brochures handy. A folder with plastic leaves for holding brochures is very handy as a reference book. Get to know your local history, local events and tourist spots.

The Guest Room

You must have a room especially for guests. It is not acceptable to have the room of a family member made available as required.

The most important parts of the guest room are clean comfortable beds. In our experience, a queen or king size is more popular than two singles, but if you only have one room with two singles, begin with these and see what happens. But they must be comfortable. The mattress might be one item you buy specially for your new enterprise.

There are many things you can do to make the guests' room attractive. Many hosts spend a great deal of effort to create an inviting, comfortable, or luxurious atmosphere, and they are rewarded for their efforts. The following are some suggestions which are not on our minimum list, but should be considered.

Create a welcoming feeling by having fresh flowers or fruit in your guests' room. Even a small vase of wild flowers adds charm. Create a feeling of generosity by providing large towels, two each if possible; two pillows also. Provide extra room for luggage, such as a table. Provide a seating area in the bedroom if space allows, so that guests do not have to sit on the bed.

If the bedroom is up or down stairs, mention this in your advertising material. Spend a night in the guests' beds (before they arrive). This will allow you to check the comfort of the bed, and also to check for unwelcome night-time disturbances such as noises and lights. Be aware of unwelcome bathroom noises.

Breakfast & Dinner

Breakfast is always provided unless indicated otherwise. In our experience Australian guests prefer to take their meals in a guest dining room, whereas many overseas guests enjoy breakfast with the hosts. If you have the time, a leisurely breakfast gives a great start to the guests' day, and yours too.

In self-contained accommodation, hosts leave the breakfast ingredients in the guests' refrigerator. Although this is convenient for the host and preferred by some guests, it lacks the personal warmth associated with a traditional B&B.

Some hosts make a feature of the breakfast. Make it as lovely as you can, and never skimp. Always provide plenty of food. It need not be haute cuisine but your guests should leave on a full stomach. An extra helping does not cost a lot. Even a continental breakfast should have plenty of toast or croissants, and tea or coffee.

Discuss breakfast the night before, so that guests know what to expect and so that you can be prepared. If possible, learn to cater for special diets.

Alter the menu and table setting, especially if guests stay more than one night. Use a variety of tableware, napkins and tablecloths. This stops preparing breakfast from becoming boring for you. Set breakfast in different places - on the sunny patio, in the dining room, or in the guests' bedroom.

Many hosts provide dinner. It is not necessary if there are restaurants nearby, but it gives you a chance to sit and chat with the guests, and gives a little extra income.

Many hosts like to serve wine with dinner, and with the relaxation in regulations it is now possible in some states to serve or sell wine and other beverages to your guest. Check out your regulations, as you will most likely need to have completed a cours in the Responsible serving of Alcohol.

First Impressions

B&B is a people business and you must do all you can to make prospective guests want to stay with you, and keep returning. Your home must of course be neat and tidy and inviting. It can be a chore to keep the house looking spic and span, but it will be worth the effort.

Your own appearance is important. When guests arrive you should be looking neat and tidy. A host wearing slippers does not make a guest feel relaxed. Obviously if you are working when guests arrive it is understandable to be in work clothes, but you need to be aware of looking unnecessarily scruffy.

Be aware of the delicate balance between hospitality and over-familiarity. Although most guests welcome the opportunity to talk to hosts, it is important to allow them the opportunity for privacy. Do not burden your guests with excessive chatter about your concerns. On the other hand be aware that personalised hospitality is what B&F is about, so be prepared to give your guests a reasonable amount of your time.

The telephone is an essential point of contact. If you are going to be away from home and do not want to miss calls there are several solutions. An answerphone is one possibility, but guests who are phoning for a bed that night can not afford to wait fo you to phone back.

Call diversion is very inexpensive, and means calls to your number can be diverted to any other number, such as your mobile phone whenever you go out. A cordless phone means you can work in the garden or anywhere in the house and have the phone with you.

It may seem clichéd but when you answer the phone, smile as you speak. The smile will carry straight down the wire.

Email is fast becoming the preferred choice for guests and hosts alike. It is low cost and convenient, but it lacks the warmth and personal touch of a phone call. It is easier with email to make enquiries to several different hosts almost at the same time. We must always remember that it is the human touch that many guests like about B&Bs so make it easy for them to call rather than send an email.

Money and Business Matters

Most B&B hosts earn only supplementary income from their B&B. Some, who have been operating their B&B for a while and have established a reputation, earn quite a bit more. You should keep a record of all guests, and declare the income. You will also be able to claim legitimate expenses. Contact your accountant, The Australian Taxation Office, the Department of Fair Trading and your local council for up to date information on business regulations and registration, taxation and rules applying in your area.

What you charge will depend on your facilities, location and demand. Check with other B&Bs and accommodation providers in your area. The rate should be proportionate to the value you offer. You will have to feel what is right, but we suggest that if you are unsure you should err on the inexpensive side. Some B&Bs which are busy during weekends offer a lower rate during midweek periods. Destinations which are busy during holiday periods also have a lower rate out of season.

Guests are always advised to book well in advance. This has mutual benefit as it offers security to you in running your business and guarantees guests their accommodation. You should ensure you offer written confirmation to confirmed reservations where possible. This should show guests' dates of arrival and departure, time of arrival, the room/s booked, how many guests in the party, whether children or pets are travelling as well and any special requirements. Indicate if minimum stays are required during peak periods, how much deposit is due and when full payment is required. Lastly always show your cancellation policy.

Most B&Bs now accept credit cards and it is worth considering having the facility, because by accepting credit cards you may attract additional guests. Most guests settle their account as they are leaving. Some hosts request payment when the guests arrive, which is more formal but has the advantage of sorting out any money misunderstandings before they become a problem

Hosts welcoming guests to stay at their accommodation aim to provide their guests with wonderful accommodation and great hospitality. But you should be aware of safety and security. Most hosts keep their terms and conditions to a minimum and some may invite guests to register on arrival and agree to their 'Conditions of Stay'. Prepare a registration card for guests to complete when they check in. It could include home address details, phone number and car registration number. Likewise you should provide them with an information sheet advising any special conditions, essential information and contact details in case of emergency. This could cover you as well as the host in case of an unforseen incident. Moreover it guarantees all guests that the accommodation will always offer the finest standards.

Regulations and Obligations

Most local councils now have regulations for operating a B&B. They can vary widely from one council to another, with some being openly supportive and others mildly tolerant. Some authorities allow you to offer two guest rooms for guests under complying development; with others you may need to submit a Development Application to the council. If you are a member of your state B&B association, they should be able to offer advice on how best to negotiate your way through the regulations.

Your insurance company should be notified that you are operating a B&B. Some such as AIB Insurance Brokers, located in Queensland, offer comprehensive policies designed for B&B operators. Your premium may be higher but you will feel safer in knowing that both you and your guests are covered in case of unforseen incidents. The policy should include public liability insurance: the figure of $10-$20 million is the usual today. Discuss with your insurance broker all the services you offer, particularly any additional activities such as horse riding, bikes for hire, and so on as this may affect your policy.

You will need to install smoke detectors in the bedrooms and elsewhere in the house. Check regulations with your local council or fire service.

You need not be available to accept every guest who calls with a booking enquiry. If it is not convenient, advise that you have no availability and suggest, or better still arrange, alternative accommodation. If you are not at home when guests call, they will simply try somewhere else.

You should allow some time with your guests. After they arrive some guests appreciate the opportunity for a talk, whilst others can't wait to relax in the privacy of their own room. Some hosts offer afternoon tea or a welcome glass of sparkling wine. The ambience of your accommodation often reflects your personality and may be one of the main reasons a guest chooses to stay with you.

Some hosts are well set-up to welcome families with children; others, such as those with accommodation on rural lands with open dams, are not suitable for children to wander freely. You should indicate if your accommodation is not suitable for children or is set up for the romantic or couples market. Similarly you should mention if you have pets, so that allergy sufferers are advised.

It is now established that all B&Bs do not allow smoking in rooms but most allow smoking outside. You should advise if you do not allow smoking at all on your property.

You can specify check in and check out times. When guests are likely to be travelling on, they will probably be keen to get away early. If you accommodation is focused towards the indulgent, relaxed or romantic market, you may find that guests prefer a much later check out.

Avoid misunderstandings and establish what you will charge for if you are asked or offer to do any extras. Taking your guests for a drive might be an extra for which you charge, or it might simply be a generous gesture.

Advertising

When you make up your mind to begin offering B&B accommodation and the room is ready, the first place to advertise is at the local visitor information centre. They may make a charge to list your name, or they may ask for a commission on guests they send you. It is often best to support them as they will usually support you later. But you may find that membership fees are quite high for a small B&B operator.

Producing a brochure can be helpful, but it can also be expensive for the results it brings. It pays to get professional help from a graphic designer because the design cost is only small in relation to the total production cost, but it makes a tremendous difference to your brochure. Find brochures you like and discuss these with the graphic designer.

Probably the most cost effective advertising is in a tourist guide book. Popular guides, such as The Australian Bed & Breakfast Book, are comparatively inexpensive to advertise. In the past many hosts joined their motoring association, now AAA Tourism. They are able to assess your property and award you with a star rating. You can then choose to advertise in one of their many publications. There are an increasing number of books, magazines and travel guides advertising B&Bs. Most print media offers a web presence as an inclusive or optional extra. There are also hundreds if not thousands of websites which will promote your accommodation. You have to be selective and go with what feels right.

There are many ways in which you can promote your B&B without spending too much. A sign at your gate will keep working for you at no cost. Check with your council about permissible sizes.

Agencies are a good source of guests. There are many agencies operating throughout the country and many hosts list with them. They take a commission for sending guests, but it should not cost you to list with them and they can be very worthwhile.

There are also benefits for you in joining your state B&B Association, such as booking services, guides and web presence. Each year the state B&B associations have annual meetings and seminars at which there is a wealth of information and topical issues are discussed.

The Australian B&B Book

The Australian Bed & Breakfast Book was first published in 1989 and is published each year around October. The Australian Bed & Breakfast Book is available in bookshops, newsagents and post offices, and is distributed through some visitor information centres, car rental offices in the main cities and air Travel and Gardening Shows held in capital cities each year.

We print 20,000 copies each year for distribution in Australia, New Zealand, the United States and the United Kingdom and Europe. We keep our advertising charges and the selling price of The Australian B&B Book as low as possible by keeping our publishing costs down. We maintain the highest publishing quality we can, offering a quality publication that is attractive in layout and strong in its construction.

The B&B Book is a cooperative venture, in that we offer incentives to hosts to assist with distribution. Hosts who distribute books to local outlets receive financial benefits. We guarantee that you will not lose by advertising in The Australian Bed & Breakfast Book. Your income will cover your listing fee. Our overseas distribution ensures that you are likely to receive a number of visitors from overseas. Hosts in The Australian B&B Book maintain that it is a most effective form of advertising.

We are committed to continue as the most popular B&B guide in Australia. If you would like more information about being listed in The Australian Bed & Breakfast Book, or if you have any queries that we have not covered, write to us with your questions.

The Australian Bed Breakfast Book
PO Box 330
Wahroonga
NSW 2076

Adelaide   (08) 8464 0959
Brisbane   (07) 3118 5959
Melbourne (03) 9017 5959
Perth   (08) 6363 5959
Sydney   (02) 8208 5959

info@BBBook.com.au
www.BBBook.com.au

For more detailed information contact Stewart Whyte, who publishes Starting and Running a B&B in Australia & New Zealand - A practical guide to setting up and managing a Bed & Breakfast. He also operates courses for aspiring B&B hosts as well as offering a selection of 'Do-it-Yourself' guides to assist hosts through the set up and running of a B&B. Email probe@bnb-central.com. Web: www.bnb-central.com

QUALITY ASSURANCE

Properties included in The Australian Bed & Breakfast Book offer a Commitment to Generous Hospitality and guarantee to offer the following standards

Housekeeping
◊ The Property is well maintained internally and externally
◊ Absolute cleanliness in all guest areas
◊ Absolute cleanliness in the kitchen, refrigerator and food storage areas
◊ All inside rooms are non-smoking unless indicated in the text

Hospitality
◊ Hosts present to welcome and farewell guests (unless advised in self-contained accommodation)
◊ Guests treated with courtesy and respect
◊ Guests have contact details if hosts leave the premises
◊ Room rates, booking and cancellation policy advised to guests
◊ Local tourism and transport information available.

Bedrooms
Bedrooms solely dedicated to guests with -
◊ bedroom heating and cooling appropriate to the climate
◊ fans and heating (alternatively reverse cycle air-conditioning)
◊ quality mattresses in sound condition on a sound base
◊ clean bedding appropriate to the climate, with extra available
◊ clean pillows with extra available
◊ bedside lighting for each guest
◊ blinds or curtains on all windows where appropriate
◊ night light or torch in case of power failures
◊ wardrobe space with selection of hangers
◊ adequate storage space
◊ good quality floor coverings in good condition
◊ adequate sized mirror
◊ power point
◊ alarm clock
◊ waste bin
◊ drinking glasses

Bathrooms
Sufficient bathroom and toilet facilities for all guests -
◊ bath or shower
◊ hand basin and mirror
◊ waste bin in bathroom
◊ extra toilet roll
◊ privacy lock on bathroom and toilet doors
◊ power point
◊ soap, towels, bathmat, facecloths, for each guest
◊ towels changed or dried daily for guests staying more than one night
◊ Towel rail/hook per guest in the bathroom or bedroom

Meals
◊ Drinks: water, tea and coffee offered or available
◊ Breakfast: A generous breakfast is provided (unless advised otherwise in self-contained accommodation)
◊ Breakfast: Self Contained Accommodation indicates if Hamper/Breakfast provisions are provided or Accommodation Only.

General
◊ Roadside identification of property
◊ An honest and accurate description of listing details and facilities
◊ Hosts accept responsibility to comply with government regulations
◊ Description includes if hosts' pets and young children are sharing a common area with guests
◊ Operational Smoke Alarms
◊ Adequate Public and Product Liability under a B&B Insurance Policy

Optional extras
◊ Lock on guest rooms or secure storage facilities available
◊ Air-conditioning, particularly in hotter areas
◊ Laundry facilities for guests
◊ Bathroom/toilet - air freshener, tissues
◊ Television, radio, fresh flowers, magazines, books, fresh fruit
◊ Membership of State B&B Association
◊ Accredited Tourism Business (Green Tick)
◊ Independently inspected B&B (eg, by AAA Tourism or B&B Association)

WE VALUE YOUR COMMENTS

The Australian
Bed & Breakfast
Book

If you know B&B hosts you will realise how important they value your comments. Most leave a guestbook in the foyer or living room, some may invite you to complete a guest comment form. They are small businesses and their success depends solely on your visitation. If you enjoyed your stay, tell them . . . if you find something is not quite right let them know before you leave . . . they will appreciate the feedback.

We too value your feedback, whether about the book or about the properties included.
We do enjoy reading the comments guests send to us – all the guest comments include in this edition were sent to us by guests such as yourself.

You may also have some suggestions on how we could improve the next edition, or recommendations of new properties you have discovered.

Add your comments below.

_____

_____

_____

Your Name _____

Address or Contact details _____

_____

Return to The Bed & Breakfast Book, PO Box 330, Wahroonga, NSW 2076
Email to info@BBBook.com.au

Telephone
Adelaide   (08) 8464 0959
Brisbane   (07) 3118 5959
Melbourne (03) 9017 5959
Perth   (08) 6363 5959
Sydney   (02) 8208 5959

Booking Notes and Other Important Details

Have you ever made a booking, then forgot the name of the accommodation or the dates of your reservation? Well you can now record all the essential details below. Or have you done your research then forget to note down the name of the location or some other important details? You may have stayed at a great place, picked up a book from their library, enjoyed a bottle of wine or had a great meal and written the details down on a back of an envelope – then lost it! We have made it easy for you. You can note down all your important details below and keep for future reference.

Accommodation Name _____
Date of Reservation _____
Important Information _____
_____
_____

Accommodation Name _____
Date of Reservation _____
Important Information _____
_____
_____

Accommodation Name _____
Date of Reservation _____
Important Information _____
_____
_____

Accommodation Name _____
Date of Reservation _____
Important Information _____
_____
_____

Accommodation Name _____
Date of Reservation _____
Important Information _____
_____
_____

Accommodation Name _____
Date of Reservation _____
Important Information _____
_____
_____

Accommodation Name

Date of Reservation

Important Information

Accommodation Name

Date of Reservation

Important Information

Accommodation Name

Date of Reservation

Important Information

Accommodation Name

Date of Reservation

Important Information

Accommodation Name

Date of Reservation

Important Information

Accommodation Name

Date of Reservation

Important Information

Accommodation Name

Date of Reservation

Important Information

20th Anniversary Edition